BRECHT'S EARLY PLAYS

BRECHT'S EARLY PLAYS

Ronald Speirs

Humanities Press
Atlantic Highlands, N. J.

First published in the United States of America 1982 by
HUMANITIES PRESS INC.
171 First Avenue,
Atlantic Highlands,
New Jersey 07716

ISBN 0–391–02554–6

Printed in Hong Kong

For Sue, Fiona, Jill and Laura

"Wir brauchen eine Kunst, die die Natur meistert"
(*GW*, **17**, 1165)
"We need a form of art which will master nature"

Contents

Preface

My aim in writing this book has been to provide a guide to Brecht's early plays which will be of interest and use both to the general reader and to the student of German literature. As well as supplying a detailed commentary on the individual plays, I have tried to build up a picture of the way the young Brecht's mind worked and developed, and to indicate the general relevance of the attitudes manifested in his early writing to an understanding of his subsequent development. All notes are gathered together at the end of the volume. Although not exhaustive, the Bibliography provides an ample selection of the most useful literature on the subject of Brecht's early plays.

I should like to take this opportunity of thanking the many colleagues and friends who have helped and encouraged me. I am indebted to Michael Butler and Bernard Standring of the German Department of the University of Birmingham, Professor Robert Smith of the Russian Department, Gerry McCarthy of the Department of Drama and Theatre Arts, but my greatest debt is to Professor Arrigo Subiotto of the German Department for his unfailing help in matters both small and large. I am grateful to the library staff at the Universities of Birmingham, Aberdeen and Stirling, and to the staff of the Bertolt Brecht Archive in Berlin – particularly to Herta Ramthun, whose ability to decipher Brecht's handwriting defies emulation.

Birmingham   R. S.
September 1981

Acknowledgements

The author and publishers wish to thank the following who have kindly given permission for the use of copyright material:

Stefan S. Brecht, for the extracts from the original editions of *Baal* (Potsdam: Kiepenheuer, 1922); *Trommeln in der Nacht* (Munich: Drei Masken, 1922); *Im Dickicht der Städte: Erstfassung und Materialien* (© 1968, by Suhrkamp Verlag); *Mann ist Mann* (Berlin: Arcadia, 1926); *Die Dreigroschenoper* (Vienna: Universal Edition, 1929); *Aufstieg und Fall der Stadt Mahagonny* (Vienna: Universal Edition, 1929); *Tagebücher 1920–22: Autobiographische Aufzeichnungen 1920–1954* (© 1975 by Stefan S. Brecht), and for permission to translate these extracts.

St. Martin's Press Inc., for the extracts from John Willett's translation of *Bertolt Brecht Diaries 1920–1922* (translation © 1979 by St. Martin's Press Inc.).

Stefan S. Brecht, the Bertolt Brecht Erben and Suhrkamp Verlag, for the extracts from unpublished material in the keeping of the Bertolt Brecht Archive, and for permission to translate these extracts (translation © Stefan S. Brecht, 1981).

Eyre Methuen Ltd, for the short extracts from the works of Bertolt Brecht and for the extracts from Jean Benedetti's translation of *The Life of Edward the Second of England* (translation © 1970 by Eyre Methuen Ltd); original work entitled *Leben Eduards des Zweiten von England* (© 1953 by Suhrkamp Verlag).

Every effort has been made to trace all the copyright-holders, but if any have been inadvertently overlooked the publishers will be pleased to make the necessary arrangements at the first opportunity.

A Note on the Texts and Translations

The first obstacle encountered by anyone wishing to understand Brecht's early plays is the fact that the first published versions of these plays are mostly very difficult to obtain. The versions published in Brecht's collected works are in almost every case significantly different from the first published versions. The differences between the early and the revised texts are not mere matters of editorial detail, but reflect the major change in Brecht's ideological standpoint which intervened between the composition of the plays and Brecht's revision of the texts for re-publication. The translations of Brecht's collected plays currently being published by Eyre Methuen mostly follow the standard text of the Suhrkamp edition, but have the advantage of being supplied with notes and variant material which permit the reader who is prepared to make the effort to gain quite a good idea of Brecht's original conception. The interpretations offered here therefore are all based on the German of the first published (or performed) versions, and I have supplied my own translations of the passages quoted, except in the case of *The Life of Edward the Second*, where I was able to use the Methuen translation. Where I have quoted longer sections of dialogue, or passages where the nuance of the German is particularly important, I have given both the German and my translation, but for shorter quotations I have given only my translation. All quotations from Brecht's essays and diaries are simply given in English. This decision is a compromise which tries to satisfy both the English-speaking reader's demand for the minimum of "clutter" in his text, and that of the German-speaking reader who wants to have before him the words Brecht actually wrote. I hope that both types of reader will be tolerant of the imperfections which such a compromise entails.

List of Abbreviations

References to the texts (for details of editions, see Bibliography) use the following abbreviations:

Aj	*Arbeitsjournal* (1938–1955)
B	*Baal*
BBA	Material from the Bertolt Brecht Archive
BiA	*Brecht in Augsburg*
dbB	*der böse Baal der asoziale* (*Wicked Baal the Asocial*)
Diaries	*Diaries 1920–1922* (trans. J. Willett)
D	*Im Dickicht* (*In the Jungle*)
DGO	*Die Dreigroschenoper* (*The Threepenny Opera*)
DM	*Die Maßnahme* (*The Measures Taken*)
E	*Leben Eduards des Zweiten von England* (*The Life of Edward the Second of England*)
GW	*Gesammelte Werke* (*Collected Works*) (20 vols)
J	*Der Jasager und Der Neinsager* (*The Boy who Said Yes and The Boy who Said No*)
MI *MIIi* *MII ii* etc.	Volume of the collected plays in the Eyre Methuen translation
Mah	*Aufstieg und Fall der Stadt Mahagonny* (*Rise and Fall of the City of Mahagonny*)
Mar	Christopher Marlowe, *The Life of Edward the Second of England*
MiM	*Mann ist Mann* (*A Man's a Man*)
SzT	*Schriften zum Theater* (*Writings on Theatre*) (7 vols)
T	*Tagebücher 1920–1922: Autobiographische Aufzeichnungen 1920–1954* (*Diaries 1920–1922: Autobiographical Notes 1920–1954*)
TN	*Trommeln in der Nacht* (*Drums in the Night*)

1 Introduction

ENDS AND MEANS

In the twenty-five years since Brecht's death his plays have reached a world-wide audience and the terms "epic theatre" and *Verfremdungseffekt* (usually, but not very helpfully translated as "alienation effect") have gained wide currency. Yet while the plays of his maturity – *The Life of Galileo, Mother Courage and her Children, The Caucasian Chalk Circle, The Good Woman of Szechwan* – continue to be produced quite successfully both in Germany and abroad, a certain weariness with Brecht, a feeling of over-familiarity with his themes, techniques and style has made itself felt in recent years, with the result that his later work is sometimes talked about with more respect than enthusiasm. Even the Berliner Ensemble, the company he led in East Berlin after his return from exile and which scored brilliant successes both under his direction and that of his disciples, has found difficulty in developing fresh and exciting approaches to his plays. On the other hand, there has lately been a growing interest in his earlier work which previously tended to be over-shadowed both in the theatre and in critical discussion by his later plays and theory. New productions of *Baal, Drums in the Night, The Life of Edward the Second, A Man's a Man, The Threepenny Opera* and *The Rise and Fall of the City of Mahagonny* have been received with interest and enthusiasm, and one English newspaper felt it was worth publishing lengthy extracts from his early diaries when these appeared here in translation. The present study aims to meet and perhaps further stimulate this increasing general interest in Brecht's early work. It also sets out to redress an imbalance in the academic discussion of Brecht by subjecting the body of his early plays (excepting the one-act plays) to the kind of detailed examination which has normally been reserved for his later plays.

A pioneering study by Ernst Schumacher of Brecht's early plays was published just before Brecht's death. His *Die dramatischen Versuche Bertolt Brechts 1918–1933* (Berlin, 1955) provides much background information of a literary–historical kind, but it concentrates on demonstrating the relevance of Marx's and Engels's analyses of capitalist society to an understanding of the content of the plays. Schumacher argues that Brecht's early plays develop towards an increasingly accurate reflection of the reality of life under capitalism. According to this view Brecht began as a "naïve" realist and materialist but progressed towards a dialectical– materialist understanding of society as his immediate observations became enriched by his reading of the classics of Marxism. Although Schumacher's study was a courageous attempt to extend the canon of Marxist literary criticism in the German Democratic Republic, where Brecht's innovations initially met with hostility from entrenched proponents of a rigidly conceived doctrine of "socialist realism", his approach remains too normative for the non-Marxist reader.[1] Unless one agrees with the Marxist *Widerspiegelungstheorie* ("theory of reflection") it is difficult to accept Schumacher's interpretation of the plays as "mirroring" social reality, or his judgements about the accuracy of the young Brecht's understanding of the world. Schumacher also introduced into Brecht studies an unfortunate tendency to view Brecht's early work as if he had written it in order to prepare himself for his later, "mature" creations. To approach the early plays on the assumption that they are "proto"-Marxist is a sure way to misunderstand them. With regard to both form and content Brecht's early plays need to be interpreted in their own terms.

Quite apart from such general disagreements about method, which lead to considerable differences about points of detail, there are other reasons for advancing an alternative view to that of Schumacher. The first is that a good deal of new material has become available since he wrote his study. The texts and manuscripts collected in the Bertolt Brecht Archive in East Berlin enable scholars to compare the first published versions of the plays with later editions and to bring knowledge of Brecht's working notes, diaries, fragments and textual variants to the study of his plays. Examination of the different versions of the plays makes it clear how important it is to distinguish sharply between the first performed or published version and subsequent editions. This is not a matter of quibbling about editorial minutiae, but of recognising that most of Brecht's later revisions of his texts stemmed from his changed ideological position in the interim. His Marxist "corrections" of his early work are an obstacle to any understanding of these plays in their own terms and in relation to the views he held at the time of writing them. We also know more now about Brecht's life, particularly about his early years in Augsburg which have been the subject of extensive research that has yielded facts, reminiscences and the texts of early literary efforts, all of which are helpful in understanding his development.

As well as incorporating textual and factual material which was not available to Schumacher, any re-appraisal of Brecht's early work needs to take account of the variety of other interpretations which have opened up perspectives ignored by Schumacher. Even before the publication of Schumacher's study Herbert Lüthy had already advanced an interpretation which stressed the subjective element in Brecht's writing.[2] This approach has found the greatest number of adherents amongst English-speaking critics. Lüthy's central proposition, which was given wide currency by the publication in 1959 of Martin Esslin's controversial *Brecht: a Choice of Evils*, was that Brecht's imaginative work and political development issued from a divided personality. According to this view, Brecht's fundamental experience was of the chaotic irrationality of the world, and this impelled him to take refuge in an excessive respect for rationality and discipline. The argument that Brecht's adoption of Marxism, although parading as a rational choice, was really an expression of the "irrational forces within him" and represented the outcome of "the struggle between subconscious impulse and conscious control" (Esslin, p. 217) earned Esslin the opprobrium of critics committed to upholding a view of Brecht as a mentor of the modern world. Although Esslin's study is still readable and stimulating, it can fairly be objected that, like Lüthy, he spoiled his case by overstating it. To reduce Brecht's commitment to Marxism to the status of a "wholly irrational" impulse merely served to strengthen opposition to *any* suggestion that subjective factors need to be taken into account when assessing Brecht's work. Esslin also laid himself open to attack by writing a wide-ranging essayistic study which was light on the detailed analysis of texts. The unjustly dismissive attitude too often taken towards his commentary demonstrates that, no matter how suggestive certain lines of interpretation may be, they need to be closely argued and supported by textual detail if they are to gain acceptance. A good deal of detailed analysis of this kind has now been done, but it needs to be consolidated. The interpretation put forward here incorporates the findings of some critics and takes issue with those of others.

However, because this book addresses itself to a wider readership
than a purely academic one, explicit scholarly debate has been kept
to a minimum. I hope that the lines of the *implicit* debate will be
clear to the reader who knows the literature in the field.

The present study analyses the imaginative structure of Brecht's
early plays. Although the approach taken could broadly be classed
as psychological, it is certainly not psychoanalytic, and makes no
claim to have penetrated to the "heart" of Brecht. As it is difficult
enough to understand even those people with whom one is in daily
contact, one cannot expect things to be easier in the case of a person
whom one only "knows" through fictions and fragmentary biographical evidence. The concept of "mastery" which is used here to
describe the way Brecht's mind worked is simply an interpretive
construct based on observations primarily of the themes, characters,
plots, style and form of his plays, but also of his "behaviour" in
other, non-fictional contexts, whether in commenting on his own
personality or on his relations with others, or on politics, art and
literature. In addition to its principal function of defining the
characteristic structure of Brecht's various dramatic experiments,
the concept is also intended to provide an account of the underlying
continuity in the widely different ideological stances adopted by
Brecht at various stages in his career.

The method of play-by-play analysis which I have adopted
recommended itself for various reasons. The first was that I felt this
approach was most likely to suit the needs of the student reader. The
second was that a chronological arrangement of the material
allowed me to deal with the question of Brecht's development
within the period under consideration. As one moves from play to
play between 1918 and 1929 it becomes clear that, although there is
a general tendency towards a more complex grasp of things,
Brecht's attitudes remain remarkably consistent throughout these
years; in fact it is this consistency that allows us to define his first
period as such. In other words, as far as his playwriting was
concerned, his much-cited reading of *Das Kapital* in 1926 seems to
have made little impact. Another advantage of the play-by-play
approach was that it permitted each play to be treated as an
independent artistic whole. By looking at the internal relations
between form and theme within each play I was seeking deliberately to avoid the approach which treats these plays as
storehouses of themes, characters, situations or techniques plun-
dered by Brecht when writing his later plays. It is clear, for example,

that the chronicle play *Life of Edward the Second of England* with its geographically and historically distant settings, its long time-span, its panoply of characters and episodes, its bald announcements of the time and place of events, shares a certain family likeness with such later historical plays as *Mother Courage* or *Galileo*. But Brecht's view of history changed enormously in the intervening years, and the uses to which he put the form of historical drama were accordingly quite different. If the term "epic theatre" is applied to *Edward II* it must be made clear that the term does not signify in this case what it signified in Brecht's later usage.

All this should not be taken to mean that I wish to isolate Brecht's early work from his subsequent development. On the contrary, I shall argue that an understanding of these early plays contributes to our overall understanding of the way his mind worked. But the relationship I wish to establish is of a general kind. Both before he became a Marxist and afterwards Brecht's imaginative writing aimed at achieving mastery of life in various ways. The quotation which I have used as a motto for this study was taken from a late essay, but it aptly characterises his approach to writing in the period with which we are concerned: "Wir brauchen eine Kunst, die die Natur meistert" ("We need a form of art which will master nature"). Both early and late, Brecht practised his art, not as a dispassionate recorder and analyst of life, but passionately, with a will to mould life into the kind of shape that would suit the demands he made on it. The tension between this desire to master life and his underlying doubts about the attainability of such mastery generates the characteristic structures of his early plays which it is the aim of this study to analyse. The concluding chapter will consider the application to his later work of the insights gained from the examination of the early plays.

As I shall be concerned mainly with the internal organisation of the plays themselves, I shall not have much to say about Brecht's place within the literary history of the Weimar Republic, but there will be some discussion of the contemporary background and of certain aspects of the German literary tradition, where these are relevant to the analysis of the plays. Brecht's fondness in later life for collective artistic work is well-attested. During the 1920s, too, he worked on a film project with Arnolt Bronnen (which did not get very far), sought the help of Lion Feuchtwanger for the versification of *The Life of Edward the Second* and helped Feuchtwanger in turn to re-write his play *Warren Hastings*; he co-operated with Kurt Weill on

The Threepenny Opera and *Mahagonny*, and contributed to Erwin
Piscator's theatrical adaptation of *The Good Soldier Schweyk*. Despite
these contacts with other writers, however, neither Brecht's plays
nor his poetry in this period had much in common with what was
being written around him. Where parallels occur they are usually
only partial, so that the observed similarity between Brecht and the
other writer or trend in question has to be extensively qualified. For
all his (occasional) conviviality Brecht kept out of any literary
grouping throughout the twenties, and only began to work closely
with those interested in developing a new, collective and revolutionary form of theatre at the end of the decade. The independent single-mindedness with which he developed his own
dramatic vision throughout this period even makes it difficult to
classify his work in terms of broad literary historical categories such
as Expressionism or *Neue Sachlichkeit* ("New Sobriety").[3] Brecht's
rejection of the idealistic pathos of a certain type of Expressionist
drama is well known, yet his work has a generality of symbolic
reference which is Expressionist in character, and quite distinct
from the trend towards a superficially realistic reflection of
contemporary life which is typical of much "New Sobriety" writing.
As compared with the modest ambitions of "New Sobriety"[4]
Brecht's determination to create for his age a form of drama which
would be as great (*groß*)[5] as that of previous ages is comparable with
the aims of the Expressionists, although his attitudes and methods
were notably different from theirs. Sub-categories such as "black
Expressionism"[6] are of little help, since Brecht's work, with the
possible exception of *Baal*, was almost as different from that of
Arnolt Bronnen, say, as it was from the earlier, idealistic type of
Expressionism. The emotional complexity of Brecht's early plays,
which could accommodate moments of "New Sobriety" cynicism
alongside moments of intense Expressionist subjectivity, simply
resists easy categorisation.[7] Thus, where comparisons are made
between Brecht's plays and those of his contemporaries, they will
draw attention to differences as often as they point to similarities.

COMPLEXITY AND MASTERY

Both in his own view and that of others Brecht's personality was full
of contradictions. His diary entry for 17 June 1921 reads as follows:

Eating cherries today in front of the mirror I saw my idiotic face. Those self-contained black bullets disappearing down my mouth made it look looser, more lascivious and contradictory than ever. It contains many elements of brutality, calm, slackness, boldness and cowardice, but as elements only, and it is more changeable and characterless than a landscape beneath scurrying clouds. That's why so many people find it impossible to retain ('you've too many of them' says Hedda). (*Diaries*, 112)

This type of contradictory personality brings its own problems. Being so labile and capable of responding in such a variety of ways to life, a person with this kind of personality is likely to find it difficult to make clear and simple decisions, or to be contented with himself for long, or with any particular course of action he decides to follow. One way of coping with such contradictoriness would be simply to drift along in various directions, abandoning oneself to whatever impulse was momentarily dominant. On occasion Brecht would feel attracted to this solution:

A man with one theory is lost. He needs several of them, four, lots! He should stuff them into his pockets like newspapers, hot from the press always, you can live well surrounded by them, there are comfortable lodgings to be found between the theories. If you are to get on you need to know that there are a lot of theories; a tree too has several, but only masters one of them, for a while. (*Diaries*, 42–3)

But although Brecht accepted that in theory "the soundest policy is just to keep on tacking" (*Diaries*, 34) he was also aware that to live in such a directionless manner would entail great costs of an emotional kind:

The question of costs has to be settled by discussion. All that's needed in order to be happy, to work well, to be able to idle, to back oneself up, is just one thing, intensity. To be intensely unhappy means not believing in the cause. Making an operation of it. Amor fati. To do everything with all one's body and soul! Never mind exactly what! (*Diaries*, 34)

Thus, the possibility of simply "tacking along" through life proves not to be an acceptable attitude because, by a paradox of character, the mind which acknowledges, with considerable irritation, its own changeability and vacillation considers that happiness must lie in intensity, in whole-hearted commitment to any given experience or course of action. Yet such self-absorbing intensity of experience is necessarily very difficult, if not impossible for this type of personality to achieve, particularly when the person has a mind as self-aware and self-critical as Brecht's was. The sigh is almost audible when Brecht remarks, "Again and again the intellect undermines the position" (*Diaries*, 71), or when he asks, "Could my accursed hankering for intensity be a sign that there's a weak point somewhere in the system?" (*Diaries*, 35). Thus the vicious circle closes: complexity of mind and feeling demand that life be mastered through unqualified commitment, but the attempt to achieve this confronts the mind, frustratingly, with its own complexity as the main cause of its inability to achieve such mastery.

The dichotomy outlined here expresses itself in various ways in Brecht's early diaries. It is at work, for example, in his admiration for Napoleon, the single-minded man of action, whose campaign-maps and death-mask Brecht kept in his study. It also underlies his attraction to a quite different type of personality, which in its own way is equally self-contained, namely that of Jesus, whom Brecht described as "a man quite without a navel, a successful creation, aimless, whose back doesn't need any sort of stiffening (fulfilment of obligations or what have you). An invulnerable man, because he puts up no resistance. Wholly prepared to tack, pliable, cloud-like, full of starry skies, gentle showers, wisdom, cheerfulness, trustfulness, possibilities" (*Diaries*, 36). The common factor in Brecht's admiration for such contrasting types was attraction to his own opposite, for each of these men seemed to have achieved an enviable wholeness and their own personal mode of living successfully. The same kind of attraction to quite different ways of achieving mastery over life is also evident in Brecht's early reading. He was equally capable of becoming enthusiastic about Nietzsche's *Thus spake Zarathustra*, a hymnic celebration of the will to power (*T*, 197), or about the work of Lao-tzu, an Eastern philosopher who taught denial of the will as the means to achieving oneness with essential reality (*Diaries*, 50). In this connection it is interesting that at one stage in his life it is reported that Brecht could always be seen with a volume of Schopenhauer's philosophy under his arm (*BiA*, 114).

If one expression of Brecht's divided mind can be seen in his interest in various types of unified personality or philosophy, another more direct expression of his problem is to be found in the fragmentary sketches for a proposed dramatic biography of the biblical King David. His conception of David is of a man divided against himself, a great king with many practical achievements to his credit who is denied happiness by his doubts about the worth of a life devoted to the rational pursuit of concrete goals. One scene of the play was to show him haunted in his old age by visions of the heroes and companions of his youth, Saul, Jonathan and Absalom, who laugh at the decay that has befallen David's practical achievements. These visions express David's feelings of guilt and anxiety at having failed to be true to his deepest convictions about life: "He is worried because he failed to do the right thing. Did he not realise that the right thing was to be idle, to want to change nothing, be human? Why didn't he do that?" (*Diaries*, 46). Despite his deeply ingrained suspicion of the rationally directed will David had been incapable of taking a relaxed, passive attitude to life: "On no account did David want to let things stay as they were, go on as they were going" (*Diaries*, 46). At the root of David's sense of failure is the feeling that, although he has long survived the departed heroes, their lives were more successful than his because they had followed their passions unreservedly and without regard to the self-destructive consequences of their inclinations. David's self-division not only makes him feel cut-off from the passionate figures of the past, but also alienates him from his own son, Solomon, an entirely cool and calculating politician, the man of the future, whom David can only despise for his flexible, pragmatic rationality. What he hates in his heir is the image of the political schemer he has himself become. But if David fundamentally doubted the value of attempting to achieve mastery of life through rational practicality, why did he devote his life to such goals? This question was to be answered in another scene, where a younger David is shown alone, brooding, as Absalom's irrational rebellion is spreading rapidly through the kingdom. David's mind turns to such problems as the provision of grain and cattle for the peasants, improvements in the marriage laws, poverty, the need for better roads, the delays in the construction of a water-pumping system. Difficult though these problems are, they provide some refuge for the king's troubled mind since they are concrete and, unlike the problems of human behaviour, at least theoretically manageable:

Realities were fine. They were consoling, despite all. You could get a footing there. People had too many faces and too few, they had two kinds of head, two kinds of feet, they couldn't be relied on. Started senseless insurrections, which wasted time and material. Aqueducts decayed, fell into disrepair or didn't work, but they were visible, distinguishable, able to be repaired. (*Diaries*, 72)

The compulsion felt by King David to pursue some form of mastery over life despite or indeed because of his doubts about its attainability is a pattern of behaviour clearly related to habits of mind revealed in Brecht's early diaries. It is a great pity that this play remained fragmentary since it might well have been one of Brecht's most interesting psychological studies.

Brecht's play about King David was to have analysed the divided mind of a politician. If one turns to Brecht's own early views on politics one finds more evidence of his contradictoriness. On one occasion he noted in his diary after attending a lecture on the conditions of life in Russia under the Bolsheviks, "What alarms me about that place is not the disorder actually achieved there but the order actually aimed for. At present I am very much against Bolshevism: universal military service, food rationing, controls, conspiracies, economic favouritism. On top of that, at best: equilibrium, transformation, compromise. I say thanks a lot and may I have a car" (*Diaries*, 45). Here speaks the anarchist in Brecht. The resistance to external authority and social discipline is the "political" counterpart to his reluctance to impose order on his unruly mental and emotional life. On the other hand, there were occasions when Brecht exhibited a quite contrary attitude to politics: "Politics too are only good if there are enough thoughts around (how bad the gaps are in this area too!), the triumph over mankind. To be able to do the right thing, ruthlessly, with severity!" (*GW*, **20**, 15). These conflicting attitudes to politics only become important for Brecht's imaginative work at the end of the 1920s; in the plays with which we are concerned the conflict between the will to master life and his doubts or reluctance about pursuing such mastery expresses itself in different ways.

The domineering streak in Brecht appears to have made itself evident in his personal relationships from an early age, as one of his erstwhile playmates recalls:

Eugen [as Brecht was known in his childhood] demanded that we should each bring along our lead-soldiers. We then heaped-up

little earthworks and posted the soldiers in exact accordance with
Eugen's battle plans. It was always he alone who dictated how we
should play, sometimes as Napoleon, at other times as Frederick
the Great. We were his generals and did what he commanded.
Eugen was always the boss. He was domineering and arrogant
towards his playmates. We thought he wanted to show us that he
was the son of the chief clerk.   (*BiA*, 33)

As an adult Brecht continued to behave in this manner on occasion,
as his close friend Caspar Neher and various mistresses knew to their
cost. Yet there was also a soft, sentimental streak in Brecht which
responded readily to the gentleness of Paula ("Bi") Banholzer and
of Frank, Brecht's illegitimate son by her:

He is slim, with delicate limbs and a fine clear face, curly red hair,
but smooth in front, he's lively and has big dark brown eyes. He
likes a joke, laughs a lot, keeps running around and playing with a
whole succession of things; but he's never violent and never noisy,
just friendly and gentle all the time.   (*Diaries*, 91)

The conflict between the desire to dominate others and his
underlying softness drew Brecht into an increasingly complicated
relationship with Marianne Zoff, the beautiful opera-singer who
became his first wife. When their affair began, his vanity and
arrogance led him to believe that he could dictate the terms of their
relationship. Despite his initial insistence that he could not possibly
marry and settle down, however, he ended up marrying this rather
difficult woman because his feelings towards her were actually far
too complicated for him to control in the way he had once fondly
imagined he could.

Brecht's first adult play was *Baal*, written at the end of the First
World War, but his literary career actually began some years
earlier, in the year when the war broke out. While still a sixteen-
year-old schoolboy he published a short play, poetry and essays,
both in the school's literary magazine, *Die Ernte* (*The Harvest*), and
in local Augsburg newspapers. Some critics would prefer to have
these juvenilia excluded from consideration, or at least treated very
dismissively as the products of a still immature mind. I do not take
this view. While it may be something of an overstatement to claim
that all a writer's formative experiences have been made in
childhood,[8] it is surely presumptuous to dismiss as opportunistic or
as an aberration the products of a sixteen-year-old's imagination

simply because they express views which at first sight are difficult to
reconcile with the writer's later attitudes. Although one may have
reservations about the literary quality of Brecht's early efforts, they
provide a useful insight into the way his mind and imagination
worked from the very beginning.

In January 1914 *Die Ernte* published a one-act play by Brecht
entitled *The Bible*. The action of the play, set in a Protestant town
under siege from Catholic troops during the Thirty Years War,
presents the dilemma of a family torn between humanitarian
considerations and loyalty to their religious convictions. The
Catholics, who are certain of victory, offer to spare the lives of the
town's citizens provided that they abjure their Protestant
confession, and provided also that the mayor of the town surrenders
his daughter to the lust of the enemy commander. The play shows
an apprehension that extremely painful, possibly even quite
intractable problems exist in the field of moral choice. The brother
of the girl fiercely argues that the survival of the town's inhabitants
takes precedence over religious principle, and demands the sacrifice
of the girl's virginity. The girl's grandfather, on the other hand,
resolutely maintains that no temporal considerations can justify
condemning even a single soul to eternal damnation for a mortal sin.
No less interesting than the play's perception of a moral dilemma,
however, is the way the problem is resolved. Instead of trying to
arrive at some rational solution to the questions it raises, the play
focuses attention on the personal qualities of the characters
involved. The central figure is the grandfather, whose importance is
underlined by the fact that he speaks both the opening and the
closing lines of the play. As the curtain rises, his troubled mind finds
an outlet in reading aloud Christ's cry of dereliction on the Cross;
when the curtain falls he is heard declaiming lines which show him
once again steadfast in his faith:

> *Großvater*:   [*laut und hallend*] Herr, bleibe bei uns, denn es will
> Abend werden und der Tag hat sich geneiget.
> [*Der Vorhang rauscht über dem brennenden Gemach
> zusammen*]
>
> (*GW*, **7**, 3038)

> *Grandfather*:   [*loudly and resoundingly*] Lord, stay with us for it is
> toward evening and the day is now far spent.
> [*With a swish the curtain closes on the burning chamber*]

With this focus on the grandfather the action takes the form of a drama of temptation. During the old man's progression from initial doubt to regained certainty he acquires an increasingly heroic stature as his iron will and commanding presence are contrasted with the distracted timidity of the girl, the depressed vacillation of her father and the ineffectual hysteria of her brother. In this way the play comes over as a drama of conflicting wills, which leaves as the strongest impression on the mind and feelings of the reader not an awareness of the insolubility of the moral dilemma, but admiration for the old man's integrity, strength and *Größe* ("greatness"), to use Brecht's favourite term of praise in those years. Precisely because of its lack of sophistication this playlet illustrates well the contrary pulls operating on Brecht's mind: his awareness of life's painful, difficult aspects on the one hand, and his attraction to an ideal of personal strength as a way of achieving mastery over life's problems on the other.

Whereas *The Bible* was a relatively innocuous literary exercise, the patriotic poems and *Kriegsbriefe* ("War letters") published by Brecht in the *Augsburger Neueste Nachrichten* and the *München–Augsburger Abendzeitung* at the beginning of the First World War are a positive embarrassment to those who like to stress Brecht's opposition to the Establishment. These publications reinforce the impression gained from reading *The Bible* that the young author's imagination was enthralled by notions of strength and greatness. Again and again one comes across sentiments such as the following:

Batallion um Batallion marschiert hinaus, am Königsplatz vorüber, die Schrannenstraße durch zum Bahnhof. Mit festem, ruhigem Schritt ziehen sie hin, umwogt, umdrängt von einer begeisterten Menge, in den großen Krieg. . . . Und unter den blütengeschmückten Helmen leuchten die Augen in dem schweißglänzenden Gesicht.   (*BiA*, 229)

Batallion after batallion march out, past the Königsplatz and along the Schrannenstraße to the station. With firm, calm step they make their way, surrounded and pressed by an enthusiastic crowd, into the great war. . . . And under the flower-decked helmets their eyes are bright, though sweat glistens on their faces.

Es ist doch schön, daß wir in der Not sehen, wie stark Deutschland noch ist, stark bis ins Innerste, bis in die Verhältnisse des einzelnen.   (*BiA*, 233)

Yet it is fine that we should see in our extremity how strong Germany still is, strong to its innermost heart, right into the life of the individual.

One of these newspaper articles took the form of a prose "ballad" which depicted a company being led into the attack by its young ensign. The piece celebrated the unifying experience of combat:

> Man fühlte sich als Gesamtheit. Aber das sahen, wußten, fühlten sie alle: Der Fahnenjunker war ihnen voran. Seine helle, schmale Gestalt, der klingende, blitzende Degen in der Hand, die wehende Schärpe, das waren alles Teile, Erscheinungen ihrer Seele, ihrer aller Seele. (*BiA*, 266)

> They felt themselves to be one body. But this they all saw, knew, felt: The ensign was out in front. His light, slim figure, the ringing, flashing sword in his hand, the fluttering sash, all these were parts, manifestations of their soul, of the soul of all of them.

Several emotions were fused in Brecht's patriotic enthusiasm. One important element, which was also present in the responses of other poets to the outbreak of war, was a sense of grandeur which had swept aside the pettiness and dissension of everyday life:

> Wir sehen, daß alles verwandelt ist. Daß Streit, Haß, Kleinlichkeit verschwunden sind. Es hat alles gleichsam größere Maße angenommen. (*BiA*, 241)

> We see that everything is transformed. That quarrelling, hatred, pettiness have disappeared. It is as if everything had assumed greater dimensions.

Also important were the sense of belonging to a unified community and of being led by a single, purposeful will:

> Das ist so schön, daß alle Stimmen schweigen
> Und still vor dieser *einen* Stimme sind,
> Die sich erhob mit Donnerton im Reigen
> Der Zeit, die sonst so größelos zerrinnt.
> (*BiA*, 236)

It is so beautiful that all voices are silent, quiet in the presence of this *one* voice, which has been raised with thundrous tone amid the dance of time, usually so lacking in grandeur as it passes into nothingness.

Because it appealed to his imagination to think of life as having some clear order and direction, the young Brecht was even capable of presenting Kaiser Wilhelm II as a great leader, and of accepting and promulgating the current ideology that the German nation, in committing an act of war, was in the process of "purifying" itself morally by carrying out God's will in an act of "frommer, heiliger Begeisterung" ("pious, holy enthusiasm" –*BiA*, 230). All this is evidence of a strong capacity in Brecht for idealising a course of action because it purported to make sense of life and even of death. Even during the early months of the war, however, when Brecht's enthusiasm for an ideology which promised such complete mastery of life was at its height, his underlying tendency to scepticism could not be completely stifled. From the beginning his "war letters" mention the "*Opfer*" ("sacrifices" or "casualties") of the war, dwell on the sorrows of bereaved mothers and express the hope that those who do not have to go to the front will show themselves worthy of those who do. For a surprisingly long time Brecht continued to accept the view that the dead and wounded had made sacrifices which were sanctioned by the higher purpose of the war. Eventually, however, as the illusion that the war had any such purpose dwindled, he began to see only the waste of life and so became as ardent an opponent of the war as he had once been an advocate of it.[9]

Knowing the high hopes once invested in the "German mission" by the schoolboy Brecht makes it easier to understand the ferociously anti-idealistic view of the world he adopted when his illusions were shattered. Broadly speaking, he rebounded from a totally ordered view of his place in the world, with the self embraced by the community and the nation guided by the hand of the Lord, to the opposite extreme of a chaotic, discordant vision of life. Whereas he once wrote of the "holy" character of the war, he now regarded it as entirely unholy and spoke of God only in cynical, grotesque terms, ironically regarding him as an arch-traitor, and describing the world as "the excrement of our dear God" (*GW*, **1**, 53). Having once been a propagandist of "higher" values, he now denounces such notions as mere delusions, designed to obscure the finality and pointlessness of death. Now, far from believing in bonds of community between men, he asserts that each individual lives in a state of utterly impenetrable existential isolation.

Yet Brecht's need to master experience did not simply disappear during his "anarchic" period. Rather, his literary work now took the form of trying out various strategies for achieving some degree of personal, emotional mastery over a hostile and complex world. At the end of the 1920s Brecht turned away from the pursuit of this limited kind of mastery and towards the ideology of revolutionary Marxism as the means of achieving a form of practical political mastery of life which would also realise the dream of a morally ordered world.[10] I would not wish to claim that the German war ideology of 1914 had actually been formative for Brecht's mind, but his Augsburg "war letters", when seen in the light of his subsequent development, surely deserve to be regarded as important first documents of the way his imagination characteristically worked: the same imaginative tendencies which first expressed themselves in the terms of one ideology in 1914 continued to shape his work when he moved on to quite different ideological positions. This study will examine the emotional structures through which these tendencies manifested themselves in the plays of the period 1918–29.

2 *Baal*

Brecht's first full-length play, *Baal*, was written in the closing
months of the First World War. The destruction in the war of
countless lives and of a whole way of life elicited a great variety of
responses. For some it was a cause of utter despair, for others a
chance for civilisation to make a brave new beginning. As a civilian
for most of the war Brecht had direct experience only of the
privations it caused, but the deaths of so many of his contemporaries
at school kept him constantly alive to the terrible waste of young
lives "out there". For him the central question arising from this
experience was: how should the individual respond to a world that
will eventually, inevitably destroy him? After his disillusionment
with nationalist ideals at the beginning of the war he had come to
distrust all idealism as a guide to life. He now insisted that ideals
were merely ridiculous attempts to erect defences against the harsh
realities of life; in the hands of the strong ideals were a means of
exploiting the weak, a task which was ironically made easier by the
need felt by the weak for ideals to prop up their crumbling lives:

> If one only had the courage, it would be as easy as pie to ascribe
> nearly every ideal and institution . . . to the human race's
> desperate need to conceal its true situation. Respect for the
> family, glorification of work, the lure of fame, likewise religion,
> philosophy, art, smoking, intoxication, aren't just isolated,
> clearly calculated and generally recognized means (moyens) of
> combating mankind's sense of isolation, abandonment and moral
> outlawry; but visible guarantees of an immense stockpile of values
> and securities. It is from this seductive cosiness that man's
> enslavement springs. (*Diaries*, 158)

Baal, the dramatic biography of an anarchic poet modelled on
François Villon, attempts to envisage a life lived positively although
without the prop of faith in an ideal. The play is a fantasy of mastery
achieved over a destructive world by accepting that life is a matter

17

of strength or weakness (as opposed to good or evil) and by
extracting the maximum intensity of pleasure from each passing
moment.

The immediate stimulus for the drama was Brecht's dislike of a
play entitled *Der Einsame* (*The Lonely One*) by the minor Expressionist dramatist Hanns Johst. Johst's play took as its subject the life of
the late (or post-) Romantic playwright Christian Dietrich Grabbe;
its theme was the clichéd one of the poet as a misunderstood genius.
When Grabbe's wife dies in childbirth his idealism is diverted into
self-punishing immorality, by means of which he hides his injured
sensitivity behind a façade of cynicism, brutality and debauchery.
Essentially his life is full of pain, remorse and self-pity which issues in
repeated comparisons of his situation with that of the suffering
Christ. In the end Johst has him die – in verse – with his hands
folded in childlike humility, well rid of a world in which there is no
room for souls like his. Brecht countered this tear-jerking display of
self-hating, perverted idealism with a vision of a life of self-indulgent
amoralism. Johst's play was, however, not the most important
object of Brecht's scorn in *Baal*. By giving his hero the name of an
ancient god of fertility who was abominated and defeated by
Jehovah, Brecht was aligning himself with a tradition of modern
paganism which included amongst its deities Nietzsche's Dionysos
and Wedekind's Lulu.[1] This cult of vitality was intended by these
writers as a challenge to their contemporaries to overcome the
decadent fear of life evident in their attachment to convention and
in the other-worldliness of their religion and philosophy. It was
characteristic of Brecht's aggressive will to master life that he should
turn to this particular tradition for help in confronting the physical,
social, moral and emotional devastation wreaked by the First World
War.

The most direct approach to Baal's mind is through his poetry.
The "Ballad of the Adventurers", the last song Baal sings before his
death, contains a protest against the limits of human existence. The
adventurer of the poem searches restlessly for "the land where it is
better to live", but is bound to fail in his search because what he is
looking for is a state of existence in which there are no reminders of
transience: "he dreams from time to time of a little meadow with
blue sky above it and nothing else" (*B*, 85). Having on the one hand
abandoned the security of unconscious life in his mother's womb,
while on the other having no access to any transcendental world
("driven from Heaven and Hell"), the adventurer cherishes the

dream of a form of existence that would be physical yet timeless. Because he knows that his dream cannot be realised his wanderings take the form of self-exposure to the fiercest ravages of transient experience so that its intensity may compensate him for the tranquillity he cannot have.

The angry awareness of the limits of human existence is only one element in Baal's consciousness. It is balanced by more relaxed moods when he calmly enjoys the richness of the world. The permanence of the sky which in the "Ballad of the Adventurers" was a goading reminder of human transience is seen in the "Chorale of the Great Baal" as a reassuring symbol, a guarantee that the individual's life partakes for a while of eternity:

> nur der Himmel, aber immer Himmel
> deckte mächtig seine Blöße zu.
>
> (*B*, 7)

> only the sky, but *always* the sky
> covered his nakedness with its might.

> Als im dunklen Erdenschoße faulte Baal
> war der Himmel noch so groß und still und fahl.
>
> (*B*, 9)

> As in the earth's dark womb lay rotting Baal
> the sky was still as great and calm and pale.

Baal is able in this mood to savour his taste of eternity by refusing to be distressed by the thought of his own transitoriness. Viewed with such equanimity transience can even appear to be a blessing. Not only does the death of others mean less competition for the favours of *Frau Welt* ("Dame World")[2] but transience also prevents pleasure becoming stale. Thus the Baal of the "Chorale" simply abandons any woman when he has had enough of her and thinks of death simply as the "full stop" at the end of a satisfied life: "Was ist Welt für Baal noch? Baal ist satt" ("what is the world to Baal now? Baal has had his fill"). A life of such undisturbed, bovine tranquillity as is conjured up in this poem is, of course, as one-sided a fantasy of wish-fulfilment as the "Ballad of the Adventurers" was one of raging intensity. Taken together, however, the poems reveal the tension between opposing attitudes to which Baal's consciousness is subject.

In other poems the opposing pulls in the poet's mind between calm enjoyment of the world as it is and angry awareness of life's inadequacy expresses itself in a variety of tones, ranging from the metaphysical lavatory humour of "Orge's Favourite Place" ("A place that humbles, where you ascertain/that you're a man who nothing may retain" – *B*, 22) to the mixture of sensuous lyricism and harshness in the elegaic "Ballad of the Drowned Girl" (*B*, 74). Baal's poetry does not always succeed in controlling the conflict between his perception of life's harshness and his dreams of transcending the limits of existence. Thus, in the poem "Death in the Forest" there is an awkward change of focus from a close-up of a man's desperate death-agonies to a distant, sentimental vision of the early sun lighting the crown of the tree under which the man is buried. This lapse into false pathos was originally Brecht's, but it is put to good dramatic use in the context of the play, since the loss of poetic control is presented ironically as a symptom of the hero's apprehensions about the approach of death; his companion Ekart comments drily, "Well. Well. So that's how far things have gone" (*B*, 80).

Baal's poems show him as having both a reflective and a determined cast of mind. He is constantly aware of his own transience, yet always bent on mastering the problem. With this degree of self-consciousness he cannot simply be regarded as an "animal" or as a mythical figure, since gods and animals are presumably spared either the fore-knowledge or the experience of personal death. On the other hand, Baal is larger than life in so many respects, particularly in his ruthless ability to live with the contradictions in his own nature, that the play cannot be read as a consistently realistic character-study. Baal is an embodiment of vitality which is of such enormous proportions that it often exercises a strange, almost magical fascination over men and women alike, but which also, very occasionally, has to struggle to assert itself against his own human weaknesses. He is a symbolic hero whose imaginative function is to exorcise the existential fears in the mind from which he sprang. The wish-fulfilling fantasy of *Baal* lies in its offering as an answer to the problems of conflict and transience, not a flight into a conflict-free existence, but a dream of transience accepted, of conflict enjoyed and of contradiction sustained with equanimity.

At first sight *Baal* can give the impression of being a formless, loose play in which the protagonist just seems to drift in and out of a number of more or less unconnected situations and meet a variety of unrelated characters. While it is certainly true that it does not have anything like the economy and inner necessity of sequence characteristic of classical drama, it does have a unifying pattern of action which holds together the variety of his experience. As Eric Bentley puts it, the play presents a variant of "the archetypal battle of life and death, Eros and Thanatos".[3] To perceive this underlying unity we need to consider the imagery of the play, the music accompanying Baal's "Dance with Death".[4]

The play opens with a party given in Baal's honour by Mech, a capitalist who would like to publish Baal's poetry. The party ends in disarray after Baal has insulted his would-be patron and blatantly attempted to seduce his wife. There is more to Baal's treatment of Mech than the Bohemian's dislike of bourgeois convention or the anarchist's revolt against capitalist exploitation. The clash of two social types is also a clash between a figure of life and a figure of death. Mech has made his fortune in the timber business: "Whole forests of cinnamon-wood swim down Brazilian rivers for me" (*B*, 11). Throughout the play trees figure as life-symbols, while rivers, by an ancient tradition, represent transience, the force of death. Thus from the moment Mech introduces himself to Baal he is presenting himself in the role of an embodiment of death. His party therefore has macabre implications which are hinted at by the words with which he offers Baal food: "That is the corpse of an eel" (*B*, 11). The celebration which is to lead to Baal's commercial exploitation is thus revealed as a threat to kill him spiritually by making his poetry an object of use (like the trees felled for Mech's profit) and consumption (like that other delicacy, the eel), and foreshadows his eventual literal submission to the power of death. Baal's response to this challenge, his seduction of Mech's wife Emily, also has symbolic overtones: faced with the advance of his enemy, death, Baal wrests from his hands an object of beauty and pleasure which he might otherwise have allowed to pass him by. From this first encounter it can be seen that death is both enemy and ally to Baal, since every confrontation with it stimulates him to extend his vital energies and appetites to the full before death claims its eventual victory. Although he will cling to life to the very last Baal is not concerned with mere survival. Not only does he accept the fact of his transience, he even accelerates his own destruction by his pursuit of the utmost intensity of experience.[5] Knowing that he can do nothing to increase the quantity of life ceded to him, Baal is willing to side with his enemy in the task of attrition in exchange for the heightened quality of life thereby achieved. Baal is strong enough to face up to the paradox that the "blossoming" country of life is also the "hostile territory" of death.[6] Whereas many are dismayed by the knowledge that in living they are dying, Baal is able to rejoice in the fact that in dying he is living, that death, as Hofmannsthal put it, is a "great God of the soul".[7]

Baal's need to experience constantly the transitoriness of his life is the impulse that governs all his behaviour. All Baal's encounters with other individuals or with nature form part of a symbolic confrontation between the protagonist and his constant but hidden antagonist, death. It is this underlying symbolic action which links such public scenes as "In the all-night café Cloud of the Night" (*B*, 42–6) or "Village pub. Evening" (*B*, 47–51) with scenes of a more intimate kind. In the scene in the all-night café Baal, who is employed to sing to the guests, breaks his contract with the owner of the establishment, ostensibly because he is not given enough schnapps, but the backdrop of the scene ("When the door is open the blue night can be seen" – *B*, 42) suggests that the deeper reason for his behaviour is his need to be free of any ties with a routine way of life in order to be able to hold at the centre of his consciousness the conflict between eternity (represented by the sky) and the brevity of his own life. There are similar symbolic overtones in the scene in the village pub where Baal persuades some greedy peasants to bring all the bulls from the surrounding district into the village that evening by promising to buy the bull with the most powerful loins. The bull is a traditional symbol of the fertility-god whose name Baal bears. Besides the superficial "Till Eulenspiegel" pleasure of duping the peasants, Baal's motive in making this arrangement is his desire to stage a celebration of vitality against the background of the evening sky:

> Baal: [*lehnt sich zurück*] In der Dämmerung, am Abend – Es muß natürlich Abend sein und natürlich muß der Himmel bewölkt sein, wenn die Luft lau ist und etwas Wind geht, dann kommen die Stiere. Sie trotten von allen Seiten her, es ist ein starker Anblick.
>
> (*B*, 50)

> Baal: [*leans back in his chair*] At twilight, in the evening – It has to be evening, of course, and of course the sky must be cloudy,

when the air is mild and a slight breeze is blowing, then the bulls will arrive. They will trot in from all sides, it will be a powerful sight.

The pleasure aroused by the sight of the bulls' vitality is inseparable in Baal's mind from the fact that they will be seen in a setting of wind, clouds and evening sky, the beauty of which heightens and is heightened by the mood of transience it expresses. Baal's overriding preoccupation with death informs all his behaviour, even where this is not clearly indicated by scenic or verbal symbolism. His brutality towards his lovers of both sexes, for example, is rooted in his determination to allow nothing to set premature limits to his pursuit of pleasure. For his will to accept any form of inhibition would mean the impairment of his vitality. When he murders Ekart for flirting with a barmaid, Baal's motive is not simply sexual jealousy, but stems from long-seething anger at Ekart's resistance to his domination. He is prompted to violence because Ekart's refusal to submit to his will at a time when Baal's vital energies are beginning to ebb is a painful reminder of the final limit which the world will set to his self-assertion.

Baal's ambivalent experience of transience, as a threat and as a source of intensified pleasure, pervades the imagery of the play. Both the river and the wind are traditional symbols of transience. In Baal's experience, however, both become sources of sensuous pleasure and vital renewal. As Baal walks through the fields at the height of summer he revels in the sensations it gives him:

Baal: [*langsam durch die Felder*] Seit der Himmel grüner und schwanger ist, Juliluft, Wind, kein Hemd in den Hosen! [*Zu Ekart zurück*] Sie wetzen mir die bloßen Schenkel. Mein Schädel ist aufgeblasen vom Wind, in dem Haar der Achselhöhle hängt mir der Geruch der Felder. Die Luft zittert wie vom Branntwein besoffen.

(*B*, 46)

Baal: [*walking slowly through the fields*] Since the sky is greener and pregnant, July air, no shirt in my trousers! [*Calls back to Ekart*] They whet my bare thighs. My skull is filled by the breeze, in the hair of my armpits hangs the smell of the fields. The air is trembling as if it were drunk on brandy.

Baal's love of the wind becomes identification with it at certain moments:

> *Baal*: Und jetzt gehörst du dem Wind, weiße Wolke! [*Rasch zu ihr, reißt die Türe zu, nimmt Sophie Barger in die Arme*]
>
> (B, 37)

> *Baal*: And now you belong to the wind, white cloud! [*Goes to her quickly, flings the door shut, takes Sophie Barger in his arms*]

The suicide by drowning of Johanna, a girl whom Baal seduces, establishes early in the play the sombre aspect of the river symbolism. Its sensuous aspect, on the other hand, is brought out in scenes where Baal lies in the sun after soaking in the warm water of a stream, or when he advises the young Johannes to revel in life instead of wasting it writing poetry:

> *Baal*: Was mußt du auch Gedichte schreiben! Wo das Leben so anständig ist: wenn man auf einem reißenden Strom auf dem Rücken hinschießt, nackt unter orangefarbenem Himmel und man sieht nichts als wie der Himmel violett wird, dann schwarz wie ein Loch wird.
>
> (B, 26)

> *Baal*: What do you have to write poems for anyway? When life's so decent: like when you lie on your back on a tearing current, shooting downstream, naked under an orange-coloured sky and you see nothing except the sky as it turns violet and then becomes black as a hole.

In the "Ballad of the Drowned Girl", a poem inspired by Johanna's suicide, Baal's imagination manages to hold together the beautiful and the deadly aspects of this symbol in its sensuous evocation of a corpse's slow drift down a stream. On two occasions Baal goes off to bathe in the river after particularly repulsive encounters with death – at a Corpus Christi procession and in the paupers' hospital. His immersion in the stream, by virtue of the ambiguity of the river symbol, is both a ritual surrender to death and at the same time a renewal and purification of his will to go on living.

Colours are much used in the play to convey the fullness of experience Baal derives from his confrontation with transience.

His favourite colours – white, black, red – all acquire the same ambiguity, as they are variously applied to images of life at one moment and of death at the next. White is the colour of appetising young flesh *and* of corpses, while black is associated both with growth in the womb and with rotting in the grave. These are not simply contrary associations, but mutually enriching ones. The whiteness of young skin is made the more appetising rather than less by the fact that its pallor conveys a message of *memento mori* which intensifies Baal's pleasure in the passing moment.[8] While Baal enjoys the sheer fact of the sky's permanence, he also enjoys it as a constantly changing showplace of colour and movement: were it not for the passing of time Baal would not be able to relish the sight of the sky sometimes filled with clouds, sometimes with stars, sometimes empty, or variously pale, dark, green, orange, purple, yellow, violet, apricot. These striking, but truly observed colours convey the intensity of Baal's perception of his world. The simple sentence-structures in which they occur give full weight to each individual image, just as, on a larger scale, the "balladesque" composition of the play as a sequence of short scenes also helps to suggest the repleteness of Baal's life, because it picks out only moments of particular intensity which, taken together, give an impression of kaleidoscopic variety. As well as giving his hero a sensuousness of language (what one of his victims describes as his "verflucht wundervolles Geschwätz" – "his bloody wonderful chat", *B*, 20) to convey the vividness of Baal's perception of the world, Brecht also creates a richly textured environment for him to respond to. Most of the people he meets are what one would call "colourful" characters – the indignant but understanding landlady with her earthy, comical mixture of metaphor, slang and dialect, the particularly vulgar and cynical exploiters, Mech and Mjurk, the tough lumberjacks in whose hut he dies. The play operates with stark contrasts: in one scene Baal is shown composing a poem in celebration of summer as the zenith of life ("Red. Scarlet. Voracious" – *B*, 34) while in the background there can be heard a beggar's hurdy-gurdy, symbol of life's monotony and exiguousness. The contrasts in Baal's consciousness acquire an almost Baroque grotesqueness and antithetical sharpness in the poor-house scene, where a baby cries in the background as a group of cancerous, mad or syphilitic adults carouse, squabble and attempt to fornicate in the foreground. By these various means Baal is given a heightened, at times melodramatic, world to live in, in order to suggest the

intensity of experience which Brecht imagines could be achieved by
a man who never for one moment forgets that in living he is dying.[9]

Baal challenges the traditional emphases of *Vanitas* poetry.
Whereas the sinful, ugly or impermanent features of temporal
existence were once cited to persuade men to turn their minds away
from the delusions of this world and towards the glory of the next,
Baal urges positive acceptance of the transitoriness, ugliness and so-
called evil of life as sources of pleasure, amusement and heightened
awareness. Brecht's presentation of Baal's life aims to unhinge our
normal moral judgements. The various ways in which he suggests
the exciting texture of Baal's experiences are part of this strategy.
The constant focus on the fact of his transience also contributes to
the task of moral subversion, as does the lack of morality in many of
Baal's competitors, since this makes him appear to be simply more
successful at playing life's dirty games than others. Where his
victims are not seen to merit rough treatment because of their moral
faults, the characters' own weakness or stupidity make it seem that
they share at least some of the blame for Baal's exploitation of them.
This applies to Johannes and Johanna, Emilie, Sophie and Ekart
who are all willing victims in the sense that they all feel a degree of
erotic attraction to Baal's animal vitality. Ekart's fate is that of a
Pied Piper who is killed by a rat, since it is he who first challenges
Baal to shake off the last vestiges of attachment to life in the city in
order to confront fully the oneness of life and death in nature. In the
event he proves not to be strong enough to live with the ruthless
vision of life which he himself conjures up at the beginning. Yet it is
not the case that no strong objections are raised in the play to Baal's
conduct. The scene where he leaves the pregnant Sophie completely
alone in the dark forest, for example, ends with her screams of terror.
Baal's later desertion in *his* extremity by the woodcutters, however,
does not so much suggest that some kind of natural moral order is
punishing Baal for his deviancy from its laws, as confirm that he was
right in believing that no individual *really* cares for another. The
callousness of the woodcutters towards the dying Baal seems only to
be a particularly clear instance of existential isolation and mutual
indifference. Yet Baal is himself not completely immune from
remorse. The drowning Johanna stays in his memory for a long
time, so that he is compelled to write the "Ballad of the Drowned
Girl" to exorcise this particular "Gespenst" ("ghost", *B*, 74). His
murder of Ekart both produces an immediate sense of shock in him
and returns to haunt him in his dying minutes. Yet these "scruples"

are only introduced into the play in order to be trampled down. Taken as a whole, the play argues that moral considerations are simply a means of evading the imperative of the appetites, a form of weakness which must be overcome if the human animal is not to be prevented from living life to the full by the spurious illusions of communal bonds conjured up by his fear of existential isolation.[10] This movement "beyond" morality is very clearly the effect achieved through the presentation of Baal's dying moments:

> [*Stille*]
> *Baal*: Mama! Ekart soll weggehen, der Himmel ist auch so verflucht nah da, zum Greifen, es ist alles wieder tropfnaß. Schlafen. Eins. Zwei. Drei. Vier. Man erstickt hier ja. Draußen muß es hell sein. Ich will hinaus. [*Hebt sich*] Ich werde hinausgehen. Lieber Baal. [*Scharf*] Ich bin keine Ratte. Es muß draußen hell sein. Lieber Baal. Zur Tür kommt man noch. Knie hat man noch, in der Tür ist es besser. Verflucht! Lieber Baal! [*Er kriecht auf allen Vieren zur Schwelle*] Sterne . . . hm. [*Er kriecht hinaus*]
>
> (*B*, 92)

> [*Silence*]
> *Baal*: Mamma! Tell Ekart to go away, the sky's so damned near, close enough to touch, everything's dripping wet again. Try sleeping. One. Two. Three. Four. You can't breathe in here. It must be bright outside. I want to go out. [*Raises himself*] I shall go out. Dear Baal. [*Sharply*] I am *not* a rat. It must be bright outside. Dear Baal. One can still reach the door. One still has knees, it's better at the door. Damnation! Dear Baal! [*He crawls on all fours to the threshold*] Stars . . . hmm. [*He crawls outside*]

Although Baal experiences familiar human conflicts he does not allow them to destroy him. At the last he is given heroic stature by his ability to push aside his fears and remorse and to devote his last strength to crawling out of the hut for a last glimpse of the stars. His dying grunt of satisfaction is the reward for the brutal consistency of his life.[11]

Baal has strengths and weaknesses which are connected with its nature as a fantasy of mastery over life. The task of imagining a life which would succeed in transforming what are usually the causes of pain into sources of pleasure produced a play of varied, nuanced moods and richness of texture. The underlying symbolic action of a duel or dance with death meant that the biography had thematic unity. Whether this unity, which is conveyed through the ambiguities of the imagery, can be successfully rendered in theatrical performance is, however, questionable. The adoption of Baal's perspective on life, which is the source of the play's colour and intensity, unfortunately resulted in too little attention being paid to the development of the other characters. All too often the dialogue lacks any true dramatic tension because Baal's *Größe*, his strength, vitality and capacity for intense experience are not matched by equal qualities in those around him or sufficiently challenged by opposing forces. Dramatic balance is best achieved in those scenes where Baal's powers are clearly confronted by those of his true antagonist, Death, as in "Trees in the Evening" (*B*, 51), where Baal's confidence is shaken by the sight of the felled trees (the mighty who are fallen), or in the poor-house scene where the ravages of death and decay leer at Baal from all sides, eventually putting him to flight. Although the size of the problems Baal confronts calls for a figure of superhuman stature to master them, and although the oppressive experience of transience makes it attractive to suspend disbelief in his ability to get the better of the problem, the fantasy is ultimately unsatisfying. Casper Neher commented aptly to Brecht, "Dein Baal ist so gut als wie 10 Liter Schnaps" ("Your *Baal* is as good as ten litres of gin" – *dbB*, 99); it is a play which offers temporary intoxication but leaves behind a nasty hangover. Precisely because it would take a character as implausible as Baal to achieve the imagined mastery over life, the play only serves to magnify the lack of such mastery attainable by normal men. Despite its celebration of human vitality, an important thing to do in the dark months of the war and its aftermath,[12] the play does not in the end leave one any better equipped to cope with the complicated muddle of egotism and altruism, desire and apathy, strength and weakness which is what constitutes real experience for most of us, as it did for Brecht himself.

Despite its faults the emotional vigour of Brecht's first play has lasted well, and it continues to enjoy successful productions. It is also indispensable reading for anyone who would understand Brecht's development. It is interesting, for example, that the fascination with *Größe* ("grandeur") evident in his earlier nationalist enthusiasm was capable of detaching itself from an abstract and general object and attaching itself to a particular individual. If this was possible, the process could presumably be reversed, as indeed happened some ten years later. It is also worth knowing that Brecht began, not as a realist first and foremost, but as a subjective rebel both against the limitations of an imperfect world and against the constraints, compromises and complexities of psychological reality. The emotional energy apparent in *Baal* enabled him later to create effective characters and situations which manage to live theatrically despite the intellectual burden they have to bear as agents of the historical dialectic. Brecht's early sympathy with the transient individual, and his understanding that men may be ruthless in the pursuit of happiness simply because they are "only here once"[13] provided a counterpoise to the tendency of ideology to encourage a person to take an abstract, oversimplified view of behaviour. It is also important to appreciate the independence and irreverence of Brecht's early attitudes to prevailing literary trends and tastes, since it is these qualities of spirit which later enabled him to resist pressures to conform to the formulae of "socialist realism". On the other hand, the powerful will to master reality which works *with* Baal in this play was equally capable of turning against him and his like when a different kind of mastery became the goal.

3 *Drums in the Night*

THE PROBLEM OF UNITY

Drums in the Night, although written after *Baal*, was the first of Brecht's plays to be performed. The première at the Munich Kammerspiele in September 1922 was such a success that the production was quickly followed by another, in December of the same year, at the prestigious Deutsches Theater in Berlin. The influential Berlin critic, Herbert Jhering, declared that this play had changed the literary complexion of Germany overnight and, on the strength of it, awarded Brecht the coveted Kleist Prize for the most promising young dramatist of 1922. While most reviewers agreed that it was an important play, they were generally more qualified in their praise than Jhering.[1] The commonest criticism directed against the play was that it lacked unity, either thematic, stylistic or dramatic. It was variously objected that the play began as a symbolic representation of the class conflicts which erupted in the revolution of 1918–19, but then lost its symbolic clarity in the later acts; or that the play initially contained a dynamic dramatic conflict, but later petered out in static declamation; or that the style was realistic or even naturalistic at first, but later veered towards Expressionism. If these various charges of disunity were correct, Jhering surely cannot have been justified in awarding the Kleist Prize to the author of the play. In view of such criticisms, which have been repeated by later, usually Marxist critics,[2] any discussion of *Drums in the Night* must clearly centre on the question of the play's artistic unity.

What distinguished Jhering from the majority of contemporary reviewers was his responsiveness to innovation and his relative lack of preconceptions and prejudices. Underlying the complaints about the alleged lack of unity in *Drums in the Night* one can detect the unease of the critics who, confronted with the novelty of Brecht's work, tried to assimilate it to themes, methods and developments with which they were familiar. The fact that many Expressionist plays had dealt with the themes of revolt and revolution, for example, created a predisposition to regard a play set against the background of the recent revolutionary disturbances in Germany as a "drama of revolution" – and then to complain that the action lacked clear and coherent significance as a political allegory. In fact, however, Brecht had written a drama of personal relationships as these were shaped by the pressures of the times, which is something quite different from attempting to symbolise the political conflicts of the revolution through the conflicts of a love-triangle. *Drums in the Night* did have a general statement to make about the times, but its concern was with the "hysteria of the German Revolution",[3] a mood affecting people of quite contrary political persuasions, rather than with the political analysis of the course of the revolution. The plot, which turns on the efforts of the ex-infantryman Andreas Kragler (who has spent the last four years as a prisoner-of-war in Africa) to win back the love of Anna Balicke (now pregnant by and engaged to marry the successful young businessman, Friedrich Murk), brings Kragler into contact with people from opposite ends of the social scale and of diametrically opposed political attitudes. What unifies this plot is Kragler's struggle to gain control over the hysterical tendencies in those around him and within himself which threaten to frustrate his reunion with Anna. Those critics who, for quite understandable reasons, were preoccupied with the outward social and political differences between the groups with which Kragler collides, were thereby prevented from perceiving that the unifying action of the play was of this inner, emotional kind.

Inappropriate preconceptions in the minds of the reviewers also account for the complaints that the play lacked stylistic unity. At the time there was a widespread hope and expectation amongst critics and audiences alike, who had grown tired of the static, declamatory manner of Expressionist plays, that the drama of Expressionism would be superseded by a more dynamic type of play: one that would reinstate the neglected conventions of realism. What many critics saw, or thought they saw, in *Drums in the Night* was an attempt to make the desired turn away from Expressionism and towards realism. These critics praised the supposed realism of the early acts, but added, condescendingly, that the young author had failed to shake off the bad habits of Expressionism as thoroughly as they would have liked, to the detriment of the second half of the play. In fact, Brecht's play did mark a break with the declamatory, hortatory type of Expressionist play,[4] even in those acts where the critics complained that it did not, but the break did not take the form of the expected and desired return to a conventional type of realism. Both in its supposedly realistic and its "Expressionist" scenes the diction is stylised and handled ironically, with the purpose of characterising and criticising the speakers. In other words, where Expressionism apparently intrudes into the play, it is a manner which belongs to the characters, and not to the author. What the puzzled critics took to be an involuntary mixture of styles was in reality a conscious technique for the distanced presentation of different types of behaviour, a first example of the deictic method for which Brecht was later to become famous but which caused quite understandable confusion at its first appearance.

The focus in *Drums in the Night* on individual emotions rather than on political issues, which must also come as a surprise to any present-day reader whose picture of Brecht has been formed from a knowledge of the later plays or theories, is quite typical of the way the young Brecht looked at the world. At that time he regarded politics, particularly those of a revolutionary nature, with indifference, even disdain. His personal "bolshiness" (during his short period in the army he came on parade wearing yellow gloves!)[5] made him more sympathetic to people on the political left than on the right, and led to his giving temporary refuge to a revolutionary fleeing from the Bavarian White Guard and to his being elected to serve very briefly on a local "workers' and soldiers' council" during the revolution. By his own confession, however, he lacked political convictions, enthusiasm or understanding at that time (*GW*, **20**, 25). The strict regime and the rationing introduced by the Bolsheviks in Russia held no appeal for him: "Ich danke für Obst und bitte um ein Auto" ("You can keep fruit; I want a motor car" *T*, 61) – and he dismissed revolutionary devotion to a principle as a ridiculous, "schoolmasterly" approach to life (*GW*, **20**, 7). But if politics did not fire his heart in those days, love did. In particular, his love for Paula ("Bi") Banholzer, the pretty mother of his first illegitimate child, was, as he put it, the "centre" of his life.[6] This early preference for the private over the public sphere of life was also reflected in his current views on theatre. While working on the revision of *Drums in the Night*, for example, he recorded his dislike of the tragedian Hebbel's practice of using conflicts between individuals as a means of illuminating the operation of historical laws. Brecht wanted to "turn on its head" what he took to be Hebbel's conception of the relative importance of the general and the particular in drama. He argued that an individual's reactions to events were much more interesting than any impersonal principles which his case might serve to illustrate: "what is important is not to create dramas of grand principles and ideas, which reveal the mechanisms of the world and the habits of fate, but simple plays which narrate the fates of individuals, individuals who should be what we gain from the plays" (*GW*, **15**, 50). What Brecht formulated abstractly here, he put into practice in *Drums in the Night*. Ironically, Brecht was later to move towards a position similar to the one he decried so vehemently in this early note, for his "mature" plays resemble Hebbel's in as far as they too contrive to analyse the large-scale historical and social processes operating on the lives of individuals. However, as far as understanding his early plays goes, it is best to put one's knowledge of this subsequent development to the back of one's mind.

"GHOSTS"

Brecht considered that his fellow countrymen were possessed of a fateful tendency to romanticise reality. This had led them into the First World War, eager to die in "grand opera" (*GW*, **20**, 11) for the theatrically-inclined Kaiser Wilhelm II. At the outbreak of the war the schoolboy Brecht had shared in the patriotic enthusiasm which swept through the country, and had even done his best to nourish such sentiments through his poems, short stories and articles in newspapers. But whereas his attitude changed when he began to understand the reality of war, it did not seem to him that other Germans had learned the same disillusioning lesson. After the war was over they continued to exhibit the same romantic tendency in their readiness to die for equally grand phrases on the barricades of the revolution. In order to concentrate attention on the emotional life of his characters, rather than on the events going on around them, Brecht had to devise some way of giving their inner life striking theatrical expression. The means he employed in *Drums in the Night* to emphasise and define his characters' tendency to get carried away by a hysterical, melodramatic view of their "fate", was that of constructing the plot as a parody of a familiar, traditional ghost-story which had been recreated for the modern public by the writers of romantic ballads.[7] The best known example of the ghostly tale travestied in the play is probably Bürger's "Lenore", which tells of the return from the wars of a ghostly soldier to claim his faithless bride. In Bürger's morally edifying version the ghostly soldier returns to punish the girl for her loss of faith *in God*. In Eichendorff's more truly romantic version, "Die Hochzeitsnacht", the vengeful knight carries off, on the very night of her wedding, the woman who has been unfaithful *to him*. This is the variant of the tale Brecht follows when he has Andreas Kragler, who has been reported dead, return from the war on the evening of Anna Balicke's engagement to Friedrich Murk. The premonitions, the moonlit night, the idea of spectral revenge, the "ride" in the dark, all these elements are taken over by Brecht from the ballad tradition, but his treatment of them is characteristically ironic, even grotesque. Because the parody of the ghost-story is such an important means of conveying the unity of the inner action of the play, it will require rather detailed analysis.

The ghost motif is introduced unobtrusively in the opening lines of the play,[8] when Herr Balicke, Anna's father, rants about the "bloody sentimentality" of his wife and daughter whose attachment to the memory of Kragler has made them resist Balicke's plan to marry off Anna to Friedrich Murk, a man whose talents and money would be useful to the Balicke family business. In reply to Balicke's angry assertion that Kragler has "rotted away" by now, his wife exclaims "Wenn er wiederkommt!" ("What if he comes back!" - *TN*, 9). The ambiguity of the verb *wiederkommen* which can simply mean "to return" or, more ominously, "to return from the grave", carries the first hint of superstition, which is quickly reinforced by her next question: "But what if he *does* come back – this corpse you say is rotting now, back from heaven or hell? 'The name is Kragler' – who's going to tell him then that he's a corpse, and that his girl is lying in someone else's bed?" (*TN*, 10).[9] The strong undertow of superstition in Frau Balicke's feelings needs to be borne in mind, in order to appreciate her hysterical reaction when Kragler *does* actually appear in her living room at the end of the act.

Anna Balicke shares her mother's superstitious anxiety about taking Murk in place of Kragler. This is made clear when Balicke becomes angry with her: "That's just your damned fear of ghosts! Get yourself a man, and you won't need to be afraid of ghosts at night any more" (*TN*, 12). The psychological basis of her anxiety is guilt and an inability simply to bury the past. Her memories of Kragler make her half-hearted about her relationship to Murk, to whom she confesses her fears: "Hush! There goes a train, travelling through the night! Do you hear it? Sometimes I'm frightened he's on his way. It gives me shivers all down my back" (*TN*, 16). Murk too thinks of Kragler as a "ghost" whose presence haunts the Balicke household and threatens his relationship with Anna. At one juncture he points angrily at Kragler's picture on the wall and exclaims, "Aber da hängt er und da ist er und da geht er um" ("But there he hangs and there he is and there he prowls about" – *TN*, 15); the verb *umgehen* is the one used to describe the haunting of a ghost. The worry underlying Murk's anger at the continuing influence exerted by the "ghost" Kragler has a different nuance from Anna's. When he arrives for the engagement he is already "cheesy faced" because of the shooting that has broken out in the city. As someone who is clearly identifiable as a bourgeois, he is naturally afraid of the revolutionary violence that is spreading in Berlin with the return to the city of thousands of weary, discontented soldiers, many of them still armed. This general anxiety about "Spartacus" (as the Communists dubbed themselves) is given an acute personal focus when he thinks that Kragler, whose girlfriend he has made pregnant, might be among the returning soldiery. Because of Murk's double guilt, as an exploiter and as a usurper, Kragler is firmly linked in his mind with the revolution. Thus, when he sees a figure standing in the dark yard between Balicke's home and factory, Murk's first thought is of "Spartacus". Through this association, the ghost motif, as used by both Murk and Herr Balicke, acquires overtones of the "spectre of Communism".[10] This link is expressed most clearly in the second act when Balicke refers to the revolutionaries outside as Kragler's "dark companions", and Murk comments, "Close the curtains! Ghosts!" (*TN*, 47).

Throughout the first act the ghost motif is used cleverly to define the emotional state of Anna, Frau Balicke and Murk. As in Ibsen's tragedy *Ghosts*, it serves as a metaphor for the continuing influence of the supposedly dead Kragler on their lives, but it is also used in its literal sense to indicate how their feelings of guilt shade off through barely suppressed hysteria into actual superstition. During this act Herr Balicke appears to be alone in not sharing the superstitious tendencies of the others. But Brecht subtly undermines the impression of confident cynicism which Balicke is at pains to create. Thus, when Murk directs his attention to the man in the yard and expresses his own association of the figure with Spartacus, Balicke retorts with a brusque "Nonsense, there's none of that sort of thing here" (*TN*, 19), but then turns away from the window, "disagreeably affected". Just as his action gives the lie to his words here, so on other occasions the manner of his speech subverts its overt meaning. The very assertiveness of such statements as "Nobody comes back from Heaven" reveals the unease it is intended to conceal and dispel. It is clear that the urgency with which he presses for a speedy engagement of Anna and Murk – and for a speedy marriage to follow – is motivated by a double anxiety: that Anna may be pregnant by Murk, and that Kragler may very well return along with the other discharged and "missing" soldiers. Balicke's all-too-jolly toasts are accompanied by frequent mopping of sweat from his brow. In other words, Balicke's closeness to hysteria is suggested throughout the act by the manner of his attempts to suppress it in himself and others. It therefore comes as no surprise that he is the first to exclaim, "The ghost, Mother" (*TN*, 32) when Kragler enters the "Picadillybar" in Act II.

Although he does not appear in person until the end of the first act, Kragler "haunts" the whole Balicke household from the beginning. In addition to its simple expositional function, the ghost motif is used in this act to introduce two important elements into the play before Kragler's first entrance. The first of these is irony: we are encouraged to doubt the words of the characters, to look beneath the surface of behaviour for hidden contradictions, and to suspect that things will not turn out as they plan. The other main function of this motif here is to foreshadow the main conflict of the play, the conflict Kragler experiences between his tendency to emotionalism and his attempts to control it, by introducing it through the behaviour of other characters. The value of this technique is twofold. First, it enables us to recognise the main conflict as such when it appears: Kragler's inner tensions conform to and confirm an already established pattern. Second, by showing that these other characters, principally Balicke and Murk, are caused considerable difficulties by this conflict of emotionalism and control, Brecht makes us aware of their vulnerability. This in turn prepares the ground for an ironic presentation of Kragler's failure to perceive his antagonists' weaknesses, but it also holds out the hope that Kragler can win his battle against them if only he can win his struggle with himself.

Kragler appears in the Balicke household just after Murk and Anna have left, in indecent haste, for the safety of the bright lights of the "Picadillybar". The first person Kragler meets on entering the home is Frau Balicke. Immediately, the ghost motif is introduced, first implicitly through Frau Balicke's terror, then explicitly in Kragler's attempts to ease the situation with humour:

Der Mann: Mein Name ist Kragler.

Frau Balicke: [*stützt sich mit schwachen Knieen auf den Spiegeltisch*] Herr Je . . .

Kragler: Na, was schauen Sie denn so überirdisch? Auch Geld für Kränze hinausgeschmissen? Schade drum! Melde gehorsamst: habe mich in Algier als Gespenst etabliert. Aber jetzt hat der Leichnam mörderisch Appetit. Ich könnte Würmer fressen! . . . [*Schenkt Wein in ein Glas*] Wein! Nierensteiner! Also für ein Gespenst bin ich doch ziemlich lebhaft!

(*TN*, 24–5)

The Man: The name is Kragler.

Frau Balicke: [*goes weak at the knees, supports herself against the dresser*] Holy Jes . . .

Kragler: What's this then, why the supernatural stare? Have you chucked money away on wreaths too? Pity! Please to report, Ma'am, set myself up as a ghost in Algiers. But now the corpse has a murderous appetite. I could eat worms! . . . [*Pours a glass of wine*] Wine! Nierensteiner! Well, for a ghost I'm pretty lively, don't you think!

Despite his jocularly macabre tone, Kragler's references to himself as a ghost have a foundation in real anxiety. As the play progresses it becomes increasingly clear that he is afraid that his long period of absence and the privations of a prisoner-of-war camp may have made it impossible for him to take up his former existence again. In particular, he fears that he may have "died" as the object of Anna's love. He also fears that his old self may have been destroyed by his terrible experiences, because in order to cope with the onslaught of the war on his sensibility he had to allow all his normal moral and emotional responses to atrophy: "One man goes mad in the sun; it's not me. Two men fall into a water-hole; I carry on sleeping. I shoot niggers. I eat grass, I'm a ghost" (*TN*, 46). In Kragler's usage, the ghost motif denotes his fear that he may have lost his identity in the war. This is why his first words on entering the Balicke home are an assertion of identity – "The name is Kragler". But, as with Balicke's assertiveness and forced jollity, Kragler's words are an expression of concealed anxiety; he is really whistling in the dark. Thus from the moment Kragler enters he is involved in a struggle between his emotions and his attempts to control them. The remainder of the play develops this conflict.

During the confrontation between Kragler, the Balickes and Murk in the second act, the ghost motif is used to mark ironically the constantly shifting balance of power as the characters variously gain and lose control over their emotions. When they arrive in the "Picadillybar", the Balickes and Murk are already in a state of nervous excitement. The women tremble, Herr Balicke sweats through yet another shirt and Anna narrates an ominous incident that occurred during her journey here with Murk: the horse pulling their carriage "froze" with terror and refused to move off until forced to do so by Murk. Their overheated imaginations are further inflamed when Kragler appears in the doorway of the café, accompanied by an icy blast of wind that blows out the candles. Not surprisingly, they panic, fleeing to the other side of the room and leaving Anna, who is too frightened to move, seated alone at the table. The outward tumult created amongst the panicking bourgeois is a quite farcically inappropriate response to a character who is himself in an equal state of turmoil internally. Ironically, however, it is their fear that Kragler has come to play the part of an avenging spirit that forces the reluctant Kragler further into a role which, for different reasons, neither he nor the others want him to play. Faced with their response, Kragler's first and only thought is to prove, particularly to Anna, that he is *not* a ghost. But one ironic consequence follows from another for the unfortunate Kragler. Because he is so preoccupied with assuring Anna, and being assured by her, that he is no ghost, he fails to register, far less discuss, the fact that Anna has a problem which may be a greater obstacle to their being united than the physical and emotional changes which Kragler has undergone, namely the fact that she has become pregnant by Murk. As a consequence he is taken completely by surprise when, at the end of the act Anna, who has been drawing closer to him, suddenly rejects him without explanation, because Murk reminds her, by a hint, of the fact that she is pregnant. Thus Kragler's fear of being treated as a ghost makes him unable to grasp and control the situation he is in, and so exposes him to the very experience of being thrust back into limbo which has been obsessing him all along.

The action of these first two acts follows quite closely the main lines of the traditional tale it travesties. Traditionally, the soldier who returns as a ghost is taken for a real person; Kragler, by contrast, is a living man who is desperate not to be taken for a ghost, but who discovers to his distress that everyone seems determined to force him into just such a role. In the ballad tradition the ghostly soldier carries off his unfaithful bride without any difficulty; Kragler, on the other hand, has first to plead with Anna to go away with him, and, when she refuses to go, it is he who is physically carried off. The parody continues in the following acts with Anna having to pursue Kragler in a grotesque "Ride of the Valkyries" that replaces the moonlit ride of the traditional ballad in which the ghostly soldier gallops off to the grave with his bride mounted behind him.

Acts III and IV focus attention on Anna and Kragler respectively. In Act III Anna is subjected to opposing pulls by Murk, the waiter Manke and the reporter Babusch. Anna's aim is to find Kragler and to tell him about her pregnancy, but not with the intention of making a fresh start in their relationship. Because of her feelings of guilt she is intent on committing suicide or, as she puts it, "*Ja zum Nichts will ich*" ("I want to go into the void" – *TN*, 61). This continues the parody of the ballad tradition, since, instead of being carried off forcibly to the grave, she not only has to run through the streets in pursuit of her "ghost" but also intends to take her *own* life! The romantically inclined waiter Manke encourages her indulgence in melodramatic emotions, whereas the reporter Babusch tries to counteract this tendency by introducing a tone of ironic reasonableness. The act is weak because it is emotionally static. The conflict between reason and emotion is expressed through a simple confrontation of characters with opposing tendencies. The conflict of emotionalism with control does not run through any single character, as it does in the case of Kragler, and so is less interestingly presented than it was in Act II. Brecht himself tacitly admitted the weakness of Act III when he permitted any producer to omit the act "if it fails to work fluently and musically and to liven up the tempo" (*M*I, 394). On the other hand, without this act the audience would not be aware of the parallel between the attitudes of Anna and Kragler when they meet again in Act v.

The central conflict between emotion and control is more successfully developed in Act IV, where Kragler is shown trying to drown his sorrows in a cheap pub. The ghost motif is introduced as soon as he enters the bar, accompanied as in Act II by a rush of cold wind. Asked who he is, he replies with a "malevolent grin", "*Niemand*" ("Nobody" – *TN*, 69) thus retracting the assertion of identity he made when he first entered the Balicke household. This retraction signifies his resigned acceptance of the ghost-like status which the others appear to have accorded him. Kragler's bitter grin as he speaks this line is the first of many expressions in this act of the conflict between his emotions and his desire to control or disguise them. Under the promptings of the other drunks in the pub, Kragler begins to recount his experiences in Africa, drinking heavily as he does so. As he tells his story, his mood of self-pity finds varying forms of expression, sometimes as undisguised pathos, more usually as bitter cynicism.

The tensions in Kragler's mind are reflected in and affected by the attitudes of his audience, some of whom respond with greedy excitement to his "story", while others, particularly the bar-owner, a disillusioned revolutionary by the name of Glubb, try to play down the emotional effect of his account. This counterpoint of excitement and irony creates a parallel between this act and the previous one. But, whereas in Act III there was a simple confrontation of characters who embodied the opposing attitudes, Act IV is psychologically more complex and more interesting. Not only is Kragler's state of mind more contradictory than Anna's, so also is that of his principal antagonist in this act, Glubb. Underlying Kragler's cynical tone is a current of real pathos which occasionally forces its way to the surface. Equally, Glubb's sarcastic commentary does not spring from a lack of emotion, but from a desire to exacerbate and then harness both Kragler's bitter self-pity and the angry sympathy of the other drunks so as to redirect these feelings into the channel of violent action. Glubb is driven along by a sense of personal injury just as powerful as Kragler's, but he is more in control of his feelings, and so is able to use the feelings of others to suit his own ends. He allows Kragler to lead the group out into the streets, but it is really Glubb who, through his emotional manipulation, has established his leadership over this band of unlikely revolutionaries.

At the end of the act, when Kragler goes off to find the street-fighting, his motive is not a revolutionary desire to change the world for the better. Indeed, he does not believe that it is possible to remove the deep-seated causes of the suffering in the world:

Kragler: Hast du Unrecht gesagt, Bruder roter Herr? Was für ein Wort das ist! Unrecht! Macht euchs bequem auf dem Stern, es ist kalt hier und etwas finster, roter Herr, and keine Zeit für das Unrecht, die Welt ist zu alt für die bessere Zeit und Schnaps ist billiger und der Himmel ist vermietet, meine Lieben.

(TN, 74–5)

Kragler: Did you say injustice, Brother Red? What a word that is! Injustice! Make yourselves comfortable on this star, it's cold here and rather dark, Mister Red, and no time for injustice, the world is too old for things to get better and gin is cheaper and the heavens are rented out, my dear ones.

Kragler joins in the revolution because it offers him an opportunity for suicide in the grand manner. The barricades he regards simply as the best available place to express his self-pity in a romantic, nihilistic gesture:

Kragler: Pfeift es schon wieder? [*Duckt sich*] Ist es Spaß? Auf die Barrikaden mit dem Gespenst! [*Steht fest, zieht tief Luft ein*] Schlußmachen ist besser als Schnaps. Es ist kein Spaß. Verschwinden ist besser als schlafen.

(TN, 78)

Kragler: Are the bullets whistling again? [*He ducks*] Is it a joke? Onto the barricades with the ghost! [*Stands steady, takes a deep breath*] Making an end of things is better than gin. It's no joke. It's better to disappear than to sleep.

(TN, 78)

Only in one phrase does he show anything resembling a positive commitment to the struggle, and even this is immediately undermined by a series of words and gestures which stress the suicidal nature of his motive:

Kragler: [*auf dem Stuhl, hantiert an der Lampe, einem vorsintflutig-lichen Fossil*] Jetzt pfeift es wieder, meine Lieben.

Oben in der Frühe oder wie ersäufte Katzen auf
dem Asphalt.

Die Anderen: [*schreien*] Oben in der Früh, Andree!
Kragler: [*löscht die Lampe aus*] Oder wie ersäufte Katzen!
Manke: Vorwärts, Auguste!
Der besoffene
Mensch: [*deutet mit dem Finger auf Marie*] Eine Kanaille
engelsgut schwamm mit ihm durch die Tränenflut.
Kragler: [*läßt sich herabgleiten*] Ich bin ein Leichnam, den
könnt ihr haben! [*Bös*] Her mit euch, an die Brust
mit euch, in die Zeitungen mit uns.

(*TN*, 78–9)

Kragler: [*on the chair, fiddling with the lamp, an ancient relic*]
They're whistling again, my dear ones. On top by
dawn, or like drowned cats on the asphalt.
The others: [*shouting*] On top by dawn, Andree!
Kragler: [*extinguishes the lamp*] Or like drowned cats!
Manke: Forward, Auguste!
The Drunk: [*points with his finger at Marie*] A ratbag sweet and
good swam with him through the tearful flood.
Krager: [*lets himself slide down*] I'm a corpse, you can have it!
[*Angrily*] Come here, come to my breast, into the
newspaper district with us.

The re-appearance of the ghost motif at this crucial juncture
underlines the existential nature of Kragler's decision to join the
fighting. Now that he has given up his hopes of re-establishing his
identity as Anna's lover, he intends simply to throw his life away.
The travesty of the traditional ballad is quite clear: having failed to
carry off his bride, this ghostly soldier is resigned to going back to the
grave to which everyone including Anna appears to want to consign
him.

Act V brings Kragler's reunion with Anna and his parting from
the revolutionaries. Even before his meeting with Anna Kragler has
already lost interest in making the romantic gesture of dying on the
barricades, and is inclined instead to take the more direct and sordid
course of simply hanging himself. On seeing Anna, however, his first
impulse is to revert to the notion of going along with the
revolutionaries, possibly because the sight of her makes him feel the
need to give his apparently ruined life some semblance of dignity, if

not purpose. Yet Anna is really more important to him than any such vapid, self-destructive gesture. When he hears that she is pregnant, the shock almost makes him have recourse to another romantic gesture, that of committing a crime of passion by stabbing her. Anna's feelings of guilt make her equally disposed to melodramatic posturing, so she exaggerates the extent to which her feelings have changed towards Kragler in order to provoke him into just such an act of revenge. Thus even Anna, like Murk and Glubb, plays on Kragler's sense of injury in order to drive him into the romantic role of an avenging spirit. Both are jerked out of this mood of romantic hysteria when the other revolutionaries, fearing that Kragler's preoccupation with Anna will prevent him from going along with them, attempt to murder her. In the ensuing turmoil the deeper feelings of the couple force their way out through the clutter of clichés which have obscured or distorted these feelings up till now. Having regained real emotional contact with Anna, Kragler has no further interest in the revolution which he now scorns as a pointless romanticisation of reality:

Kragler: Fast ersoffen seid ihr in euren Tränen über mich und ich habe nur mein Hemd gewaschen mit euren Tränen! Mein Fleisch soll im Rinnstein verwesen, daß eure Idee in den Himmel kommt? Seid ihr besoffen?

Anna: Andree! Es macht nichts!

Kragler: [*sieht ihr nicht ins Gesicht, trollt sich herum, langt sich an den Hals*] Ich hab's bis zum Hals. [*Er lacht ärgerlich*] Es ist gewöhnliches Theater. Es sind Bretter und ein Papiermond und dahinter die Fleischbank, die allein ist leibhaftig. [*Er läuft wieder herum, die Arme hängend bis zum Boden und so fischt er die Trommel aus der Schnapskneipe*] Sie haben ihre Trommel liegen lassen. [*Er haut drauf*] Der halbverfaulte Liebhaber oder die Macht der Liebe, das Blutbad im Zeitungsviertel oder Rechtfertigung eines Mannes durch sich selbst, der Pfahl im Fleisch oder Tiger im Morgengrauen.

(*TN*, 93–4)

Kragler: You almost drowned in your tears for me and I've just washed my shirt in your tears. Is my flesh to rot in the gutter so that your idea can get into heaven? Are you drunk?

Anna: Andree! It doesn't matter!
Kragler: [*doesn't look her in the face, slouches around, puts his hand to his
             throat*] I've had it up to here. [*He laughs in annoyance*] It's
             just the usual playacting. There are boards and a paper
             moon and behind it all the butcher's bench, that's the
             only thing that's real. [*He runs around again, his arms
             hanging to the ground and thus hooks up the drum from the pub*]
             They've left their drum lying here. [*He beats it*] The Half-
             rotted Lover or The Power of Love, The Bloodbath in
             the Newspaper District or A Man's Justification of
             Himself, The Thorn in the Flesh or Tigers at Dawn.

Through this attack on the melodramatic illusions to which the
others are still subject, Kragler is very gradually gaining control
over the emotionalism in himself which has so nearly led him into
senseless destruction and self-destruction. As one might expect, the
speech contains, in the phrase "the half-rotted lover", the last
explicit allusion to the ghost-story from which Kragler is now finally
dissociating himself. The last image of the play, which shows the
lovers walking off to begin a new life together, tacitly completes the
travesty of the gloomy ballad tale that has structured the plot
throughout.

The transition from emotionalism to self-control is not an easy or
a quick one for Kragler. Even as he pours scorn on the romanticism
of his companions and of the audience who he believes would gladly
send him to a romantic death, Kragler is in the process of fighting
against the tendency to romanticism in himself. His beating on the
drum both punctuates in fairground style his sarcastic list of
melodramatic subtitles for his "story" and expresses anger, as much
with himself as with his companions and would-be exploiters. His
struggle to overcome emotionalism is itself evidently strongly
coloured by emotion. Thus his mocking laughter almost chokes him
as he stumbles about before hurling the revolutionaries' drum (torn
from the orchestrina in the cheap pub) at the red paper-lantern
which has glowed throughout the play to suggest a connection
between the hero and the romance of revolution or bloody revenge.
As he turns away from the revolution, he says of himself, "I'm a
swine and the swine's going home". The epithet echoes insults
which have been showered on Kragler from various directions
during the action, but also his own descriptions of the physical and
moral degradation he had to endure in Africa. His "cynical" words,

his choking laughter, his stumbling movements, his beating of the drum, all express a mixture of reasonable self-justification for choosing survival, and the self-mockery of a man who still feels the attraction of romantic nihilism even as he is committing himself to the compromises and imperfections of everyday reality. Only by stages does Kragler's tone change from overheated cynicism to one of real tenderness for Anna, and only gradually do they come closer to one another physically before walking off in an embrace. This final exit, which completes the parody of the romantic ghost ballad, also marks the completion of the unifying action of the play, the conflict between emotionalism and control, which it was the function of the ghost motif to articulate.

Several functions are performed, then, in the play by the parody of the ballad tradition of the ghostly soldier. It structures and unifies the action, it gives enlarged, theatrical expression to the inner life of the characters, and it ensures a distanced, critical portrayal of the hysterical mood of the times. It is both unfortunate and illuminating that Brecht's later emendations of the text included the excision of certain important passages in which the ghost motif appeared. The most crucial of these omissions is in Kragler's speech just before he leaves the cheap pub with the other drunks. In the original the speech ran as follows:

> *Kragler*: Are they whistling again? [*He ducks*] Is it a joke? Onto the barricades with the ghost! [*Stands steady, takes a deep breath*] Making an end of things is better than gin. It's no joke. It's better to disappear than to sleep.

In the 1954 version all that remains of this speech is the simple question, "Are they whistling again?". By this omission Brecht obscured both the suicidal and the romantic nature of Kragler's decision to join the fighting. The change enabled him to suggest that Kragler's refusal in Act V to go on with the revolutionaries was an act of betrayal, a retraction of a moral commitment rather than a common-sense decision to live with Anna rather than be mown down while offering pointless resistance to the heavier fire-power of the government's artillery. This suppression of Kragler's existential motives for going to the barricades also inevitably obscured the dramatic unity of the play as a conflict of emotionalism with control. Brecht's commentaries on *Drums in the Night*, also written out of embarrassment at the sceptical view of politics taken in the original version, have only added to the confusion.

FUNCTIONAL FORM

Apart from obscuring Kragler's motivation, the alterations made
by Brecht in Act IV to reduce the level of hysteria amongst the
"revolutionaries" also did serious damage to the structure of the
play, for they blurred the many carefully drawn parallels in the
original between the behaviour of the bourgeois and that of their
enemies. Act II and Act IV are both set in bars, the one opulent, the
other not, in both acts the clients of the bars are very drunk. Because
they are so drunk both bourgeois and down-and-outs alike respond
very emotionally to Kragler's story, but no member of either group
is really able to share Kragler's experiences. While the Balickes are
only able to see Kragler as a resentful front-line soldier, his drinking
companions in the cheap pub regard him, with more sympathy but
just as little understanding, as a victim of injustice. Because the
others generalise his experiences, converting them into terms with
which they are themselves familiar, Kragler remains emotionally
isolated from both groups, trapped inside the circle of his painful,
obsessive memories, experiencing with personal immediacy sufferings which his words cannot re-create in his audience. But not only
does the incomprehension of the "revolutionaries" parallel that of
the bourgeois, it is also made clear that both groups in their different ways exploit Kragler's sufferings. In Act IV the colporteur
Bulltrotter plies Kragler with gin in order to encourage him to talk,
and thus to have the pleasure of listening to his "real life story"
"leibhaftige Geschichte". Although the nature of the exploitation is
different, Bulltrotter's treatment of Kragler is no better than
Balicke's in Act II, when he, too, poured gin into Kragler so as to
make him talk about his sufferings in Africa rather than act to
revenge them. Kragler is aware of the lack of true consideration for
his feelings underlying the drunks' interest in his tale. His resentment at the eager fascination aroused by his pain comes out in such
phrases as "You know, you only need to throw cats down from a
wall" or, later, "Have you got free tickets?" The attitude of the
"red" bar-owner Glubb, although different from that of the drunks,
is also presented critically, as being a form of exploitation of
Kragler. Glubb, whose motive in joining the revolutionaries' fight is
his personal desire to repay the destruction of his property with the
destruction of the property of others, seditiously manipulates the
emotions of Kragler and the drunks listening to his story so that they
will come and risk their lives fighting alongside him.

The parallels between Kragler's experiences at the hands of the bourgeois and at the hands of their enemies produce even fiercer ironies in Act V. The cat image quoted above is only one of a series of such metaphors for Kragler's sufferings which are an important means of linking different areas of experience. It occurs in Kragler's description of life in the prisoner-of-war camp off the coast of Africa where he spent three years cut off completely from the outside world. He likens the experience of isolation to being drowned like a cat in a sack: "Three years. Three years, that's over one thousand days. They held us under water, you see, like cats in leather sacks, they don't want to die" (*TN*, 71). The experience of drowning almost becomes reality for Anna when the revolutionaries try to force her into the water, merely because she represents, from their hysterical point of view, an obstacle in Kragler's path to the barricades. Ironically, however, it is Anna's scream for Kragler's help when they try to drown her, that breaks through the emotional barriers which have been keeping Anna and Kragler apart. Their common experience of acute fear, which is underlined by the recurrent imagery, provides the basis of their reunion. The imagery of drowning is not the only means used to draw parallels between Kragler and Anna. There is a structural parallel between Acts III and IV, which show first Anna and then Kragler responding in their different ways to the conflicting pulls of emotionalism and control. Gesture is used to create a parallel between them in Act V, where the revolutionaries' attempt to force Anna down and into the water echoes their earlier pinning-down of Kragler when he became angry with Anna. At both points the aim of the revolutionaries is to separate the lovers so that their drunken march to the barricades will not be delayed. The rapid change from their "protection" of Anna to their persecution of her shows that they are not really concerned with what happens to her, but only with ensuring that Kragler goes along with them. The holding down first of Kragler, then of Anna contains a further irony: it suggests that these "revolutionaries" are quite willing to suppress the individual, whether enemy or ally, in their eagerness to fight – supposedly in order to avenge the oppression of the individual. These various streams of imagery – of cats, of drowning, of lying prostrate – flow together in the repeatedly used phrase "like drowned cats on the asphalt", which is how Kragler imagines the fate of the re-volutionaries who go on to defy the government's guns. As far as the suffering individual is concerned, so the imagery implies, civil war is as callous as imperialist war.

As in *Baal*, the imagery of *Drums in the Night* forms a network which adds to the cohesion of the play. On the other hand, *Drums in the Night* differs from *Baal* in that its images lend themselves much better to theatrical realisation. In fact they demand it. Thus, the consideration of the cat metaphor for example quickly led into a discussion of the significance of two parallel pieces of stage business (the holding down of Kragler and of Anna). Such transitions from the verbal to the visual plane of expression are bound to occur repeatedly in an examination of the play's imagery. The central metaphor of the play, the ghost motif, is a case in point. The dialogue is peppered with the vocabulary of death: "to stink", "to rot", "carrion", "corpse", "cadaver". As well as revealing the preoccupations of the characters, such vocabulary indicates the quality of their feelings, their common tendency to go to extremes of hatred or fear. In this way the verbal imagery determines the way the characters will be realised theatrically. The idea of ghostliness also pervades other areas of theatrical expression. When Kragler enters a room he is accompanied by a cold rush of air and his entry causes the other characters to tremble and shiver. As well as giving theatrical presence to Kragler's "ghostliness", the wind becomes a palpable and powerfully suggestive symbol not only of the unrest in the mood of the times, but also of the experiences of transience and exclusion from the warmth of life which make Kragler so desperate to re-establish his relationship with Anna.

The psychological state which Brecht sought to conjure up by means of the ghost motif was hysteria. This condition he translated into theatrical terms by means of a range of gestures and movements. The tempo of the play, for example, is generally fast, and the movements of the figures frequently quick and agitated; the play abounds in such stage directions as "restless", "in haste", "fleeing", "fleeting". As the bourgeois become increasingly worried about the possibility of Kragler's return in Act I, the tempo of their actions rises steadily until it becomes virtually a headlong dash to get away to the bright lights of the "Picadillybar". This produces a comic reversal at the end of the act, when Kragler appears before Balicke, who has been rushing the others out, has himself had time to leave. It also sets in train a counterpoint of fast and slow movement, since Kragler is last seen moving slowly and clumsily (because he is stunned by the news of Anna's engagement) when the curtain falls for the end of the act. Similar contrasts of tempo are indicated for the speech of the characters. Whereas Kragler often has to grope and stumble after words in the second act, the rhythms of Murk's speech to Anna in Act I, as he tries to reassure himself that he has at last achieved security in life, indicate that his unease and uncertainty are stronger than his belief that he has overcome them:

Murk: [*auf Anna zu, faßt sie nicht, steht schwankend vor ihr*] Jetzt wächst das Fleischgewächs. Jetzt fließt der Rotspon. Jetzt bin ich da! In Schweiß gebadet, die Augen zu, Fäuste geballt, daß die Nägel ins Fleisch schneiden. Schluß! Sicherheit! Wärme! Kittel ausziehen! Ein Bett, das weiß ist, breit, weich! [*Am Fenster vorbei, schaut er, fliegend, hinaus*] Her mit dir: Ich mache die Fäuste auf, ich sitze im Hemd in der Sonne, ich habe dich.

(*TN*, 23–4)

Murk: [*goes up to Anna, doesn't take hold of her, stands swaying before her*] Now the fleshy plant [i.e. the foetus] is growing. Now the red biddy's flowing. Now I've arrived. Bathed in sweat, my eyes shut, fists clenched so hard my finger-nails are cutting into my flesh. It's over! Security. Warmth. Overalls off. A bed that is white, wide, soft! [*Looks fleetingly out of the window in passing*] Come here with you: I'll unclench my fists, I'm sitting in my shirt-sleeves in the sun, I have you.

During most of his speech Murk stands "swaying" before Anna. As well as indicating his state of inebriation, his physical unsteadiness is a visual expression of his continuing emotional insecurity. This gesture occurs repeatedly throughout the play when characters are experiencing shock or instability. Kragler, for example, is made to sway at crucial points in the action – when he first hears of Anna's engagement, when he first confronts Anna, when he enters the cheap pub, when he learns that Anna is pregnant. A variant of the gesture is indicated by stage directions requiring "schwerfällig" ("clumsy") movement, which is similarly suggestive of diminished powers of control. The language of gesture can be an important means of presenting a character's complex and contradictory emotional state. Balicke's profuse sweating during the engagement party is one instance of the body betraying what a character's words would conceal. Another example of this ironic technique is the contradiction between Kragler's cynical words and his agitated movements as he takes leave of the other revolutionaries. His subsequent change to gentleness in both gesture and words is one of a number of such details designed to create an effective theatrical contrast marking the caesura between the agitation of the struggle for Anna and the lovers' return to emotional balance and control.

Brecht's tendency to reinforce his verbal metaphors by visual means in *Drums in the Night* is also evident in his handling of the animal imagery. At two points in the play he shows characters making animal-like gestures. This occurs first in Act I when Murk is alone with Anna, and again in Act V when Kragler is alone with her. In both instances their behaviour is reminiscent of an ape's: Murk faces Anna "like an Orang Utang with his arms hanging down" (*TN*, 23), and Kragler picks up the drum while running around "with his arms hanging to the ground" (*TN*, 94). These ape-like gestures distil the essence of the play's many animal metaphors, and also reveal the symbolic significance of choosing Africa as the place of Kragler's captivity. Kragler's competition with Murk for Anna is presented as a primitive combat for a mate, an expression of instincts which continue to exert a powerful, unchanging influence on human behaviour beneath the changing surface of civilised manners.[11] Kragler's unconscious adoption of this gesture in the last act echoes Murk's similar behaviour in the first act, so that it is made clear that Kragler is now emerging as the victorious animal from the age-old struggle for dominance. But because Kragler's ape-like behaviour occurs during his farewell from the revolutionaries, it also performs the further function of showing why he (and others like him) could not go on with the revolution: the instinct for survival and animal comfort is a more powerful and fundamental influence than the fleeting attraction of making any grand romantic gesture, political or otherwise.

The grouping of the characters on stage was clearly also conceived with an eye to expressive effect. Kragler's existential isolation is conveyed by his being presented as a lone figure or as a figure separated from the others on stage. At the end of Act I he is left alone but for the maid; when he enters the "Picadillybar" in Act II all the other characters flee to the opposite end of the room; in Act IV he dances alone after entertaining the audience of drunks with his story; in Act V he begins to hurl clods of earth at both Anna and the revolutionaries. The frequency of this arrangement also makes for a striking resolution of the conflict in the closing moments of the play, when Kragler gradually draws closer to Anna and eventually puts his arm around her as they walk off. This is another of the devices used by Brecht to suggest that the behaviour of Kragler and Anna at the end of the play is qualitatively different from all that has preceded it.

The dialogue is also carefully patterned to create specific effects. Kragler's physical isolation has an aural counterpart in the frequent silences which suggest the gulf separating characters from one another. A related effect is created at the end of Act IV, when the dialogue breaks down into a series of monologues in which the characters talk to the deaf ears of the others about the several causes of their misery. The obstructive interference of the other characters, both bourgeois and revolutionary alike, in Kragler's relationship with Anna is symbolised by having the lovers conduct a dialogue in Acts II and V across lengthy interruptions. In general the dialogue is managed more skillfully in *Drums in the Night* than it was in *Baal*, where there was little possibility of true dramatic interaction between the disproportionately larger-than-life hero and the other characters, and where in consequence the dialogue frequently degenerated into an opportunity for Baal to demonstrate his strength, or his lyrical soul or his fatal attractiveness to lovers of either sex. Even those passages in *Drums in the Night* where Brecht appears to slip back into the earlier involuntary tendency to write monologues rather than dialogues are really dramatic in conception. Thus, the longer speeches by Murk or Balicke in Act I, where they congratulate themselves on their achievements, are spoken under the shadow of Kragler's feared return, and so represent attempts to find or spread reassurance. In fact, the whole exposition in Act I would do credit to any traditional dramatist, in that facts are stated and decisions taken under the pressure of recent events and imminently expected change. Long before he appears on stage, indeed from the moment the first curtain rises, Kragler is already an active dramatic figure.

Stage sets and properties also contribute to the expressive effect of *Drums in the Night*. Brecht wanted the action played before walls that were visibly made of cardboard, the flimsiness of which contributes to the idea that modern civilisation affords only meagre protection from the forces of nature.[12] The effect is strengthened by the incongruity of Kragler's mud-caked uniform in the Balicks' lace-curtained parlour – Kragler is a walking reminder of the earth's threats to human dignity, order or even bare survival. The red moon, with its associations of romance and revolution, is here a markedly artificial contraption that lights up automatically when-

ever Kragler appears on stage. In the end he knocks it down and
reveals it for what it is, a mere paper lantern which is as
insubstantial as the romantic ideas associated with Kragler's
"destiny". The false moon is not the only ironically deployed
lighting effect. On two occasions Kragler causes the lights to go out:
once accidentally when entering the "Picadillybar", and once
deliberately when leaving Glubb's gin bar. In neither case does the
subsequent action bear out the apparent symbolic significance of
the plunge into darkness. In Act II Kragler does not prove to be the
revolutionary threat he seems, and in Act V he abandons his suicidal
resolve when he meets up with Anna again. The frequent references
in the dialogue to the pallor of the characters' faces ("pale and
swollen", "cheesy faced", "pale as linen") suggest that Brecht may
also have favoured the use of stark white make-up to convey the
general mood of fear and tension.

RHETORIC

Drums in the Night is a rhetorically organised play. In other words,
Brecht sought to persuade his audience to take a particular view of
the action and to control its emotional responses to the events on
stage. Brecht's rhetorical strategy was related to the play's main
concern, the mastery of emotionalism. In the course of the action
Kragler undergoes an exemplary development: he is thrown into
emotional turmoil by Anna's rejection of him, his emotionalism
then makes him unequal to the challenge of winning Anna back, he
finally learns to control his feelings and becomes master of his own
fate. Although Brecht's moral and emotional sympathies lay with
Kragler, there were various reasons why he felt it necessary
to temper his sympathy, and control carefully the audience's
emotional identification with the hero. He wanted the audience to
understand the causes of Kragler's suffering and to recognise where
the remedies for it lay. He therefore had to ensure that the audience
did more than feel *with* Kragler, indeed, wherever the hero lost the
ability to grasp and control his situation, the audience had to be
made to dissociate from him emotionally, in order that they might
perceive the importance of control even where he could not.
Sympathy which was vague or not tempered by critical distance
Brecht considered to be morally suspect.[13] For this reason he
recommended that placards be hung in the auditorium during

performances of *Drums in the Night*, bearing mottos taken from Kragler's last long speech, such as "Don't gape so romantically" or "Every man is the best in his skin". This last slogan has at least two connected meanings. First, it demands the recognition of and respect for individuality: Kragler's behaviour should be judged and understood in terms of the concrete situation he is in, bearing in mind that there are limits to the ability of one individual to grasp another individual's experience. The play contains ample illustration of the characters' misinterpretation of each other's inner worlds, and of the consequences of such misunderstanding. Second, the motto is a defence of sheer survival: it is better for a man to carry on living in his own skin, than for him to throw it away for the sake of some "higher" value. In Kragler's case, it is better for him to go home with Anna, who needs him, than to allow himself to be killed in the revolution in order to gratify the romantic demands of his companions or of the audience. Having clarified why Brecht wanted to control the audience's emotional responses, we need to consider *how* he did so.

Brecht establishes sympathy for Kragler and antipathy towards his bourgeois antagonists by simple and conventional means in the first act. The self-centred and hypocritical materialism of the Balickes and Murk makes them morally unattractive. Being coarse, devoid of any warmth of feeling for one another, and lacking in any personal courage (they have exploited Kragler in his absence and are terrified at the thought of his return), they are also emotionally unattractive. One might also say that their behaviour is aesthetically unpleasant, in that they lack the substance to match their style. Murk and Balicke ape the diction of Sternheim's bourgeois heroes, but do not possess any of the tough, vital resourcefulness which makes the Maskes' villainy curiously appealing. Brecht frequently has Kragler's antagonists behave in a clown-like manner in order to make the audience dissociate from them emotionally. Thus Balicke is comical when, in his fury at his stubborn womenfolk, he cuts himself shaving and then, in a rising paroxysm of temper, has difficulty in applying sticking plaster to his self-inflicted wounds. Here the central conflict between emotionalism and control takes on the quality of farce. Frau Balicke is equally ridiculous when she 'swishes" into their utterly prosaic parlour dressed in a black hooded cloak and burbles that the moon is "so big, so red", while all the time admiring her appearance in the mirror. It is just as important for the rhetoric of the play that Kragler's antagonists are as comically inadequate as they are unscrupulous. Brecht needed to establish this double view of them, as both threatening and vulnerable, from an early stage, because Kragler was to be shown so often as suffering at their hands. Unless his persecutors were seen from the outset to be vulnerable and insecure, and therefore liable to have their momentary triumphs turn into eventual defeat, it would have been difficult to control the pathos of certain scenes, and to maintain the audience's awareness, in keeping with the overall comic character of the piece, that everything will eventually work out to Kragler's advantage.

Kragler's first entrance is calculated to win immediate sympathy for him. In his old-fashioned and mud-caked uniform, he represents a challenge to the smug cosiness of the bourgeois parlour, and a reminder of the ugly past which they would like to think is dead and buried as they return to "business as usual", gleefully anticipating the profits to be made from manufacturing baby carriages for the children of those men who for the past four years have dragged the ammunition-carriages made in the same factory. Kragler's appearance is welcomed by the audience as a sign that the Balickes are to receive the retribution which they deserve. Our moral sympathy for Kragler is reinforced by his emotional appeal. Kragler's calm, pipe-smoking manner provides a brief but gratifying relief from the hysterically strained atmosphere in the Balicke household. His behaviour seems a much more natural and proper state for a man to be in than the melodramatic emotionalism affecting the others. This initial impression, although brief, is an important element in the emotional economy of the play. It provides a yardstick by which to measure the behaviour of the characters, including that of Kragler himself, a sense of normal emotional equilibrium from which the mood of the times has deviated and to which life, in the nature of things, ought to return. Thus, both the notion of poetic justice and our idea of what is natural and dignified in man predispose us to hope, to believe even, that Kragler will confound his persecutors and win back Anna. When, at the end of the play, Kragler once more pulls out the pipe which he has neglected throughout the action, there is created the satisfying effect of a circle closing, as normality is restored – for Anna and Kragler, at least.

At bottom *Drums in the Night*, like so many of Brecht's plays, draws on the simple emotional appeal of melodrama. What makes it more than melodrama are the rather more unconventional and recognisably Brechtian techniques he employed to keep the audience's sympathies for Kragler within certain limits. Whenever Kragler's emotions get out of control Brecht counteracts the intensity of the mood by injecting an element of the ridiculous into the scene. Thus, when dramatic irony begins to make Kragler seem increasingly pathetic, as, ignorant of the extent of Anna's unfaithfulness, he believes that there are no more barriers to their being reunited, Brecht has the action interrupted by a waiter who has been watching the scene with growing emotional excitement, and who now stammers that "the main question is . . . whether she still has her lily" (*TN*, 37). Similarly, near the end of the second act, the same waiter is made to exchange clichéd romantic observations on "the story so far" with a voice offstage at the very moment when Kragler is devastated by Anna's announcement that they cannot after all be reunited. The effect produced by these crude interjections of cliché is grotesque, and probably counter-productive, since the emotional dissonance is so intense as to distract attention from the intellectual point which the technique is supposed to help clarify, namely that the hero's emotionalism repeatedly puts him at a disadvantage in life's struggles.

A technique which produces a better mix of sympathy and ironic detachment is that of introducing an element of parodic stylisation into a character's diction, notably that of Kragler and Anna. Brecht subjects Kragler's speech to such stylisation whenever the protagonist's mind is dominated by painful memories which diminish his ability to master present difficulties. At such points Kragler's speech becomes highly metaphorical, even to the point of bordering on the incoherent, and recognisably Expressionist. The difficulty of following Kragler's meaning is itself a means of inhibiting the pathos, but such inhibition is mainly achieved through the ironic contrast of Kragler's words with other elements of the scenic presentation. In Act IV, for example, Kragler's "Expressionistic" incoherence increases as he becomes more and more inebriated, while in Act II the obviously artificial red moon dominates the darkened set as Kragler launches into his metaphorical style. Brecht does not "lapse" into Expressionism at such points, rather he quotes Expressionist style in order to *define* Kragler's behaviour as belonging to a recognisable type. In the same way he quotes the style of the Psalmist in Act III in order to undermine, by exaggeration, the self-importance Anna feels as she turns her back on bourgeois respectability in order to follow Kragler. The parody of Expressionist style gives an added topical edge to the play's sardonic commentary on the Germans' tendency to emotionalism, by suggesting that the Expressionist Messiahs far from helping men to create a new world had merely strengthened the bonds of an outworn romanticism.

Brecht was already a Marxist when he expounded his now famous theory of "alienation". From this later standpoint he looked back at *Drums in the Night* and expressed regret that, at the time of writing it, "the technique of alienation was not yet at my disposal" (*GW*, **17**, 946). In terms of his own definition of the technique as one which presents an image of reality in such a way as to challenge established assumptions about what is "natural" *and* to promote a sense that the world can and should be changed, Brecht was right in making this comment about *Drums in the Night*. On the other hand, it is rather letting the later Brecht have things his own way if we simply accept the link which he claimed existed between a theatrical technique and the political ends he wanted to put it to. In fact he was using the technique, in *Drums in the Night* and elsewhere, long before he defined it as an instrument of Marxist political theatre. Although *Drums in the Night* does not call into question an audience's whole understanding of life under capitalism, the play challenges a range of assumptions about the psychological and moral disposition of the returning soldiers and about the way the theatre ought to respond to the condition of post-war Germany. In order to do so the playwright employed a series of devices, as we have seen, to ensure that the audience, beyond feeling sympathy for the hero, was led to a clearer understanding of the problems affecting him and his society. The interplay of empathy with ironic distance used in this play was to become the method of presentation most consistently favoured by Brecht throughout his career as a dramatist, both before he became a Marxist and after. The technical differences between his early and later works are differences of degree, not of kind, and they arose from the desire to adapt a structure that had grown naturally out of his mixed feelings about his early heroes' passions, to the particular political purposes which he later embraced. In other words, neither "epic theatre" nor "alienation" were originally or essentially part of a political or so-called "scientific" conception of theatre.

Brecht's choice of the vulnerable Kragler as the hero of his second play benefited his development as a dramatist. In *Baal* Brecht's will to mastery had issued directly in the almost entirely uncritical portrayal of a figure possessed of near-mythical strength and invulnerability. Because Baal's imaginative function was to triumph over life's difficulties by finding pleasure where lesser mortals find only pain, the play was inevitably undramatic. *Baal* is also difficult to stage because insufficient thought was given to the problem of how to make Baal's various encounters with other characters symbolically transparent, or, to put it the other way round, how to give theatrical (as opposed to verbal) presence to Baal's true, but hidden antagonist, Death. Although far from perfect, *Drums in the Night* is a more mature play than *Baal* in a number of respects. Firstly, it begins to grapple with the problems of suffering and inadequacy which *Baal* had imperiously swept aside – and left unanswered. It has a better dramatic balance than *Baal*, since the vulnerable individual Kragler has real internal and external obstacles to overcome before he can be reunited with Anna, and is made to suffer defeat before he experiences victory. The choice of an imperfect hero also meant that *Drums in the Night*, unlike *Baal*, contained the possibility of development of both plot and character. In fact, at one stage of its composition Brecht had conceived two possible endings, one tragic, the other comic (*Diaries*, 14). Kragler's imperfections also meant that the playwright had mixed attitudes to him, and this in turn led to the play eliciting more complex and interesting responses. Because he had limited the extent to which his own will to mastery could find satisfaction in simple identification with the hero, Brecht found that he had to develop formal means of distancing the characters' behaviour, including that of the hero, in order to achieve the desired imaginative mastery of experience. This increased interest in formal questions went hand in hand with an improvement in the theatrical concreteness of his work.

The advance in maturity between *Baal* and *Drums in the Night* is considerable, but there are still faults in Brecht's second play which are symptomatic of the way his imagination worked. Like *Baal*, *Drums in the Night* was more of a determined effort to master problems than an attempt to explore and define them honestly – hence its "rhetorical" organisation. While it is true that Brecht makes his hero more vulnerable and his antagonists more powerful than in *Baal*, the presentation of the action is prejudiced from the outset by the playwright's sympathy for his hero and, equally important, by his determination to point a moral. Because of the playwright's prejudices the handling of character is not always consistent or plausible. The susceptibility of Murk and the Balickes to hysteria is not entirely convincing, and serves too obviously the purpose of equalising the dramatic balance of power between Kragler and his enemies. The journalist Babusch is a striking example of vague characterisation. When this character first appears, in the role of a friend of the Balicke family, he seems to have the cheerfully cynical attitude of a hardened newspaperman with a taste for good living. His ironic tone provides a welcome contrast to the excitability of the Balickes. In the second act, however, he stops being an amoral and rather malicious *provocateur* and becomes a supporter of Kragler in his struggle for Anna. In the third and fifth acts his function is to counteract the emotionalism of Anna, the waiter Manke and the revolutionaries respectively, but when Kragler and Anna have been reunited he is simply forgotten about, no directions being given for the when, where or why of his exit. In this case psychological plausibility has simply been subordinated to the exigencies of maintaining an emotional balance in various situations.

Another flaw which arises from the playwright's determination to demonstrate that life's problems can be mastered occurs in the closing moments of the play. After taking pains to show that Kragler and Anna experience considerable emotional difficulties in re-establishing their relationship, Brecht all but ruins their last scene by prescribing that a streak of rosy dawn light should appear in the sky ("Ein kleines Fähnchen, Frührot oben in morgengrauen rauchigen Himmel", *TN*, 95) as the lovers walk off to begin a new life. The effect would have been only marginally more acceptable if, as he had originally planned, the sky was to show a more neutral yellow streak on the horizon (*Diaries*, 47). Although the hope for the lovers is contrasted with the continuing shouting in the newspaper district, where the revolutionary battle is being fought out, this ending taints the play with the very same vague emotionalism against which much of its energy is directed. Clearly, Brecht's will to master experience had to be made to face up more honestly to the harsh aspects of life if he was to progress further as a dramatist.

4 *In the Jungle*

Brecht's third major play, *In the Jungle*[1], marks a return from the relatively realistic depiction of contemporary events in *Drums in the Night* to the more freely fantastic vein of writing in which, as the author of *Baal*, he had begun his literary career. As in *Baal* and many other Expressionist works, fantasy is used here by the playwright as a source of symbolic figures and actions which give shape and expression to aspects of the mind which normally remain hidden in everyday life. The setting of the action, "in an unreal, cold Chicago" (*D*, 134), is an inner landscape, the world of urban civilisation as experienced by the existential self.[2] The action, a wild "metaphysical struggle" (*D*, 52) between a Malayan timber merchant named Shlink and the much younger George Garga, a bookseller by profession, is a vehicle for exploring imaginatively the nature of the existential self and its relations with other selves. This action, which was intended by Brecht to create a certain degree of puzzlement,[3] has prompted some critics to describe the play as downright incomprehensible.[4] It is therefore best to begin with a fairly detailed analysis of the plot, in order to establish that the struggle between Shlink and Garga, although admittedly strange and idiosyncratic, does have a coherent meaning.

THE METAPHYSICAL STRUGGLE

The struggle between Shlink and Garga opens thus:

> *Garga*: Das ist ein Kriminalroman, kein gutes Buch. Das da ist ein besseres Buch, eine Reisebeschreibung.
> *Moti*: Sie tun einfach sagen: das ist ein schlechtes Buch?
> *Shlink*: Ich möchte Ihnen diese Ansicht abkaufen, wenn es Ihnen beliebt. Sind zwei Pfund zu wenig dafür?
> *Garga*: Ich schenke sie Ihnen.
>
> (*D*, 13)

Garga: That is a detective novel, it's not a good book. This one
          here is a better book, a travelogue.
Moti: You mean you're saying "That's a bad book", as simple
          as that?
Shlink: I'd like to buy that opinion from you, if you please. Is two
          pounds too little to offer?
Garga: You can have it for nothing.

The ensuing dialogue gradually adds meaning to this strange
opening exchange. Shlink's offer of money in exchange for Garga's
opinion of a book (which book is not important) is a symbolic
gesture of challenge, nicely calculated on the basis of what Shlink
has been able to discover about the young man's character to draw
out Garga's aggressions by prodding him on a sensitive spot. Shlink
has found out that Garga is the sole but unwilling breadwinner of a
poor family which has recently moved "from the plains" into the big
city. Although he is prepared to work in a dingy lending library to
support his family he secretly dreams of escaping, like his hero
Gauguin, to a life of freedom in the South Seas.[5] As a compromise
between his obligations to his family and his personal desires he
spends three weeks in every month at work and the fourth in the
company of his mistress, Jane Montpassier, drinking heavily and
nourishing his dreams of Tahiti with information gleaned from the
encyclopaedia. This monthly indulgence in bohemianism is an
attempt to preserve for himself an area in which he can be free of his
ties with the everyday world. Shlink's offer of money is an attack on
Garga's belief that it is possible to retain at least one's inward
freedom in the face of the outside world's encroachment on the self.

As he gradually increases the amount of his offer Shlink points out
the various ways in which Garga could use the money: he could help
his family with it, or spend it on the pursuit of pleasures – on Jane for
example, or on "Cook's travelogues" or even on a ticket to Tahiti.
Shlink's "generosity" recalls Satan's when tempting Christ to sell
his spirit in exchange for all the kingdoms of the earth. In reality
Shlink's offer is a mocking reply to Garga's ingenuous opening
remark that one book is "better" than another: if Garga is so sure of
his ability to perceive the greater or lesser value of things, he implies,
he surely ought to be able to put priorities on his various
attachments to family, travel, his girlfriend, literature, his opinions.
As Shlink puts it, "One has to know which is better: a pound of fish
or an opinion" (*D*, 14). What Shlink is also implying is that in all

aspects of his life Garga is dependent on money in any case: he needs it to support his family on the one hand, or to indulge in "private" bohemianism on the other. To believe in "higher" and "lower" values is to fall prey to the delusions of mere words in a world which is "flattened" ("abgeplatter"), where all values are reducible to material terms, and where there no longer exist any fixed points of orientation ("The polar explorers have difficulty in not missing the pole" – D, 21).[6] Thus, Shlink argues, since Garga's inner "freedom" is really spurious, because of its dependence on the everyday, material world, he might as well admit the fact and openly accept money in exchange for part of this "private" self, namely one of his literary opinions. He ought to sell the words which will "give pleasure" to Shlink just as readily as he takes money for the words of the authors whose books he sells. Underlying this suggestion in turn is the even more menacing insinuation that it is possible for one man to gain access to and control over another man's freedom of choice. Fully to buy Garga's opinion of a book must also mean buying his ability and freedom to make choices. What Shlink has already been able to discover about Garga's private life and dreams is in itself a demonstration that his inner world can be invaded; in the ensuing struggle the Malayan's governing strategy is to anger his chosen opponent by taking possession of his inner world, depriving him of his freedom of choice by anticipating and fulfilling – even before he has expressed it – his every wish.

Garga's initial response to Shlink's attack is to assume an air of detachment. However, when Shlink increases the pressure on him by degrading him in front of his employer and having Jane brought in drunk on the arm of a pimp, Garga decides that he must demonstrate that he *is* spiritually free by breaking all ties with his previous way of life. He replies to Shlink's symbolic challenge by discarding, with a martyr's gesture, the clothes which signify his social role. He then counters Shlink's offer with an ironic reversal of that offer:

Garga: Hier meine Stiefel. [*Er wirft sie auf den Ladentisch*] . . . ich bitte um meine Freiheit! [*Er läuft in Hemd und Hose hinaus*]
(*D*, 22)

Garga: Here are my boots. [*He throws them onto the counter*] I'm asking for my freedom! [*He runs out in his shirt and trousers*]

Whereas Shlink had offered money in exchange for something Garga regards as unsaleable, namely his spiritual freedom, Garga now offers to sell all those things which he considers are venal – including Jane! – but his price is something which he believes Shlink cannot give him, namely his freedom. Thus, as far as Garga is concerned, this encounter has ended in an absurd impasse, with each man demanding of the other something which the other cannot give. As he leaves the library declaiming some of Rimbaud's poetry – in defiance of Shlink's scorn for mere words – Garga clearly believes that he has demonstrated the obvious, namely that he does indeed have the spiritual freedom he has always cherished. However, he soon discovers that things are not as simple as that.

Garga's departure from his place of work is not the unambiguous assertion of his independence he believes it to be in the heat of the moment. This is an action which, although he may often have contemplated it, he had never actually carried out until Shlink forced his attentions on him. His departure could therefore be regarded, not as an act of free will, but as an action which he has been coerced into by his attacker. The real lack of freedom in his decision to leave for Tahiti manifests itself in his inability to carry out his plan of going there, and in his "choosing" instead to retaliate against Shlink's attack. Garga explicitly acknowledges this loss of freedom in conversation with his sister Marie who is present in Shlink's office when he comes to deliver his counter attack:

> Garga: [*geht herum*] Ich weiß nicht, was sie mit mir vorhaben. Sie haben mich harpuniert. Sie zogen mich an sich. Es scheint Stricke zu geben.
>
> (*D*, 25)

> Garga: [*paces around*] I don't know what they want with me. They harpooned me. They pulled me towards them. There seem to be ropes.

It is the very fact that Garga does not understand the motives of his assailant that makes him unable to free himself from Shlink's "harpoon" and "ropes". This sense of having lost his freedom is confirmed by his discovery that, contrary to his expectations, Shlink has been expecting him to come to the office. In coming to fight with Shlink, Garga is both facing up to the loss of freedom involved in his emotional bond (of hatred) with his enemy and taking steps to regain his independence. His aim is now to regain the freedom he has surrendered in taking on the fight, by defeating his enemy, for only a decisive victory will set him free of the painful emotional fetters which now bind him to his attacker. What Garga has not yet realised is that even such a recovery of emotional freedom can be no proof of the absolute freedom of his will, since *any* action deliberately taken in relation to Shlink is evidence of some kind of need to take action.

Garga's first onslaught is the most obvious one to make on a man who appears to look upon money as the sole value in life: he sets out to destroy Shlink financially. But when he draws a revolver and demands that Shlink hand over his timber business, he meets, not the resistance he had expected and hoped for, but a readiness on Shlink's part to give up his property. As Erich Engel, with whom Brecht collaborated closely on the first production of the play, noted at the time: "Garga, who had expected resistance, is disarmed by co-operation" (*D*, 120). Garga is disappointed and disoriented by Shlink's acquiescence in every humiliating demand made on him, because unless Shlink resists his attacks, he has nothing to overcome and no opportunity to emerge from the fight with the knowledge that he has crushed his opponent. At the end of the encounter he pretends that Shlink's "cowardice" has given him moral victory so that he is now justified in regarding the fight as over, but his sister Marie points out that this is really only cowardice on *his* part, an attempt to disguise his fears that he may not be able to defeat such an opponent (*D*, 32–3).

By the end of this encounter Garga is thoroughly at a loss to understand Shlink's behaviour. The audience is in a slightly better position to understand Shlink, having heard his opening monologue in which he reveals something of his motives for fighting:

Shlink: [*am Tischchen sitzend*] Glatt bin ich, rund, satt. Alles ist so geringe Mühe, alles bekommt mir. Wie leicht ich verdaue! [*Stille*] Zehn Jahre war es leicht, so hinzuleben. Bequem, seßhaft, jede Reibung war zu überwinden. Jetzt gewöhne ich mich an die Leichtigkeit und alles ist mir zum Überdruß.

(*D*, 24)

Shlink: [*sitting at the small table*] I'm smooth, round, sated. Everything costs so little effort, everything does me good.

How easily I digest! [*Silence*] For ten years it was easy to live like this from day to day. Comfortable, sedentary, all friction could be overcome. Now I'm accustomed to the ease and I've had enough of it all.

Equipped with this clue that Shlink's motives for fighting are boredom and loss of sensitivity,[7] it is left to the spectator's "delight in solving puzzles" (*GW*, **15**, 55) to understand why he conducts the fight in the way he does. Much later, almost at the end of the play, more explanation is given for Shlink's behaviour:

> *Shlink*: Das Leben ist ein Spaß. Wie es spüren? Man müßte den Geschmack des Todes auf die Zunge bringen, die Essenz! Man fällt ab wie ein reifer Apfel, ohne daß man es merkt.
>
> (*D*, 24)

> *Shlink*: Life is a joke. How is one to feel it? There ought to be some way of getting one's tongue around the taste of death, its essence! One falls like a ripe apple, without even noticing it.

For him the fight is a "last sensation" (*D*, 137), a struggle fought for the pleasure of fighting, an attempt to enjoy every last minute of living – including the moment of death – as intensely as possible. Since he is interested in the experience of the fight itself, his aim must be to continue the struggle to the very point of death. By his tactics of passivity and impassivity he seeks to keep up his opponent's interest in the fight and to taunt Garga with his inability to find some way of wounding him. Thus he hopes eventually to provoke Garga into killing him, like a "scarab, hired to bring me under the earth" (*D*, 100).[8] In short, Shlink, who regards himself as "something unique" (*D*, 88), is determined to die "his own" death rather than allow fate or chance to determine the manner of his demise.

If Garga were able to carry out the threat which he makes at the end of their second encounter, to sail away to Tahiti with Shlink's money, he would win the fight outright, on an emotional level at least, for such an action would demonstrate that he is unfettered either by his ties to his past way of life or to his enemy, and would also frustrate Shlink's masochistic ambitions. However, when he tries to put this plan into operation, it becomes clear that he lacks such complete emotional freedom, for he feels that he cannot simply desert his mother. Caught between his desire for freedom and his attachment to his mother, he at first attempts the compromise solution of asking her to go away with him. Such a solution would not really meet the problem, of course, for if he has to admit his lack of emotional independence in relation to his mother, then merely to break free of his ties to Shlink would not be a *complete* assertion of freedom or strength. When she refuses to go away with him, he has to face up to the need for a total sacrifice of his family if he is to realise his plan. Ironically, when he then decides to abandon his family completely, he merely worsens his situation, for this allows Shlink, who knows that Garga would really like to have his family provided for, to take over his position as breadwinner. This move of Shlink's is a good one for a number of reasons: because he has done no more than carry out one of Garga's – admittedly unexpressed – wishes, he has again demonstrated that he can penetrate into the young man's most private thoughts and anticipate the movements of his will; also, his presence in the family will add to Garga's feelings of hatred towards him, making him jealous of Shlink for having usurped his place in the home and angry at the thought of being obliged to his enemy for the provision of his family; finally, he has burdened himself masochistically with the physical strain of labouring in the coalyards to support the family and with the emotional strain of giving up his cherished isolation in order to live in close contact with others.

Shlink's success in binding Garga emotionally to him is confirmed when Garga, instead of leaving for the South Seas, comes to visit his enemy in the coalyards in order to resume the fight. Although willing to fight, Garga confesses that he is unable to find a way of getting to grips with his opponent (*D*, 41). Because Garga sees no way of making an attack, Shlink is forced to take the initiative in restarting the fight, and this initiative suggests to Garga where Shlink's "weak spot" might be. The Malayan's "attack" takes the form of offering to marry Garga's sister Marie. In so doing he is acting on the same principle as before, that of fulfilling one of Garga's unexpressed wishes (in this instance to have his sister cared for), but in such a way as to provoke only anger in the younger man. Ostensibly Shlink is simply removing another obstacle to Garga's departure for Tahiti and achievement of personal freedom (*D*, 44). But of course the real effect of such a move is to create rather than remove an obstacle. In the first place, as Shlink is perfectly aware,

Garga loves his sister and would not be happy to see her married to a man he hates. Moreover, the very fact that it is Shlink who is offering to clear his path to Tahiti makes such a course of action impossible for Garga to follow. Not only is it emotionally unacceptable for him to be indebted to his enemy, but there is also the problem that to go away now would mean acting according to decisions made by Shlink in his usurped position as arbiter of Garga's actions. If Garga wants to prove his independence, the one thing he may not do now is go to Tahiti. Erich Engel sums up his dilemma neatly: "Tahiti is only useful to Garga as a conquest, not if he flees there. Shlink ruins Tahiti for him by showing him the way there. This blocks his path" (*D*, 122). Yet the "round" does not go altogether in Shlink's favour, for in his eagerness to prevent Garga going to Tahiti by ostensibly helping him to leave, he has shown signs of fear which Garga has been quick to notice (*D*, 44). The knowledge that Shlink is afraid that Garga will actually terminate the fight becomes a weapon in Garga's hands, for it enables him to taunt and tease his enemy by adopting tactics of passivity and apparent indifference towards Shlink and the struggle. Thus, while Shlink's gambit has succeeded in hurting Garga, since it has forced him to deny his desire to escape to Tahiti, it has also damaged Shlink by exposing his "weak spot" to his opponent.

The shift in the balance of power created by Garga's discovery of Shlink's weakness, namely his masochistic interest in the fight, manifests itself in the fact that the flow of the action is reversed, Shlink now having to bring the fight to Garga rather than the other way round. The Malayan is forced by Garga's inactivity to visit him in the squalid bar where he spends his days drinking away the money he once said he would use to sail to Tahiti. Shlink exposes more of his flank when he shows indignation at this behaviour (*D*, 51). To provoke Garga into action Shlink now repeats his threat of proposing to Marie. Rather than abandon his policy of passivity Garga agrees to this sacrifice of his sister. Fortunately for him he is spared the pain of seeing Marie fall into Shlink's hands, because, despite her love for Shlink, she refuses to be "bought" like this and prefers to seek refuge with her former suitor Mankyboddle. Garga then takes his strategy of avoiding combat a stage further by marrying Jane, returning with her to his parents' home and resuming work in Maynes' lending-library. He is even prepared to tolerate Shlink's financial interference in his private affairs, by accepting shares in some cotton fields, rather than give his enemy the pleasure of having his intrusions resisted (*D*, 63-4). Now that Garga has abandoned his defence of absolute freedom, Shlink finds it necessary to forsake temporarily *his* principle of using "goodness as a means to evil" (*D*, 134) in order to force Garga to give up his tactic of passivity. When Jane misuses the share-papers Shlink gave to Garga, the Malayan threatens to have Garga put in prison. This almost has the effect of provoking Garga into the kind of violent action which Shlink has been aiming to stimulate all along. But Garga just manages to resist the temptation (*D*, 77), realising that physical violence would only satisfy Shlink, whereas Garga's absence for years in prison will cause the older man suffering and frustration by depriving him of the pleasure of fighting with Garga.

When Garga returns from prison, he finds his family broken up: Marie has become a prostitute, Jane an alcoholic, and his mother has disappeared. Only his father, for whom Garga has no affection, remains. Having lost his family and his spiritual freedom because of his determination to injure Shlink, he now finds, ironically, that the only thing left to live for is the fight itself and the promise of revenge it holds out: "I still have revenge sticking in my throat, I have hatred between my fingers" (*D*, 90). However, after a further three weeks of single combat "in the jungle", Garga has to accept that he cannot even have the satisfaction of forcing his opponent to concede defeat. Their natures are so different, he concludes, that their respective strengths simply cannot be measured: "In dem Wald ist die Antwort. Eine Eiche ist nicht stärker als ein Iltis" ("The forest holds the answer. An oak is not stronger than a polecat" – *D*, 93).[9]

Although this insight into the incomparability of their respective strengths is an important step in Garga's development, it is not in itself sufficient to set him free from the attachment to Shlink in which his enmity involves him. It helps him to decide that Shlink must simply be "disposed of" (*D*, 98) by being handed over to the lynch-mob which is out looking for him. But because he still feels the need for a last trial of strength he rejoins Shlink and tells him of the approach of the lynchers, in the hope that Shlink's fear of death will make him give up the struggle.[10] However, Shlink has already anticipated this move and has even had a horse made ready for the escape of the one whose will breaks first. Shlink then deals the final blow to Garga's remaining illusions of independence by stating that he has known all along that Garga would survive him and has even "hired" him specifically with this end in mind (*D*, 100). Yet the fight between Shlink and Garga ends without either man gaining a clear victory. Formally, Garga is the loser of their "metaphysical struggle", since he has not been able to devise any course of action which has not been anticipated by Shlink. In arranging to have Shlink "disposed of" by a lynch-mob, Garga has also had to admit to his own lack of resourcefulness in discovering a way of penetrating to the core of Shlink's personality and forcing him, as he has forced Garga, to injure himself by his own actions. To leave the scene of the fight on the horse provided by Shlink is also to concede that he lacks Shlink's courage and determination to "outface" his enemy, even at the cost of his life. As he departs, leaving Shlink to face the lynchers alone, Garga concedes defeat in terms which are a direct answer to Shlink's original challenge, "I'm selling, Shlink" (*D*, 101). Paradoxically and ironically, however, Garga's admission of defeat brings a form of victory to him and a substantial defeat to Shlink. Although he provided a horse for Garga's escape, Shlink did not really want Garga to abandon their fight. He hoped, rather, that by providing the means of escape he would actually make it emotionally impossible for Garga to leave (just as he had managed earlier to prevent him fleeing to Tahiti). He had also hoped that the news of Jane's murder on Shlink's orders would provoke Garga into violent retaliation against Shlink. This would have satisfied not only Shlink's masochistic ambitions, but also his sadistic ones, since Garga would then have had to suffer the consequences of killing Shlink – possibly even at the hands of the lynch-mob which he had drummed up himself. In this way Shlink would have died with the satisfaction of knowing that he had determined the manner of his death, and also that he had succeeded in binding Garga's life completely to his own. However, Shlink made a serious "error of calculation" (*D*, 102) in his assessment of Garga's likely reaction to the news of Jane's murder. Instead of being enraged, Garga is sickened suddenly by the pointlessness of the whole struggle. He realises that he is simply not so obsessed with their fight as Shlink, and that for him "it is not important to be the stronger before God, but the one who is alive" (*D*, 100).

Because of his miscalculation Shlink's sado-masochistic strategy founders in the end, for he is left to die by his own hand, without Garga even being present at the last. The imagery of his dying speech, which is of fish rotting and stinking despite the care taken to preserve them,[11] expresses Shlink's disgust at the substantial failure underlying his formal victory. Garga, on the other hand, although defeated in his deliberate efforts to demonstrate his absolute freedom of action, has gained his *practical* freedom of action by simply giving up the fight, and thus taking a course of action which Shlink failed to predict. The crowning irony is, however, that the action which gives Garga practical victory cannot give him emotional or "metaphysical" satisfaction, because he did not actually abandon the fight with the deliberate intent of hurting Shlink or of doing something unexpected. Because deliberate victory eluded him, Garga is left with a feeling of dissatisfaction after his enemy has been "stamped into the ground". He looks back with some nostalgia to the fight, "It was the best time. Chaos is all used up, it left me unblessed.[12] Perhaps work will comfort me. Doubtless it is very late. I feel abandoned" (*D*, 105). Shlink would no doubt have been delighted to know that he continued to preoccupy the mind of his beloved enemy even after his death; but, of course, this is a satisfaction he could not have. The gains and losses are perfectly balanced.

PARALLELS AND CONTRASTS

Closely interwoven with the action which unfolds between Shlink and Garga is the fate of Garga's sister Marie, whose relationship with Shlink is so designed as to provide an ironic contrast with that of her brother. The function of this parallel is to qualify the validity of the cynical conclusions which Garga learns to draw from his encounter with the Malayan. Whereas he slowly learns that the art of self-preservation involves abandoning any notions of absolute value (freedom of the will), or any ambition to establish that his personal worth is greater than that of another man's, Marie's fate emphasises what is lost in human terms when a sensitive individual's need for an absolute value (in her case, love) is frustrated.

The pattern of contrast between brother and sister begins when they meet in Shlink's office. Whereas Garga had refused to sell part of himself to Shlink, Marie has gladly accepted his offer of work as a washerwoman because this will help provide for the family. This point of difference is a sign of a deeper contrast in their natures: Garga's main value is his independence, but Marie cherishes the values of allegiance and security. Whereas Garga's values lead him into hatred for Shlink, Marie's admiration for what she mistakenly sees as Shlink's virtues of kindness, patience, diligence, leads her to love him. Her subsequent experiences at Shlink's hands are an exact

inversion of Garga's: while he is drawn against his will into a close
relationship with his enemy, she, who deeply wants to enter into a
love-relationship with Shlink, is forced by his treatment of her into
repeated assertion of her independence.[13] This first happens in the
scene where Shlink offers to marry Marie simply in order to gain an
advantage in his fight with Garga. Marie's refusal represents a first
defeat for Shlink's belief in the predictability of human behaviour.
Rather than be bought and sold in this way she turns to an unloved
suitor by the name of Mankyboddle. She continues to love Shlink,
however, and eventually abandons her loveless relationship with
Mankyboddle. When she later meets Shlink again she allows him to
seduce her, realises immediately that this is for him again only a
tactic in his struggle with Garga, and again unwillingly asserts her
independence by leaving Shlink after demanding payment from
him for her "services". After this she becomes a prostitute, but this of
course only increases her misery and underscores the tragic waste of
a love denied fulfilment. After one last desperate attempt to win
Shlink's love, which is frustrated by his suicide, she resigns herself, in
a travesty of the conventional happy ending of comedy, to a loveless
marriage with Mankyboddle. In this concluding scene brother and
sister are brought together in a last illustration of the double face of
lost idealism: the cheerless monotony of Marie's future with
Mankyboddle effectively counterbalances Garga's anticipation of
the pleasures of the simple life – "I'm moving to the South. I'll
cultivate land" (*D*, 104).[14] Here, as throughout the play, the
contrast between brother and sister is a pointer to the tensions
within a single experience, tensions which are clearly expressed in
the rapidly shifting moods of Garga's last speech:

> Jetzt frische Wolken her, Ostwind! Wir fahren in einer Schale an
> den Südküsten hinauf, das ist gefährlich. Auf den Wind warten
> wir noch. [*Er setzt sich an das Tischchen*] Es war die beste Zeit. Das
> Chaos ist aufgebraucht, es ließ mich ungesegnet. Vielleicht
> tröstet mich die Arbeit. Es ist zweifellos sehr spät. Ich fühle mich
> vereinsamt. (*D*, 105).

> Now bring on fresh clouds, East Wind! We shall sail in a shallow
> boat up the southern coasts, that's dangerous. We're still waiting
> for the wind. [*He sits down at the little table*] That was the best time.
> Chaos is all used up, it left me unblessed. Perhaps work will
> comfort me. Doubtless it is very late. I feel abandoned.

A study of the behaviour of Shlink, Garga and Marie indicates that, far from being chaotic or incomprehensible, the play does have a coherent theme, namely the question of the place and nature of values in life. Just how tight the thematic control in this work is, becomes apparent if one also examines the presentation of the minor characters. Their function is to contribute to the "balance of power" between the need for spiritual values and scorn for them, which underlies the main action of the play.

Towards the end of Garga's second confrontation with Shlink he invites a group of Salvationists into Shlink's office and offers to donate the building to the Salvation Army if the young officer in charge will accept the humiliation of allowing Shlink to spit in his face. Garga's intentions are, on the one hand, to force Shlink into resisting such a challenge, and on the other, to show that he is just as tough as Shlink, by passing on to another innocent the kind of treatment he had received from Shlink when the latter "spits a little cherry-stone in my eye one forenoon" (*D*, 23). After some initial hesitation the young man accepts this personal humiliation as part of his "mission". When he next appears, much later in the play, he tries to commit suicide with the revolver which Garga, anticipating the effects of such humiliation on the young man, gave him at their first meeting. The scene of his suicide attempt is a cheap liquor store where he sits reading aloud from the list of drinks, as if from a litany, "with a hard voice, tasting each word to the full" (*D*, 81), while an orchestrina mockingly plays "Ave Maria" in the background.[15] The young Salvationist's collapse from idealism into despair, via humiliation, is clearly intended as a parallel to Garga's experiences. Equally, his suicide attempt, which occurs just after Garga has been deserted by Jane, translates into action Garga's own thoughts of killing himself as a final act of commitment to his ideals ("There's only one thing left for you, to string yourself up" – *D*, 84). The failure of the Salvationist's suicide attempt is a sardonic commentary on the pointlessness of such idealistic gestures. It shows that what the will decides is not entirely in the hands of the will to execute, because an idea, when converted into action, is subject to the interference of contingent factors. Put concretely, the Salvationist fails to aim straight. Although he murmurs the dying words of Frederick the Second, ("La montagne est passée; nous irons mieux" – *D*, 86), chance would have it that he survives. This incident is related by the theme of suicide to the earlier scene where Mankyboddle, having been deserted by Marie, contemplates, but

decides against, shooting himself (*D*, 71). The good sense of his
decision speaks for itself, but simply to reject idealism like this, in
favour of indulgence of the appetites, offers no satisfactory solution
to the despair experienced by the Salvationist or Marie, or Garga
for that matter, and the attractions of such a baldly rational,
commonsensical attitude are offset by Marie's feeling of desolation
when she has to share the boring vacuity of Manky's way of life.

Another character who has her initial altruism crushed is Garga's
mother, Maë. Her life's work has been a constant struggle to hold
together the family she loves, but when Garga and Marie become
more concerned with their respective relations with Shlink than
with the family, she gives up the unequal struggle and leaves them
to their own devices, "like a brig, slowly, slowly gnawed by the rain,
which has rubbed itself free. Into the blackness" (*D*, 68). Before she
disappears, however, she adds an important dimension to the
conflict of values in this work. When Garga rails against all the
"respectable, stupid, secure people" (*D*, 35) whose way of life he
despises, and pleads for his right to exercise "the freedom to go
under" (*D*, 35), his mother raises powerful ethical objections to his
concern only with his own existential problems:

> *Mäe*: Ja, schreie nur! Sage es nur, daß es alle hören. Wie alles
> umsonst ist und alles zuviel, was Mühe ist, und man wird
> weniger davon?
>
> (*D*, 36)

> *Mäe*: Yes, shout away! Just say it, so that everyone can hear you!
> How it's all a waste of time, and all too much trouble, and
> do we become any less of a problem by you saying it?

The practical moral force embodied in Maë Garga exerts a pull in a
quite different direction to the mutually opposed forces of idealism
(which can, as in Garga's case, be quite selfish) and cynicism.

The moral viewpoint voiced by Garga's mother is also expressed
in other less direct ways in the play. Two minor characters, Jane
Montpassier, Garga's mistress, and Moti Gui, Shlink's erstwhile
chief clerk, become casualties of the struggle between Shlink and
Garga simply because they are satellites of these adversaries at the
beginning of the fight. Jane is reduced to the level of a promiscuous
alcoholic and is eventually murdered, while Moti Gui is forced by
Garga to humiliate himself by fishing coins out of a slops-bucket

with his teeth.[16] The pathetic fates of these admittedly unattractive characters illustrate the sheer human waste which Shlink and Garga are prepared to create in pursuit of their existential goals. Their presence on stage thus adds weight to the element of moral opposition which is so important to the overall economy of the work.

"A COLD, UNREAL CHICAGO"

The actions of Shlink and Garga are undeniably fantastic. This does not mean, of course, that they have absolutely no connections with reality. Their needs and impulses are real enough, but they are given a freedom to act on these impulses and to seek to fulfil these needs which is just not part of our normal psychological reality.[17] A fantastic action of this kind requires to be presented in a way which will overcome the problem of its psychological improbability. The following consideration of the stylistic characteristics of the work can therefore best begin with an examination of the means used by Brecht to create a recognisably "special" world in which the characters may freely follow their impulses.

The scene-settings are perhaps the most obvious means of conveying the fact that the action of the play takes place in a world which is set apart from the everyday world. These settings reflect symbolically the moods of the principal characters. In the opening scene, for example, Maynes' lending-library is presented thus: "Brown. Wet tobacco leaves. Soapy green sash-window, steps. Low ceiling. Lots of paper" (*D*, 13). Almost every element in this description seems to convey something of Garga's inner world. The brown colour of the room suggests his feelings of depression at having to work here; it also creates associations with the many images of muck or excreta which recur throughout the play to suggest the feelings of disgust aroused in the characters by their relations with others.[18] The opaque window gives the impression of complete imprisonment, the low ceiling one of oppressiveness; the clutter of paper may be seen in relation to the dry, dusty, unsatisfying nature of the work, and to the unreality and bookishness of his attitudes to life. The same technique of mirroring inner states in the outward setting can be seen in the following scene, entitled "In the quarry": "A white chalk-face. Forenoon. Offstage, the rumble of the Pacific trains. Men shouting" (*D*, 23). Here the setting allegorises the depths of the mind where Garga makes his decision to fight Shlink rather than leave for Tahiti, the "Pacific trains" symbolising his desire to escape and the "Men shouting" representing possibly the life of struggle and pain which is the alternative if he remains here.[19] Finally, mention must be made of what is perhaps the most striking example of this symbolic technique, namely in the scene "Garga's attic" which is introduced thus: "Night. Snatches of shouting from below. The wooden closet seems to sway. A ship" (*D*, 87). Here Garga's room is made to rock like a ship in order to convey his inner turmoil.[20]

Another aspect of the "special" world in which the action is set is the use of symbolic gestures which express emotional events in a boldly stylised manner. For example, during the first attack on Garga, Shlink's crony "Worm" cuts up books with a knife. The meaning of this symbolic indication of Shlink's philistine (*Spießer*) attitude to literature is underlined by Garga's comment, "Man spießt die Literatur auf"("The Philistines are spearing open the books" – *D*, 18). Because of Garga's involvement with books it also suggests Shlink's plan to carve up Garga's life in accordance with his own whims. Worm's use of the knife is just one small part of a whole arsenal of underworld accoutrements, speech and behaviour which Brecht uses to symbolise the destructive, anti-social nature of the impulses in which Shlink and Garga are indulging. Just as these gangster trappings need to be understood metaphorically, so the material impoverishment of the Garga family does not lead out to a critical consideration of capitalist society as the cause of such misery; rather, the deprivation functions mainly as an "objective correlative" of Garga's feelings of disgust at the *spiritual* poverty of a life lived within the confines of everyday concerns. Brecht's perspective on capitalist society is not yet that of a materialist revolutionary, but, like so many of his contemporaries, that of a cultural pessimist.

Brecht's use of language in the play is a particularly important means of creating an awareness of the apartness of its fictional world. As usual he employs the "gestic" technique of stylising speech through the exaggeration of particular characteristics so as to give the actor clear guidance on the bold outward forms which he should use to convey a character's attitudes – as, for example, in Shlink's "Asiatic" habit of couching his speeches in elaborate formulae of politeness so as to keep his real motives and emotions hidden behind a mask. The most distinctive quality of the language of *In the Jungle* is, however, not the fact that it is gestic but the extent to which it is metaphorical. There is not a wide variety of metaphor but certain key images and image-clusters are used with striking frequency. The "jungle" or "thicket" image which occurs in the play's title will serve as a suitable point from which to start tracing the intertwined threads of metaphor. The thicket is a symbolic setting that mirrors the wild and entangled emotions which are normally hidden below the surface of the psyche. It is an area of the self which exerts an increasing attraction over men with the increasing denaturation of life in the modern metropolis. As a location it is not in but near to the city, a place to which Shlink and Garga retire in order to conduct the final, fierce rounds of their struggle. On the other hand, it is not a place where man can revert to animal forms of behaviour. During their struggle "in the thicket" Garga laments the gulf separating the simplicities of the primeval world from the complexities of fully evolved human experience:

Garga: Der Wald! Von hier kommt die Menschheit, nicht? Haarig, mit Affengebissen, gute Tiere, die zu leben wußten. Sie zerfleischten sich einfach, und alles war so leicht . . . und der verblutete zwischen den Wurzeln, das war der Besiegte, und der am meisten niedergetrampelt hatte vom Gehölz, der war der Sieger!

(*D*, 93)

Garga: The forest! This is where mankind came from, isn't it? Hairy, with the jaws of apes, good animals who knew how to live. They simply tore each other apart, and everything was so easy . . . the one who bled to death among the roots of the trees was the loser, and the one who had trampled down the most undergrowth was the winner!

In contrast to the primeval jungle inhabited by man's simian ancestors, the "thicket" in which Shlink and Garga try to engage in their metaphysical struggle is a spiritual tangle of ideas and emotions:

Shlink: Er verirrt sich in der Reflexion. Durch das Los der Jane haue ich ihn heraus. Das Dickicht wächst zu hoch. Der Sturm muß ihn erreichen können.

(*D*, 129)

Shlink: He is losing his way in reflection. I will hack him out by announcing Jane's fate. The thicket is growing too high. The storm has to be able to reach him.

The emotions binding Garga to his family are described with the same metaphor:

Shlink: Passionen sind kostspielig. Sitzen Sie noch im Dickicht? Schlagen tüchtig um sich? Schneiden Äste ab, die sichtlich wachsen?
Garga: Sie heben auf, was ich wegschmeiße?

(*D*, 42)

Shlink: Passions are costly. Are you still sitting in the thicket? Hacking valiantly about you? Cutting off branches which are visibly growing?
Garga: Are you picking up what I throw away?

Because this "jungle" is essentially a human, spiritual one, people are frequently referred to as trees; Shlink, speaking to Marie, says "Sie wollen eine Schlinge sein, ein Gestrüpp" ("You want to be a creeper, tangled undergrowth" – *D*, 71). Contrasting with this image of living, growing vegetation are metaphors of dead and processed wood, which Garga associates with the hated, dry and conventional life of socialised man:

Garga: . . . alle die vielen braven und fleißigen Leute, die an den Hobelbänken arbeiten und ihr Brot verdienen und die sauberen guten Tische machen . . . wie ich sie verachte.

(*D*, 35)

Garga: . . . all the many worthy and industrious people who work at their benches and earn their bread and make the good, clean tables . . . how I despise them.

In her attack on Garga's selfishness Maë Garga likens a human being to a piece of furniture, used for a time and then discarded unfeelingly (*D*, 36). It is as part of this very systematic pattern of imagery that Shlink, like the death-figure Mech in *Baal*, is given the profession of timber-merchant. The dead wood in which Shlink deals reflects the deadening of his emotions which has accompanied

his rise to wealth and social standing. His mastery of life has proved
to be a highly ambiguous achievement. Because Shlink has
identified himself so completely and for so long with civilisation's
exploitation of nature, he now feels the need to rebel violently
against his previous way of life and its dedication to the avoidance of
pain. After a lifetime spent acquiring the protection afforded by
power, and thereby sacrificing his sensitivity, Shlink now wants to
drag Garga down with him into the "jungle" of suppressed
emotions in the hope of experiencing life intensely once more
through self-exposure to pain.

Another important group of images centres on the idea of fishing.
Before the curtain rises, the audience is told in the programme-notes
that it is about to witness the *"Fischzug eines malaiischen Holzhändlers
in einer Leihbücherbude"* ("haul of a Malayan timber merchant in
a lending library" – *D*, 9). The thread of imagery is picked up again
when Garga describes himself as having been harpooned by Shlink
(*D*, 25), or as having lain like a fish in a pond and been attacked by a
stork (*D*, 27). It is necessary to have recognised the significance of
these images in order to make sense of Shlink's speech about the
"stinking fish" before his suicide. These images of fishing are related
to the jungle imagery by references to the "swamp" in which the
stork (Shlink) lives and preys.

Apart from the natural imagery of the jungle, the "mythical"
worlds of the boxing ring and the Wild West also provide images to
characterise the struggle between Shlink and Garga.[21] The
"Western" influence is to be seen in such words as "prairie",
"sheriff", "revolver", "lynch justice", or in a phrase like "So you
won't throw your hidden thoughts on the table" (*D*, 15), with its
connotation of card-playing in a saloon. The imagery of boxing is to
be found in such phrases as "I'll break anybody's nose" (*D*, 55),
"Fold back your shirt-sleeve over your biceps" (*D*, 64), or in the
requests for "a glass of water" at the end of a "round" (*D*, 65). A
later prologue invited spectators to view the play as a "wrestling
match" (*GW*, **1**, 126). The heterogeneity of such imagery and the
linguistic clash with the frequently uncolloquial sentence structures
in which they occur, contrive to heighten the element of the
fantastic in the work. By means of this fantastic struggle, life in the
modern city is presented from the perspective of the "savage soul",
the existential self desperately searching for fulfilment through
intensity of experience in a world which is being made increasingly
sterile and inhospitable by the advance of civilisation.

The jungle and the fishing images work on the simple principle of
providing physical correlates of emotional states or relationships. As
such, they are really only an extension of a central cluster of images
of the body which express the characters' feelings in deliberately
simple but forceful terms. A character's innermost self is symbolised
as his "Gesicht" which, conveniently, can denote either "face" or
"vision".[22] Hence the use in the play of the gesture of spitting in a
person's face to symbolise deeply wounding attacks on a person's
innermost self or "vision" of the world. Shlink's great strength lies in
his ability to keep his real self or "Gesicht" hidden behind the mask
of his physical face. The metaphorical use of the word "Gesicht"
thus produces surrealistic statements like the following:

> *Garga*: Aber ich will gern noch Ihr Gesicht sehen, Ihr milchig–
> glasiges, verdammtes, unsichtbares Gesicht!
> *Shlink*: Suchen Sie's.
> *Garga*: Vielleicht haben Sie gar keines.
> *Shlink*: Vielleicht ist es aus Luft!
>
> (*D*, 77)

> *Garga*: But I'd still like to see your face. Your milky–glassy,
> damnable, invisible face!
> *Shlink*: Look for it.
> *Garga*: Perhaps you don't have one at all.
> *Shlink*: Perhaps it's made of air.

As part of this complex of physical metaphor, images of skin (thick
or thin) convey the degree of a person's sensitivity. Because, on the
one hand, civilisation is built on "skinning" people,[23] while on the
other hand serving as an extra layer of protective hide, the walls of
buildings are talked of as co-extensive with the characters' skins:
"What kind of a joint is this? Covered with our skins! So that it does
not rain into our stomachs" (*D*, 21). As a corollary of this usage,
the skin may be described as permeable, like bad or broken walls, by
the weather, which in its turn supplies images of emotional states
(e.g. cold, lonely, miserable); thus: "that's poor Jane, she stuffs the
rags of her dress into her mouth, snow falls into her skin" (*D*, 95).
Although perhaps rather perplexing at first reading, the imagery of
the play is employed so consistently and systematically that it lends
itself quite easily to allegorical "de-coding" in this way.

The physical functions of sex and excretion also belong to this complex of bodily metaphors. As we have seen, images of excretion express the characters' disgust at the impurity of human relations. Sexuality, including the so-called homosexual relationship between Shlink and Garga, also needs to be interpreted in context. Shlink "loves" Garga because he is a young man with a strong fighting spirit, someone who embodies the attractions of the life which the older man is shortly to forsake. Through his contest with Garga Shlink can re-live, in a reflection as it were, his own lost youth. What he seeks is a trial of strength, particularly strength of spirit. Their relationship is described in sexual terms by Garga who quotes from *Une Saison en Enfer* Rimbaud's characterisation of his own un-ambiguously homosexual relations with Verlaine in terms of the attitude of a kept woman to her man:

Garga: "Ich nenne ihn: meinen höllischen Gemahl in meinen Träumen." Shlink, den Hund. "Wir sind von Tisch und Bett geschieden. Er hat keine Kammer mehr, sein Bräutchen trinkt zuviel Absinth. Er bringt weißes Brot in die Familie! Nun, die Mätresse raucht Virginias und verdient sich was in die Strümpfe!" Das bin ich!

(D, 47)

Garga: "I call him: my infernal spouse in my dreams." Shlink, the dog. "We are separated from table and bed. He no longer has a chamber, his little bride drinks too much absinth. He's bringing white bread home to the family! Now, his mistress smokes Virginias and puts her earnings in her stockings." That's me!

Garga recites these lines in a bar where he is getting drunk on the money he was supposedly going to spend on a ticket to Tahiti. Like that of the unfaithful mistress of the poem, his debauchery is an expression both of hatred and self-hatred. In both cases the act of breaking faith is an expression of resentment which attests to the strength of the continuing, but twisted emotional bond between the pair. The mixture of attachment and resentment in the sexual relationship provides an analogy for the tensions between the partners in the metaphysical struggle. To take such metaphors literally would be to introduce an inappropriate element of naturalism into the interpretation of the play.

One critic has described the language of the play as an "experimental style which hardly ever aims at creating dialogues which are comprehensible or through which the characters come to an understanding".[24] Yet, where this critic may have experienced some difficulty in following the dialogue (which is not altogether surprising in view of its stubborn opaqueness), the characters themselves evidently do not experience any such difficulty, for they move about within this "code" of metaphors in exactly the same way as people normally use everyday language. It is also inappropriate to criticise Brecht for allowing characters to speak in a style which would not be the normal means of expression of such a character in reality. The language in the play operates as an enclosed system with its own conventions, the principal one being the use of metaphors where most people would simply describe a thing directly, with the result that highly metaphorical language ceases to become an individual speech characteristic. Linguistic individualisation does nevertheless take place, although created by other means; for example, Shlink uses peculiarly "Asiatic" turns of phrase, while his henchman Moti Gui, a none-too-well-educated thug, habitually uses the loose ungrammatical construction *tun*, plus an infinitive. On the other hand, it is true to say that the "artificial language" of the work is a symbol of inadequate communication, for although the characters exchange words (or metaphors) freely enough, each is necessarily so alone with his existential predicament that he can neither express his *individual* feelings nor understand those of others. The artificiality of the language is thus a way of "estranging" and so drawing attention to the foreignness of the coins of linguistic exchange, to the fact that words generalise, deaden, simplify and codify expression so as to make it impossible for a person to communicate his feelings *directly*.[25] One character sums up the problem when he complains of "Words! Sentences without teeth!" (*D*, 71). From this perspective some light can be thrown on Brecht's statement that "In *Jungle* I wanted to improve on *The Robbers* (by proving that struggle is impossible because of the inadequacies of language)" (*GW*, **15**, 69). A common criticism of Schiller's *The Robbers* has always been the dramatist's failure to bring the warring brothers together dramatically. *In the Jungle*, by contrast, sets out to show that no dramatic struggle between two individuals is *possible*, because the existential self is essentially private and inaccessible, lacking any language to communicate its pain to others and unable to know what pain it has caused to others.

The formal aspects of the play which we have been examining, the staging, the stylisation of gesture, the peculiarities of the language, all co-operate in creating a special fictional world which is markedly different from the world in which we normally move. Herbert Ihering put this point well in his review of the première:

> A police report from Chicago's Chinatown has become a vision, a subject suitable for a penny-dreadful has become an apocalyptic parable. . . . Brecht creates an atmosphere in which unheard-of things, the air in which uninterpretable things are bound to happen. With the opening words he creates a third world, in which the struggle between people must unfold on a different level, "in the aether".[26]

The construction of a special fictional world for these characters is, on the one hand, an act of liberation, a setting-free of impulses which are repressed in reality so that the spectator may vicariously share them for the duration of the play. On the other hand, the evident "otherness" of this fictional world is also a means of containing and defining these very impulses, and so functions as a means of gaining intellectual and emotional control over them. While allowing his characters (and through them, his audience) to enjoy behaving with the brutal ruthlessness of underworld thugs, Brecht simultaneously defines as ugly and irresponsible the actions which the liberated existential self might resort to in the pursuit of its aims. In other words, this technique of giving larger-than-life expression to normally outlawed desires is ironic or ambivalent in effect.[27]

Brecht draws on a number of forms of popular entertainment in *Im Dickicht* in order to find images which will both express and "contain" the violence of the action. At the first performance of the play sensational headlines such as one might read in the yellow press were shouted out across the stage by "newspaper vendors" before the curtain rose. The intended effect, one presumes, must have been to create both an atmosphere of excitement and, at the same time, an ironic awareness of the clichéd, suspect nature of the emotions being appealed to. As has been noted already, the myths of the Wild West and the underworld are important sources of this kind of ironically deployed imagery. Erich Engel's staging also sought to incorporate something of the atmosphere of the waxworks (which traditionally included a chamber of horrors) when he prescribed "paper lanterns, so as to bring out the waxworks effect" (*D*, 120).

The ambivalence of the play's stylistic peculiarities contributes to the tension between opposing sets of values which is generated in the course of the action, for the style both yields to the violence of the content and, by defining it, resists the pull of this violence. As a final illustration of the dual function of the formal characteristics, mention may be made of one aspect of the language and an aspect of the staging which have not so far been discussed. As R. Pohl has pointed out (*Strukturelemente*, p. 88), there are moments when the passions of the characters break through the protective veil of artificial language and express themselves in freer, more fluid speech patterns than usual. Such moments as these tend to intensify one's emotional involvement with the characters:

> *Garga*: Nein, ich will nicht mehr.
> *Maë*: Du willst nicht mehr? Aber ich? Wie sollen sie hier durchkommen? Reiße mir doch nicht die Zähne aus! Ich kann vielleicht mehr arbeiten, oft schlafe ich halb beim Waschen. Und ich kann vielleicht etwas schneller laufen in der Stadt aber ich kann sie nicht allein durchbringen, das weiß ich.
>
> (*D*, 35–6)

> *Garga*: No, I don't want to go on.
> *Maë*: You don't want to go on? But what about me? How are they to survive here? Don't tear out my teeth! Perhaps I can work more, I'm often half asleep over the washing. And perhaps I can run a bit faster in the town, but I can't manage to support them alone, that much I know.

The opposite effect to that achieved here, namely that of inhibiting such involvement in the fiction, appears to be the intention underlying Brecht's desire to have the actors not actually involved in a given scene seated at the back of the stage, following the action in their scripts:

> Everything played before a circular backdrop. To the rear the actors not involved in the scene follow the text; they are in dusty illumination. The book slips from the hands of the dead Jane Garga etc. (*D*, 136)

The tension between emotional involvement in, and emotional distance from the fates of the characters is reflected not only in the style of the work, but also in Brecht's comments on it. For example, in an address "To the gentleman in the stalls", written in connection with the Berlin production of 1925, he described the play as one which would appeal to the audience's desire for irrational excitement, whilst at the same time offering an opportunity for the exercise of their rational powers:

> As a man of our times you have a need to exercise your gift of combination, and you are resolutely determined to let your talent for organisation triumph equally over life and over my image of it. That is why you were in favour of the play *"Jungle"*. I knew that you want to sit there calmly and deliver your judgement of the world, as well as testing your knowledge of human nature by backing one or other of the people up on the stage. . . . You consider it valuable to have a share in certain *senseless* feelings of enthusiasm and discouragement, which are part of life's fun. All in all, I have to aim to strengthen your appetite in my theatre. Should I be so successful, that you feel like lighting a cigar, and excel myself by having it go out at certain points, predetermined by myself, both you and I will be satisfied with me.
>
> (*GW*, **15**, 75)

"IT BEHOVES A MAN TO SMOKE AND TO FIGHT WITH METAPHYSICS"[28]

Although *In the Jungle* differs from *Drums in the Night* in many respects (style, milieu, characterisation), the two plays are related by theme. In both plays the conflict between "realism" and romanticism figures prominently. But, whereas in *Drums in the Night* Brecht realised his aim of steering the hero first into and then safely out of the dangerous waters of romanticism, there is in *In the Jungle* no clear resolution of the conflict between these attitudes to life. At the end of *Drums in the Night* Kragler simply abandons the idea of seeking a romantic death on the barricades when Anna comes back to him. However, in order to persuade the audience (and himself?) that Kragler is making the right choice by opting to compromise with an imperfect reality, Brecht lapses at the last moment into rather clumsy sentimentality. *In the Jungle* begins more or less where

Drums in the Night left off, with Garga trying to make the best of a life of compromise such as Kragler had finally opted for. Yet here Shlink finds little difficulty in loosening Garga's hold on normality when he prods the nerve of existential dissatisfaction. Throughout the fight Garga is shown to suffer considerable emotional losses because of his romantic self-abandonment to the passion of hatred, but he continues the struggle because these losses are compensated by the excitement of the struggle and the pleasure of having a specific goal in life to which he can devote his intellectual and emotional energies.

If *In the Jungle* is more honest than *Drums in the Night* in its appraisal of the dissatisfactions and tensions in a life founded on compromise, it is also more honest than *Baal* in its assessment of self-indulgent romanticism as an alternative to compromise. Whereas *Baal* was an escapist fantasy in which the hero experienced little internal or external opposition to his behaving amorally, like an "Orang Utang", Garga both finds it painful to try to sever his emotional and ethical bonds with other people, and discovers in the end that there is no way back to the simian satisfactions and simplicities of the forest. Men have become too complicated and differentiated in the course of their spiritual evolution for them to be able to experience the satisfaction of clear-cut victory or defeat in life's struggles for domination, such as apes may have achieved. Because Garga and Shlink are not content with the outward signs of power, with simply "stamping the enemy into the ground", but want rather to penetrate into each other's minds in order to *experience* what the other is feeling, particularly at moments of defeat, their struggle must end in frustration. Evolution, by giving each man an individually differentiated spiritual life has also condemned man to become conscious of his emotional isolation within a relatively undifferentiated fleshy cell.[29] Because man wants more than the animals, he has less. Although it is possible to gain control over the external circumstances of other men's lives, neither love nor hatred can produce access to the existential centre of another self. Consequently, the struggle between Shlink and Garga peters out in frustration and ambiguity.

In the Jungle is the first play of Brecht's that does not end with a hero triumphing, in one way or another, over the difficulties he encounters. In fact, although one would *probably* describe Garga as the protagonist of the play, his fate and character are not allowed to overshadow all else. Shlink is just as fascinating and powerful a personality, even more so perhaps, and the characters of Marie and Maë Garga also attract interest in their own right. This care in developing a number of characters, who all pull in different directions, but particularly the creation of an antagonist who is fully a match for the protagonist, makes for a richer and better balanced drama than Brecht had produced hitherto. Despite the subjectivity of its themes, *In the Jungle* is a much more objective, impartial play than those which preceded it.[30]

Yet, although Brecht's will to master experience was not permitted in *In the Jungle* to express itself *directly* through the triumphant actions of a hero, this does not mean that this impulse was entirely suppressed in the writing of the play. Rather, it found expression through less direct, but artistically more legitimate channels. It is evident in the creation of an "alienated" language and in the parodies of popular forms of entertainment, techniques which distance and define the emotional life of the characters. It is perhaps most palpable in the many ironies which shape the action. Irony is at work from the very beginning of the first scene, when Garga unwittingly declares a travelogue to be a "better" book than a detective novel. In the course of the next few minutes he not only discovers how uncertain he really is about where his values lie, but he also finds his life beginning to resemble the plot of one of the thrillers he so despises. In this opening scene irony follows irony: Garga, who worships the words of certain authors, finds that words fail him when he tries to convey his love to Jane; he believes himself able to withdraw into an inner realm of "Asiatic" freedom, but quickly succumbs to his passions when Shlink unleashes them. Irony also links scene with scene: whereas at the end of Scene 1 Garga departs proclaiming his right to freedom, he is unwilling, in Scene 3, to allow his sister to act independently; whereas Garga is convinced in Scene 2 that his counter-attack will take Shlink completely by surprise, he finds in Scene 3 that Shlink has been fully expecting him to appear. Shlink too is subjected to humiliation by the twists of irony. After drawing Marie, with some difficulty, into a sexual relationship with him, purely in order to harm Garga, Shlink is "rewarded" by Marie's re-appearance, bringing the gift of her love, at the very moment when he most wants to be alone with the shame and disgust of his suicide. The irony which unfolds from the beginning of the first scene is still at work at the end of the final one: the last image of the play is of Garga seated, grinning, in the chair which once was Shlink's. Garga stays seated when a voice off-stage

announces that the "East wind" has sprung up, for which he has
been waiting. Garga has removed Shlink from the scene of his
former power, but is now unsure what he should do with his life, and
has become so hardened emotionally as a result of their struggle,
that his occupation of Shlink's seat seems to signify that he has also
inherited from Shlink the insensitivity which drove the Malayan
into a pointless masochistic struggle. The closing image is,
appropriately, an ironic one, of victory and defeat in one. Such
irony was Brecht's chief means of "smoking and fighting with
metaphysics" in the writing of this play.

In the Jungle is a play in which Brecht took stock of his emotional
and intellectual position.[31] In it his desire for mastery of experience
was kept within the bounds of defining the complexities of living in
an urban environment where man is made increasingly aware of his
existential isolation from other men and from the world around
him. The "malevolent, stony consistency" of the great cities
(T, 145) becomes here a metaphor for the harsh, inhospitable face
of the world, once "Nature" has been stripped of any show of
motherliness. In the coldness of his Chicago his characters are made
to feel the coldness of empty space. The imagery and language of the
play have a new persuasiveness, and the characterisation and
interaction of the figures is subtle and fascinating. In other words,
by tying his imagination down to the task of *defining* the experience,
Brecht's work gained in poetic, dramatic and psychological worth.
Whether he also created a play which is theatrically viable is a
question which still remains to be answered. It is a play which,
although not performed frequently, has caught the imagination of
at least two distinguished producers in Erich Engel and Peter
Stein.[32] Both producers found they had to devise means of coping
with the problem of the play's deliberate opaqueness. Engel's
method (which caused heated conflict with Brecht)[33] was the
"Stanislavskian" one of helping the actors to develop an intuitive
understanding of the emotional dynamics of the scenes. His hope
was that the audience, although likely to be baffled by the
intellectual issues at stake, might nevertheless perceive the patterns
and the nuances in the characters' interaction, which, after all, is
what turns the metaphysical argument into something dramatically
interesting. Peter Stein's production, by contrast, was much colder.
Taking as his text Brecht's advice to regard the action as a sporting
event, Stein presented it as a gymnastic exercise in the theatre of the
absurd. Unfortunately, the melancholy undertone of the play could

not make itself felt in such a production. A production which succeeded in combining critical distance with a sympathetic understanding of the characters would seem to be required by the text. It remains to be seen whether, once time has brought a greater familiarity with Brecht's early work, the play will challenge more producers to attempt to stage it, or whether its metaphorical density and the demands this makes on an audience will condemn it to the fate of so many other German dramas – that of being read but not performed.

5 *The Life of Edward the Second of England*

The thematic consistency of Brecht's Marxist work is fully matched by that of his pre-Marxist writing. So insistently did his mind keep returning to his central concern, namely the individual's ability (or lack of it) to master painful experiences, that even his adaptations of the plays of other dramatists resulted in the transformation of the original into something which is stylistically and thematically of a piece with the products of Brecht's own imagination. With the ruthlessness of a self-styled "vandal" he would take over certain characters and the rough outline of a plot, and use these as a vehicle for expressing his own concerns and point of view.[1] Of course, the pieces chosen for adaptation were such as to lend themselves to his purposes. In 1923, at a time when the reaction against Expressionism had re-awakened interest in historical drama, Brecht was given a contract to prepare *Macbeth* for production at the Munich Kammerspiele. Instead, however, he adapted Marlowe's *Life of Edward the Second* in 1924, drawing heavily on the psychology of *In the Jungle* in the process.[2] Presumably the Marlowe was chosen because it could be assimilated more easily than *Macbeth* to the patterns of behaviour which Brecht had already dramatised. Later Brecht described this adaptation as "a copy, a greedy reminiscence of a more fortunate dramatic era" (*GW*, **17**, 952). In "copying" Marlowe he was able to paint on a broad historical canvas, rehearse the use of "naïve" techniques of presentation, and work in an historical milieu where the kind of brutal and arbitrary behaviour he was interested in was socially and psychologically plausible.

The adaptation of works by other authors was to remain an important aspect of Brecht's work in the theatre throughout his career, and was eventually to become the main outlet for his creativity on his return to Berlin after the Second World War.[3] His later adaptations were mainly concerned with developing in the audience a dialectical–historical understanding of social processes by presenting it with pictures of life in past ages and inviting it to perceive critically both the parallels and the contrasts between the past and the present. In contrast to this later development, Brecht's first adaptation tends to reduce the element of socio-historical narrative in Marlowe's original. In 1924 Brecht was not interested in bringing a modern audience's historical self-understanding into dialectical confrontation with a past age, but sought rather to use Marlowe's picture of feudal anarchy simply as raw material from which to fashion a dramatic image of the complex of moral and emotional tensions which preoccupied him in these early years.

"LE ROI RÉVOLTÉ"

In some remarks made a few years after his adaptation of Marlowe's *Edward II* Brecht touched, in passing, on the difference of emphasis between his own view of Edward and Marlowe's presentation of the king's character:

> The secret of the great figures of drama partly consists in the fact that they can have virtually any body and that there is room in them for many private traits. Just as, in the dramas under consideration, the poet permits one to take various views of the subject-matter, so equally, the dramatic figures are quite indeterminate. Edward II, for example, can equally well be a strong, evil man as a weak, good one. For the kind of weakness, the kind of evil he has is very deep and metaphysical and present in all manner of people.   (*GW*, **15**, 195)

Seen from the standpoint of Christian metaphysics, as in Marlowe's play, Edward II is a weak man whose mind is torn between its spiritual duties and the temptations of earthly passions. The career of Brecht's Eduard,[4] by contrast, takes place within the context of a transcendental void, and the king's spiritual freedom is restricted merely to choosing the manner of his inevitable destruction.

In Marlowe's play the frailty of the human condition is demonstrated in an action of awe-inspiring magnitude by putting a mighty ruler in the role of Everyman being tempted and having to take stock of his life when summoned by Death. The dangers besetting the soul in this mortal life can be shown with particular clarity in the case of a king, because his crown both imposes on him

particularly onerous duties, and, by the power it gives him, exposes
him to great temptations of pride and passion, both of which he can
indulge to a degree denied to most men. King Edward's death in
prison is here a case of the punishment fitting the crime, for, having
allowed his soul to become the prisoner of his passions, it is poetically
or "wittily" apt that he should end his days in literal
imprisonment.[5]

Brecht's Eduard also ends his days in prison, but differs from
Marlowe's in experiencing his imprisonment not as a punishment
but rather as a source of masochistic pleasure. Brecht took as his
starting point for this radical change a detail in the original:
Edward's pain is increased by the fact that his body, in not
succumbing to torture, seems to conspire against him:

Matrevis: He hath a body able to endure
             More than we can inflict and therefore now
             Let us assail his mind another while.

                                          (*Mar*, 100)

It seems that his body, the seat of the passions and prison of his soul,
has now become an instrument of his punishment. For Brecht's
Eduard by contrast, the resilience of his body under the duress of
torture is a source of pleasure:

Eduard: Die Grub, drin sie mich halten ist die Senkgrub,
           Und über mich her, seit sieben Stunden, fällt
           Der Kot Londons. Doch sein Abwasser härtet
           Meine Gliedmaßen. Sie sind schon wie Holz
           Der Zeder. Geruch des Abfalls macht mich noch
           Maßlos vor Größe. Gutes Geräusch der Trommel
           Läßt wachen den Geschwächten, daß ihn nicht
           Anlangt sein Tod in Ohnmacht, sondern im
           Wachen.

                                          (*E*, 224)

Edward: This hole in which they hold me is the sink-hole
           And upon me here, these seven hours, falls
           London's filth. Yet its sewage hardens
           My limbs. Now they are like cedar
           Wood. The stench of rubbish makes my
           Stature boundless. Great rolls on the drums

Keep him awake, though weak, so his death
Find him not in a swoon, but rather
Waking.

(*MI*, 261)

This last detail, Eduard's determination to meet death with open eyes, is another example of Brecht's technique of developing in a perverted form motifs already present in the original. Marlowe's Edward is shown as a penitent Christian who wants to meet his death in full consciousness in order that his soul may be prepared to meet its Maker:

Edward: Yet stay awhile, forbear thy bloody hand.
And let me see the stroke before it comes
That even then when I shall lose my life
My mind may be more steadfast on my God.

(*Mar*, 103)

By contrast, Brecht's Eduard (like Shlink) wants to see death coming so that he may continue to experience to the very last moment the fact of his existence with all the conscious intensity that he can muster. This blasphemous perversion of the Marlowian theme is intensified by having Eduard compose and sing "*Psalmen/ Weils Frühjahr wird*" (*E*, 223; "psalms/Against Spring's coming" – *MI*, 260). These "psalms" celebrate spring, not as the season of Christ's death and resurrection, but with a pagan glorification of violence and of the psalmist's own energy:

Eduard: Gut war Regen, Nichtessen sättigte. Aber
Das Beste war die Finsternis. Alle
Waren unschlüssig, zurückhaltend viele, aber
Die Besten waren, die mich verrieten. Darum
Wer dunkel ist, bleibe dunkel, wer
Unrein ist, unrein. Lobet
Mangel, lobet Mißhandlung, lobet
Die Finsternis.

(*E*, 224)

Edward: Good was rain; hunger satisfied. But
The best was darkness. All

Were wavering, many hanging back but
The best were those betrayed me. Therefore
Whoever's dark let him dark remain, who's
Unclean, remain unclean. Praise
Want, praise cruelty, praise
The darkness.

(*M*I, 262)

Whereas the repentance of Marlowe's Edward marks a turn for
the better in a sinful life, the blasphemy of Brecht's Eduard in prison
crowns a life of blasphemy. Not believing in God, he claims for
himself the powers which are normally God's alone; thus, when he
wants Anna to commit adultery with Mortimer, he mockingly and
arrogantly offers to give her absolution for her sins (*E*, 177–8; *M*I,
210). His masochistic hymns to suffering and darkness are his
response to a world which, "geht schier bald unter" ("will soon be
wrecked") and in which man consequently becomes law unto
himself.

Eduard's masochism in prison should not then be regarded
merely as the *outcome* of his experiences, but rather as the now
revealed *motive* for seeking these experiences in the first place. His
words in praise of pain finally clarify the reason for his curious
behaviour in the years preceding and culminating in his imprisonment and torture. Seen in this light, his career is a search for
opportunities to exercise and suffer violence, a search which he feels
to be the proper response to the inescapable fact of individual
isolation. In Eduard's view man neither has a God to turn to (hence
his cynical arrogation of the power of forgiveness) nor is he able to
make any spiritual contact with another human being. Even
physical contact with other men gives little comfort to compensate
for the lack of spiritual communication (*E*, 195; *M*I, 230).
Encapsulated in his individuality, the only meaning he can see in
life lies in exercising his capacities as an individual to the full.
Eduard therefore leads a life of unremitting struggle, deliberately
manoeuvering himself into dangerous situations in order to find the
measure of his personal capacity for treachery, cruelty and
suffering. His aim is to embody in his life the principle of transience
to which all existence is subject, to consume and be consumed in
turn, seeking at least to determine *how* the world shall bring about
his death, and thus to realise the limited degree of freedom which is
his within an overall existential situation of constraint. His

philosophy and strategy are similar to Shlink's in *In the Jungle*, with the difference that he succeeds where Shlink failed. Whereas Shlink was unable to force Garga to kill him and was thus forced to have recourse to suicide, Eduard does manage to maneouvre his chosen enemy, Mortimer, into murdering him and suffering in turn the consequences of this action.

The thread running through Eduard's bizarre career is his devotion to a life of unremitting and ever-widening *revolt*. The revolt begins before the action of the play, with his choice of the "butcher's boy", Daniel Gaveston, to be his homosexual "bosom friend" and favourite. This revolt is suppressed during the lifetime of Eduard's father by the latter's banishment of Gaveston to Ireland. However, as soon as his father has died, even before the requiem mass has been read for him, Gaveston is summoned back to London by the new king. Yet Eduard's revolt is much more than a rebellion against the authority of his own father.[6] It is a revolt against all father-figures, against all authorities and all conventions that would set limits to his personal arbitrariness. The summons of Gaveston to London in direct defiance of the dying wish of his father is already a deepening of his revolt from one directed against a person to one directed against the *principle* that a dying man's last wishes are sacrosanct. Aptly, then, the first person to suffer at the hands of the new king is a churchman, a representative of divine authority. Eduard incites Gaveston to duck in the gutter the Abbot of Coventry in revenge for the part this cleric played in having Gaveston banished and so thwarting the will of Eduard. Eduard then bestows on Gaveston the abbot's title, land and income. In this small example of his indulgence of his homosexual favourite Eduard can be seen to flout law, authority, convention. As a king he has a duty to preserve the peace, not to incite to violence against individuals. As the head of the court he should respect the sensitivities of his peers, not flout them by making a low-born man his favourite. As a husband, he should love his wife Anna above all others; instead, he tortures his wife by rejecting her in favour of Gaveston, defies his father (who chose his bride), and scorns the sexual conventions of his society by flaunting his homosexual passion.

In the course of the action Eduard's revolt develops from a rebellion against persons, institutions and conventions into a refusal even to be bound by the dictates of prudence. This leads to the loss of Gaveston, the freeing of Mortimer (the king's most effective enemy and murderer of Gaveston) and eventually to the king's own defeat, imprisonment, torture and death. All this, however, does not add up to a conventional tale of blind folly bringing just retribution. Rather, it is an account of a systematic, deliberate campaign against a world that is hostile to the individual. That men are born to suffer and die Eduard recognises, from the outset, all too clearly. What he will not allow, is that this malevolent world should triumph over his will. His lonely, masochistic career is an assertion to the very last of his determination to master life, to impose *his* meaning on the experiences the world would inflict on him. Eduard's masochism is the consummation of his lifelong revolt against a world where life can always be relied on to play some "dirty trick". In the following analysis of the changes made in adapting the Marlowe play, we shall see how Brecht's re-fashioning of plot, characters and themes all flow from his radically changed conception of the meaning of Eduard's life and, above all, of his death.

THE "BUTCHER'S SON"

One major aspect of the play to be altered radically as a result of the changed conception of the king's role, from that of victim of his social position and emotional needs to that of the active manipulator of his own fate, is the king's relation with Gaveston. Marlowe's Gaveston combines those qualities of aestheticism, sensuality and cunning that one might expect to find in a Renaissance poet's conception of the male "mistress" of a king. The speech in which he contemplates how he will hold his patron's favour illustrates all these qualities:

> Gaveston: I must have wanton poets, pleasant wits,
> Musicians, that with touching of a string
> May draw the pliant king which way I please;
> Music and poetry is his delight,
> Therefore I'll have Italian masques by night,
> Sweet speeches, comedies and pleasing shows,
> And in the day when he shall walk abroad,
> Like sylvan nymphs my pages shall be clad,
> My men like satyrs grazing on the lawns
> Shall with their goat feet dance an antic hay.
>   (*Mar*, 9)

This Gaveston is a schemer in politics and appears to be the active, dominant partner in his relationship with Edward. This is suggested by the imagery of the triumphant conqueror in which he voices his delight at being reunited with the king:

> Gaveston: It shall suffice me to enjoy your love,
> Which whiles I have I think myself as great
> As Caesar riding in the Roman Street,
> With captive kings at his triumphant car.
>
> (*Mar*, 13)

The imagery of the king in chains, omitted by Brecht because inappropriate to his active conception of Eduard, reinforces Marlowe's central theme of the monarch's enslavement (to his passions, to his pride, to his throne) which runs through the whole play and culminates, as has been remarked already, in the poetic justice of his physical imprisonment.

Brecht, by contrast, systematically reduces Gaveston's role to that of an uncomprehending decoy in the king's sado-masochistic game with his peers, and to this end takes away any wit and charm that he may have, so as to make him merely a boorish "son of a butcher". The frequently repeated reference to Gaveston as a butcher's son ("eines Schlächters Sohn") forms part of the pattern of blasphemy running through the play: the senseless slaughter of this man is a perversion of the saving death of Christ, "des Menschen Sohn" ("Son of Man").[7] Eduard, a self-appointed god, is shown toying cruelly with the feelings of his dependent creature in a "love scene" which takes place in the midst of a battle:

> Gaveston: Viel Volk in London sagte, dieser Krieg
> Hört nicht mehr auf.
> Edward: Höchst eigen rührt es Unser Aug, dich, Gaveston,
> In dieser Stunde, ohne Waffen, uns vertrauend,
> Ohne Schutz Leders und Erzes, nackter Haut,
> Vor Uns zu sehen, im gewöhnten
> Irischen Kleid.
>
> (*E*, 168)

> Gaveston: Many men in London say this war
> Will never end.
> Edward: Our eye is greatly moved to see thee, Gaveston,

At this hour trusting in us, weaponless
Without defensive steel or leather, bare skinned
Standing before us in accustomed
Irish weeds.

(*M*I, 200)

Gaveston's lack of protection in a dangerous situation is for Eduard
symbolic of the human condition. The death which he causes
Gaveston to suffer by his refusal to conduct the war sensibly, is an act
of sacrifice to the destructive forces which Eduard sees ranged
against Man, and with which he identifies himself. The cruelty in
Eduard's treatment of Gaveston, only implied in this love scene, is
made explicit in the following scene where Gaveston, a hunted
animal, sinks exhausted to the ground:

Gaveston: Ich rühr jetzt keine Hand mehr und ich leg
Mich einfach in den Boden da, damit
Nicht ich bleib bis ans Ende der Zeiten.
Und wenn morgen der König Eduard
Vorbeireitet, mich zu quälen, rufend, "Danyell!
Wo bist du?" bin ich nicht mehr da.

(*E*, 169)

Gaveston: I'll not move a finger but just
Lay me down on the ground here, that I
Endure not until the end of time.
And when tomorrow morning King Edward
Rides by, calling, to torment me: "Daniel
Where art thou?" I'll not be here.

(*M*I, 201)

To define Gaveston's role in the sadistic game Eduard plays with
his barons, Brecht uses again the angling imagery which he had
already employed in *In The Jungle*, and which he must have been
pleasantly surprised to find already present in Marlowe's play.
Marlowe introduces the image in a speech of Mortimer's concerning Gaveston:

Mortimer
Junior: Fair queen forbear to angle for the fish,
Which being caught, strikes him that takes it dead,

I mean that vile torpedo, Gaveston,
That now I hope floats on the Irish seas.

(Mar, 27)

In a later scene Lancaster, when asked what emblem he will bear in
the forthcoming tourney, chooses a design of a flying fish caught by
a bird of prey, which prophesies the death of Gaveston (*Mar*, 39).

The subsequently revealed significance of the fish imagery is
already present when it first occurs in Brecht's play, namely when
Eduard invites his favourite to accompany him to the pond at
Tynemouth:

Eduard: Mein Gaveston, du hast nur mich zum Freund.
Laß sie! Wir gehen an den Teich von Tynemouth,
Fischend, Fische essend, reitend, schlendernd,
Auf den Ballistenwällen Knie an Knie

(E, 157)

Edward: My dearest Gaveston, thou hast me for thy friend.
Let them be! We'll to the pond at Tynemouth
Fishing, eating fish, riding, strolling,
On the catapult walls, knee to knee.

(MI, 87)[8]

What the imagery implies, unbeknown to Gaveston, is that he is to
serve as the bait to catch the anger of the barons: Eduard's
aggressive intentions are suggested by his choice of the "catapult
walls" as the place to flaunt his dalliance with the hated Gaveston.
The king's provocation becomes more explicit in the next but one
scene where the barons watch as Eduard demonstrates his new
military machines, ostensibly to Gaveston, now Earl of Cornwall,
but in fact to the barons whose hostility he is bent on provoking, as
Lancaster wryly observes to the Archbishop (*E*, 160; *MI*, 190–1).
When Mortimer takes up the thread of fish-imagery in his "Helen of
Troy" speech in parliament, he alludes to the nature of Gaveston's
role in the king's relations with his barons. According to Mortimer's
account, the Greeks, as they lay waiting and fishing in the harbour
at Troy, were really angling for the anger of the Trojans:

Mortimer: Die Griechen weiter liegen fischend auf den Segeln,
Den herabgelassenen, bis in einer Ale-Kneipe

Im Hafenviertel einer einem
Die Nase blutig haut, ausredend sich,
Dies sei um Helena.
Vor jemand sichs versah in folgenden Tagen,
Griffen vieler Hände nach vieler Hälsen.
Von zerbrochenen Schiffen spießte man viele auf,
Ertrinkende, wie Thunfische.

(*E*, 164)

Mortimer: The Greeks still lay fishing on their drooping
Sails until, in an ale-house
On the water-front, someone bloodied
Another's nose, pretending
It was for Helen's sake.
Before they knew it in the days that followed
Many hands grasped many throats.
From broken ships men speared other men
Like fishes as they drowned.

(*M*I, 195–6)

Like Helen in this ironic account of the Trojan War, Gaveston is no more than an excuse for a conflict which, like the pub-brawl in Troy, is sought and fought for its own sake. Gaveston's passivity is further emphasised by another variant on the fish metaphor, Mortimer's reference to the weeping, terrified favourite, now the prisoner of the barons, as a "wässrigen Stockfisch" (*E*, 170). The usual metaphorical connotation of *Stockfisch*, namely "whipping-boy" (because dried fish was beaten to make it palatable), also reiterates Gaveston's scapegoat-role in the war.

Whereas for Marlowe's Edward Gaveston is the object of a blinding passion which he merely wants to preserve from the world's interference, Brecht's Eduard uses his favourite as a means of deliverately provoking his barons into war. The difference between the respective attitudes of the two kings to Gaveston is brought out by their differing responses to the news of his death. Edward immediately swears to avenge the loss of his beloved favourite in a speech which culminates in an anguished curse on "You villains that have slain my Gaveston" (*Mar*, 62). Brecht's Eduard, by contrast, swears an oath of revenge which makes no reference at all to the barons' assault on his sovereignty nor to the loss of Gaveston.

This Eduard's curse is no more than an expression of blood-lust, with homosexual overtones. His speech ends with the lines, "I will have your white/Headless trunks" (*M*I, 212), a formulation which echoes his twice repeated, "I will have Gaveston" in the first confrontation with his peers. Just as a strong measure of cruelty was involved in his homosexual love for Gaveston, so it would appear that there is an element of homosexual lust for the white trunks of the barons in his hatred of them. The lack of any lasting feeling for Gaveston is further suggested by Eduard's attitude to his corpse:

Eduard: Sorget, wird des Gaveston Körper aufgefunden,
           Für würdiges Begräbnis. Doch sucht ihn nicht.
           Er glich dem Mann, der wegab ins Gestrüpp geht
           Hinter dem die Sträucher zusammenwachsen, die
             Kräuter
           Sich wieder aufrichten, so daß ihn Dickicht
           Einfängt.

                                      (*E*, 186)

Edward: If Gaveston's corpse is found, take care
           To give it honourable burial. Yet seek it not.
           He was like a man who walks away into the wood:
           Behind him bushes close again, grass
           Springs up again and he is swallowed in the
           Undergrowth.

                                      (*M*I, 219)

The image of the "Dickicht" ("thicket") closing behind Gaveston suggests Eduard's ability to submerge his memory of him as unfeelingly as nature swallows up its own creations. Having served his purpose as a bait for the barons' anger, Gaveston simply ceases to exist as far as Eduard is concerned.

THE QUEEN

Because of the shift in Brecht's presentation of Eduard's homosexuality away from the motives of infatuation and regal pride and towards that of revolt, changes also had to be made in the role of the queen. In the original the king, after having been forced by the barons to renew the banishment order against Gaveston, asks the queen to use her influence with Mortimer and the other peers to procure his favourite's return. If she fails she is forbidden to return to court, but if she succeeds she is to be reconciled with the king. This whole episode emphasises the extent to which Edward's love for Gaveston determines his state of mind: while Gaveston is gone he is lovesick, determined to take revenge against the barons and harsh in his treatment of the queen, but when she succeeds in securing Gaveston's return, he becomes as happy as a child, kind to the queen and generous towards the peers. The incident also demonstrates his political naïveté, for it shows him as foolish enough to believe that he can rely unreservedly on the queen's love for him, simply ignore her hatred of Gaveston, and enter into a bargain with Mortimer. In fact the queen and Mortimer betray him by appearing to accede to his desire to have Gaveston back, while secretly planning to kill the favourite at the merest provocation on his return. In Brecht's version, by contrast, there is no question of the king agreeing to banish Gaveston, with the result that the scenes showing his fluctuations of mood according to the state of his relations with Gaveston simply disappear. Brecht does however find an opportunity to use the incident of Eduard's request that the queen approach Mortimer, but gives this a quite new significance. When the king hears that Gaveston has been taken prisoner, he orders Anna to prostitute herself with Mortimer to obtain his release; he also demands that she go to Scotland to find more troops for him. But whereas Marlowe's Edward had held out the promise of reconciliation in return for her help, this Eduard makes absolutely no attempt to conceal his dislike of the queen, while yet insisting that he will never free her from the marriage which his father arranged for them against Eduard's wishes (*E*, 178, *M*I, 211). In this scene, the naïveté of Marlowe's infatuated king has been replaced by malicious cunning. Maltreated as she has been and long frustrated sexually, Anna is clearly bound to seek solace with Mortimer and so betray Eduard. This is of course precisely what Eduard wants her to do, because this will not only provide a spurious cause of contention with Mortimer, behind which to hide his true sado-masochistic intentions, but will also mean that Mortimer will later have the Scottish troops with which to attack the king.

As well as changing the king's attitude to the queen, Brecht also changes Mortimer's relation to her. Whereas for Marlowe's Mortimer Isabella was a coveted prize, both personally and as the mother of the next king of England, whose protector Mortimer would like to be, Brecht's Mortimer accepts Anna in the same spirit as Eduard rejects her: she is to be courted because, like Gaveston, she can serve to give some spurious justification to the struggle between the two men.[9] Mortimer makes no pretence of his contempt for Anna even during his courtship of her, and Anna is right in feeling that there is a strong element of aggression in his sexual approach; her choice of the words "mich anspringt" ("falls on me") conveys this ambiguity:

> Anna: [*für sich*]
> Sehr elender Eduard, wie erniedrigst du mich,
> Daß ich diesem nicht ins Gesicht schlagen darf,
> Sondern muß stillhalten, bloßstehen,
> Wenn er mich anspringt in Geilheit.
>
> (*E*, 161)

> Anna: [*aside*]
> Oh base Edward, how you shame me
> That I dare not strike him in the face
> But must stand silent, naked
> When he falls on me in his lust.
>
> (*M*I, 192)[10]

Anna's union with Mortimer is based entirely on a common antagonism towards Eduard and not on mutual love. This is made clear in the scene following the Battle of Killingworth when they both swear revenge on the king and join forces to defeat him (*E*, 187–8, *M*I, 220–1). Their relationship breaks down when Anna, who needs violent struggle to compensate her for the emotional loss which separation from Eduard means to her, grows bored and impatient at the tactical struggle which Mortimer has to continue to wage after capturing Eduard. Deprived of the opportunity, first of love, then for active hatred, she becomes gluttonous, alcoholic, sexually insatiable and openly hostile to Mortimer. Her gradual descent into a state of desperate, self-hating sterility, where she "laughs at the emptiness of the world", underscores the bleak view of the "vanity" of life which forms the background to the aggressions of the king and Mortimer.

Anna's physical deterioration and emotional destruction towards the end of the play are the result of an emotional conflict which is present from the beginning, but gradually worsens. At heart she is a loving and kind person who is driven reluctantly into hatred and cruelty. Her antagonism towards Eduard is really a transformed expression of her love for him, and her sexual and political union with Mortimer is an entirely unsatisfying substitute for her failed marriage with the king. When she eventually turns against her ally Mortimer, this is only the culmination of the hatred which she has felt towards him for a long time and for a variety of reasons. She hates Mortimer because he is the enemy of the man she loves, because she knows that Mortimer's courtship of her was no act of passion but a piece of unpalatable yet necessary political "business", and she hates him because her union with Mortimer is a constant reminder both of her failure to win Eduard's love and of her guilt in transforming her love for him into hatred.

In a complicated, indirect way the spiritually broken Anna still functions as one of the voices of morality that are raised in the play against the self-regarding struggle between the king and his barons. Her double function as accomplice in violence and moral critic of violence accounts for the inconsistency of her attitude towards Gaveston during the battle of Killingworth. Whereas at the beginning of one scene she curses "this devil Gaveston", she pleads for kindness to be shown him when she meets him in the course of the very same scene. Similarly, although for long disaffected from Mortimer, she pleads with her son Eduard to temper justice with humanity when dealing with Mortimer's crimes. Generally though, her role is to present an indictment of violence more subtly, by embodying the sheer human waste which results from the antagonisms of the powerful.

THE CROWN

The new focus which Brecht brings to bear on his material is evident not only in his handling of the theme of homosexuality and the resulting changes in the roles of Gaveston and Anna, but also in his presentation of the king's attitude to his office. A central concern of Marlowe's play is with the problems and, in Moelwyn Merchant's phrase, the "ironies of kingship" (*Mar*, xiv). This subject is given ironic treatment by having the conflicting principles of legalism and divine right represented by individuals with marked personal failings. Edward's insistence on the absolute and inalienable nature of his inherited authority is made to appear questionable by placing emphasis on his personal arbitrariness and the abuse of his office for private ends; equally, Mortimer's defence of the peers' right to depose an unjust king ill conceals his own ambitions for royal power. The matter is made more complex still by the introduction of a curious see-saw-like effect whereby Edward gains in moral stature as he is weakened physically and politically, while Mortimer's initial concern for the political health of his country gradually becomes debased to purely personal Machiavellianism when he acquires power.

In Brecht's version, the problems of feudal sovereignty cease to be a focus of attention.[11] This is particularly noticeable in the changes made to the scenes where the king is asked to abdicate. In the original, Edward is troubled by feelings of guilt at the thought of relinquishing a divinely sanctioned office: "No, these innocent hands of mine shall not be guilty of so foul a crime" (*Mar*, 85). Brecht's Eduard, by contrast, absolutely refuses to abdicate, although not because of qualms about his duty to remain king:

Eduard:　[*er setzt die Krone wieder auf*]
　　　　　Unmenschliche, genährt mit Tigermilch,
　　　　　Gieren nach ihres Königs Untergang.
　　　　　Seht, Bestien, her von Westminsters Abtei!
　　　　　Ich kann sie nicht abtun, mein Haar geht mit,
　　　　　Das ganz verwachsen ist mit ihr. Oh sie
　　　　　War eine leichte Last mir alle Zeit gewesen,
　　　　　War wie die leichte obre Kron des Ahorns
　　　　　Sehr leicht und lieblich allezeit zu tragen,
　　　　　Und allezeit wird nun ein dünnes Blut
　　　　　Und Fetzlein Haut, ganz schwarzes Blut, dran kleben
　　　　　Von Eduard Ohnmacht, Armut, Tigerbeut.
　　　　　　　　　　　　　　　　　　　(*E*, 200–1)

Edward:　[*He puts on his crown again*]
　　　　　Inhuman creatures nursed with tiger's milk
　　　　　Lusting for your sovereign's overthrow.
　　　　　See, you monsters, from Westminster Abbey, see!
　　　　　I cannot take it off, my hair goes with it
　　　　　It is quite grown with it. Oh it
　　　　　Has at all times been an easy burden to me
　　　　　No heavier than the maple's crown of twigs

So light and pleasing at all times to wear
And for all time now a little blood
A scrap of skin, black blood will stick to it
From Edward the Powerless, the Poor, the tiger's prey.

                                                    (*M*I, 235–6)

Eduard feels the crown to be an organic part of his person, his
kingship an attribute which he cannot give up without damaging
himself. He clings to the crown so fiercely because it is the last
possession he can defend against his enemy Mortimer, and, by
defending it, protract the struggle which he has sought with this
man. Eduard has identified himself wholly with his role as
Mortimer's enemy, so that his crown, the ostensible object of their
contest, must from now on, by virtue of this act of self-definition
through conflict and suffering, bear the marks of all that he endured
in its defence. To intensify his sufferings and so increase the
satisfaction to be derived from enduring them, Eduard even
deliberately starves himself so as to be in the weakest possible
physical condition when pressure is put on him to abdicate. When at
last Mortimer himself comes to demand his crown (in a confrontation which has no counterpart in the original) the king reveals his
strategy:

Mortimer:	So werdet ihr also zustimmen?
Eduard:	Es ist nicht in Unserm Plan. Der Stoff
	Dieser letzten Tage klärt sich heraus. Eduard, dessen
	Zerfall unabwendbar, doch nicht fürchterlich
	Herannaht, erkennt sich. Nicht gelüstig
	Auf Sterben, schmeckt er Nützlichkeit
	Schrumpfender Vernichtung. Eduard, der nicht mehr
	Der arme Eduard ist, zahlt billig mit Tod
	Solchen Genuß am Würger. Kommt doch, wenns
	Soweit ist, Ihr selber, Mortimer!

                                                    (*E*, 220)

Mortimer:	Will you consent?
Edward:	That is not in our plan. The substance
	Of these last days starts to clear. Edward, whose
	Fall approaches, inexorable yet
	Not fearful, knows himself. Not wishing much

> To die he savours the usefulness of
> Withering destruction. Edward, who no more
> Poor Edward is, thinks death but a little price
> For such pleasure in his murderer. So then
> When it is time, Mortimer, come yourself.
>
> *(M*I, 257)

This plan of Eduard's, to make his enemy murder him and thus to bring about *his* downfall in turn, is again a development of an idea which is present as little more than a rhetorical boast in the original:

> *Edward*: He of you all that most desires my blood
> And will be called the murtherer of a king
> Take it.
>
> *(Mar*, 85)

After taking leave of Mortimer, Eduard begins to prepare himself for the next and final stage of their contest by ceasing his fast, so that he will have sufficient strength to meet the most strenuous test of all: he knows that, because he has not resigned, the next move of his enemies will be to take his life (*E*, 203; *M*I, 238).

Thus, in the remodelling of the scenes dealing with Edward's abdication the main thrust of Brecht's adaptation can again be seen to be towards presenting the theme of the vanity of life in a radically new light. Whereas Marlowe's king is initially blinded by the passions of love and pride and has to learn through suffering to loose the bonds which tie him to earthly things, Brecht's Eduard is fully conscious from the outset of death's power to render all human effort vain, so much so in fact that he bases all his actions on this certainty. In his case, however, the conviction of life's *vanitas* is nihilistic rather than Christian, and leads, not to contemplation of the heavenly, but to the desire to experience the transience of this life with the utmost sado-masochistic intensity.

CATCHING THE EEL

To complement the changes made in the king's character Brecht alters that of his principal enemy, Mortimer. Brecht replaces Marlowe's two Mortimers (elder and younger) by one, who has the aggression but not the Hotspur-like characteristics of Marlowe's younger Mortimer. One has the impression that Brecht's Mortimer is an older man than the king, which would certainly be consonant with Brecht's presentation of Eduard's behaviour as a revolt against all figures and forms of authority. He is a character in whom the alliance of aggression with intellect produces, after apparent initial reluctance to enter the political sphere, a resourceful political schemer. The first scene in which he appears shows him "in his house, surrounded by books, alone". In his opening speech he muses on the career of Julius Caesar as illustrating the absurdity of even the greatest political career. Yet the very fact that he has been studying Caesar's life betrays a positive interest in political and military affairs behind his contemptuous pose. When finally unleashed, his lust for power is all the more powerful for having been long suppressed. When told by the Archbishop that London needs his help, Mortimer replies sarcastically that "London needs flour". This should not, however, be taken as a sign that he is a man with a strong social conscience. As the dialogue progresses, his contempt for the common people is revealed in his unwillingness "to take his countenance into the market place amid the sweaty rabble" merely because of the king's attachment to his homosexual favourite, or even because of the consequences for the country of this "sport of nature". Mortimer is not a morally motivated character. Rather, he is intelligent enough to devise and use moral arguments when the occasion demands, as, for example, when pleading for his own life before parliament. When moralising has no specific purpose, he has no use for it. Thus he chides Anna for showing pointless passion when she claims, to no-one in particular, that their defeat of Edward is a divinely appointed victory for the good cause (*E*, 192, *M*I, 326).

In the words of the Archbishop, Mortimer is "cold with passion" ("kalt mit Leidenschaft"). The phrase indicates quite rightly that he is both able to remain cool even when pursuing passionate aims, and that he is passionate in his dedication to cold, deliberate action. He is fully aware of the strength of passion behind the ascetic, dry attitude he habitually adopts, and warns the Archbishop of the dangerous consequences which are likely to ensue if he once begins to indulge his appetite for violence (*E*, 159; *M*I, 190). This combination of aggressiveness with cunning makes Mortimer the ideal opponent for Edward, since he too combines these qualities in his person, although it sometimes suits him to disguise or deny the fact. When Eduard releases Mortimer, ostensibly to be a witness to the king's revenge on his barons, but actually to renew the war as a duel between himself and Mortimer, he contrasts Mortimer's character with his own in a way that is not supported by the subsequent course of events:

Eduard: Ihr Mortimers rechnet
Stumpfäugig, seid in Büchern daheim
Wie Würmer. Doch in Büchern steht nichts
Von Eduard, der nichts liest, nicht rechnet,
Nichts weiß, und der mit Natur verknüpft ist
Und von sehr andrer Speise sich nährt.

(*E*, 185)

Edward: You Mortimers reckon
Dim-eyed, are at home in books
Like worms. But Edward is not found
In books, he reads not, reckons not
Knows naught, but is nature's friend
And feeds himself on very different food.

(*MI*, 218)

Although Eduard does *appear* at times to be stupid – his "bad" conduct of the battle of Killingworth led to the loss of Gaveston, and his "poor" leadership in the later war with Mortimer results in his own defeat – these are only tactics in an overall strategy: the loss of Gaveston was followed by the wild slaughter of the barons, his "defeat" at Mortimer's hands eventually leads to Mortimer's execution by the very parliament before which he had once demanded the banishment of Gaveston. Eduard's cunning in executing his well concealed plan in fact eventually proves greater even than that of his chosen opponent, the "eel" Mortimer.

To concentrate attention on the conflict between the king and Mortimer, Brecht severely pruned away episodes and characters which had their place in the original either simply because they happened historically or because they illustrated the vagaries of historical development and thus underlined the theme of the unpredictability of *Fortuna*. Ihering has pointed out the essential difference between Marlowe's "tragical History" and Brecht's "Historie": "'History' does not mean 'historical play', it does not mean history in the temporal sense, but rather history as a mode of communication, history as in ballad or *Moritat*. The material is seen from the point of view of popular literature, or of a fairground entertainment."[12] Brecht was not at all interested in historical authenticity; in fact, as Laboulle has pointed out, "Not only does he repudiate historical facts, he perverts them, deliberately inventing a series of dates for which there is no evidence in Holinshed, Marlowe or anyone else."[13]

But he was interested, like the ballad-mongers of the fairground, in presenting lurid scenes of cunning, treachery and violence. Brecht's lack of concern for historical accuracy enables him to bring the action more swiftly to the point of war by having Eduard refuse categorically to banish Gaveston, thus omitting the unnecessary complication of his expulsion and recall. More importantly, in the scene where the demand for the banishment is made he reduces the number and importance of the other peers and increases the role of Mortimer. Whereas Marlowe's younger Mortimer had made a direct, passionate attack on the king and his favourite, Brecht's more intellectual Mortimer adopts the tactic of giving an ironic account of the Trojan War as an oblique prophecy of the consequences of obduracy on Eduard's part. The king responds to this speech by weeping. Why he weeps is not entirely clear; it may be from anger at the suggestion that his favourite is a "a whore", it may be from hurt majesty, or it might be that these are tears of sorrow that much blood will be shed. On the other hand his tears are accompanied by the strange statement, "God grant Mortimer, thy lips have not lied" (*MI* 197). What this suggests is that his tears are an expression of gratitude for a promise which he has detected in Mortimer's description of the carnage in Troy. In other words, he hears in Mortimer's warning an assurance that a war as "total" and unremitting as the Trojan War will ensue if the king refuses to abandon his favourite, Gaveston.

The ensuing conflict between the king and the barons has its meaning underlined by its symbolic location at Killingworth; the point of the battle lies in the slaughter perpetrated during it. In this battle Mortimer is again given a more important role than in the original. Whereas in Marlowe's play the barons with Mortimer amongst them act as a body, Brecht has Mortimer distance himself from the others by using the cunning which is his chief characteristic in an effort to save his own skin, should the battle turn against the barons. He (and not Warwick as in the original) takes charge of the captured Gaveston and orders his soldiers to keep him safe until eleven o'clock the following morning, when they are to rejoin Mortimer in Killingworth Wood. He also orders them to spread the rumour that they are taking their prisoner to the "knacker's yard", expecting that this rumour will reach Eduard and cause him to betray the barons with whom he has arranged to parley next morning. Mortimer then "prudently" absents himself from this parley. He thus forces the king to renew the fighting in order to capture him and so makes the king responsible for Gaveston's death. With the announcement that Eduard's execution of the peers led to the death of Gaveston, Mortimer believes he has fired the parting shot in the first round of their contest. Yet Eduard's loss is also a perverse kind of victory, for he has expected to lose Gaveston (having done nothing to protect him), and is pleased to have found one particularly able opponent with whom to fight a longer war than the other barons were capable of sustaining.

Whereas in the first half of the play Eduard's actions are openly sadistic, he begins to change over to a more masochistic course of action after the meeting at Killingworh. After executing the peers, he continues to wage war for another four years, but his conduct of his military affairs becomes increasingly strange. He tears up field reports, ignores warnings of approaching ships and of troops gathering at the port of Harwich. He neglects his army, allows it to disperse and, when he hears of villages being burnt in the North, pretends to take this as a sign that Anna is on her way with the Scottish troops he sent her for four years previously! Yet there is method in Eduard's seeming madness. He knows full well that Anna is leading the Scottish troops *against* him, not in order to support him. This hidden awareness is revealed in a brief remark he makes when his servants leave him alone to eat, "There is sorrow in my heart my son/Should be suborned to prop their wickedness" (*E*, 191; *MI*, 225). Thus, whereas in the original Edward is defeated involuntarily, simply by the greater military strength of Mortimer and Isabella, Brecht's king is himself responsible for the easy victory which his enemies gain over him. The underlying reason for this strange behaviour becomes apparent in the later scenes which reveal that his intention has been to test his own spiritual and physical resources to their limit. This he could only do if he rids himself of his army. His weakening of his own military position foreshadows his physical self-debilitation when he deliberately starves himself during the period of imprisonment and torture in order to be in the weakest condition possible when the demand is made for his abdication. Only when he has withstood the intense temptation to exchange his crown for physical comfort, does he resume eating in order to build up reserves of strength again for his final and worst ordeal, his murder (*E*, 203; *M*I, 238). On the other hand, Mortimer is intelligent enough to see that he must avoid directly murdering the king, because he knows that such a course of action would undoubtedly bring about his own downfall. Instead, he devises a plan which may make it unnecessary actually to kill the king: he has Eduard exposed to merciless deprivation and exhaustion, and kept constantly on the move, so that no-one may find him; he then simply announces that the king has abdicated. Eventually, however, this plan fails and he is challenged to produce Eduard before parliament. When his last attempt to extract his abdication from the king by intensifying his torture fails, Mortimer is obliged, as Eduard had planned, to have him murdered. Mortimer's own execution on the orders of Eduard's son follows soon after. When he is sentenced, Mortimer tries to minimise his defeat by adopting once more the cynical, apparently detached view of life which he had cultivated before his entry into the political arena. However, behind the mask of resignation to Fortune's fickleness there speaks the bitter voice of a man who has measured success and failure in terms of his ability to gain and retain real political power. Whereas the "sensualist" Eduard dies a satisfied masochist, the other-worldly-seeming Mortimer dies with his appetite for power unsatisfied at the last.

AMBIVALENCE

The presentation of violence in Brecht's *Edward II* is ambivalent. On the one hand, Eduard's pursuit of pleasure in his own destruction is undoubtedly given a heroic aura. Above all, it is suggested that his way of life is at least honest and consistent, and that his ruthlessness is an understandable response to a hostile world. The bare language and the powerful rhythm of such speeches as the king's nihilistic "Psalm to Spring" draw the reader into empathy with Eduard's exultation in his own vitality. On the other hand, a photograph of Brecht's staging of the dungeon scene in his 1924 production, shows Eduard as a barely human figure.[14] In other words Brecht presented Eduard's heroism in an "alienated" manner, so as to make the audience aware of the strangeness of the man who takes this attitude to the world. Already in this production Brecht was putting into practice a technique of presenting the actions of "great" individuals in a new, questioning light, which he formulated thus some four years later with reference to Richard III:

> It is not the task of the dramatist, when he presents the figure of Richard the Third, say, to make the actions of this man appear to us as comprehensible as possible. On the contrary, his task is to present them to us as quite monstrous, inhuman, strange, and the man who does the actions as a remarkable, but almost inaccessible animal. In this way the spectator is enriched, for he will experience the great and divine variety of the world which in no way can be exhausted by man's attempts to understand it.   (*GW*, **15**, 194)

The ambivalent attitude to violence evident in the presentation of the king can also be observed in the theatrical handling of the common people on whose backs the battles of the mighty are fought out. Brecht's sympathy for their suffering as a result of senseless wars is communicated through the satirical bite of a ballad which is sung repeatedly during the battle of Killingworth so as to maintain an awareness in the audience of the real consequences of such games of war:

> Der Peer von Cornwall hat zuviel Schilling im Strumpf
> Bitt für uns, bitt für uns, bitt für uns
> Drum hat Patty keinen Arm mehr und O'Nelly nur 'nen Stumpf
> Bitt für uns, bitt für uns, bitt für uns.
>
> (*E*, 157)

> The Earl of Cornwall has silver at his rump.
> Pray for us. Pray for us. Pray for us.
> But Pat has no arms and O'Nelly just a stump.
> Pray for us. Pray for us. Pray for us.
>
> (*MI*, 187)

During the battle of Killingworth the peers march on Boroughbridge under cover of darkness, and their soldiers sing this ballad as they march with the words "In the night" substituted for the "Pray for us". The effect is to contrast a quite different experience of the "darkness" of evil with Eduard's praise of it. The element of revolt against warmongering in the ballad was underscored in Brecht's own production by having the citizens of London sing the refrain "Pray for us" in such a way as to suggest menace.[15] To some extent, however, this sympathetic attitude towards the common people was offset by the presentation of the attitudes of the soldiers who kill and are killed in the wars. In the following reflection on his production (in which he refers to himself in the third person) Brecht's description of the soldiers draws critical attention to their passivity:

> The most peculiar feature of this production was the soldier. He went to battle to the accompaniment of monotonous drum rolls. Marched unceasingly, when the moon stood in the sky. He marched by the order of Edward II and he marched by the order of Mortimer, and the latter marched after tracing the movements of world politics on a globe one Thursday. While the soldier marched he lost all contact with time – he cheated time with his singing. When the bells of peace rang out, he laid down his weapons and laid himself on the ground. When the battle raged, his face became white as chalk, when the battle was lost he jumped over bridges and threw away his weapons. These soldiers were thousands of Tommies.[16]

The allusion to the First World War indicates that Brecht wanted to imply criticism of the fact that the exploitation of the common man as cannon-fodder had not changed from the Middle Ages to the present. On the other hand, the contradiction between the soldiers' willingness to fight senseless battles and their awareness, expressed through their songs, of this very senselessness must also raise the question of their own responsibility for their fate.

Brecht's ambivalent attitude to violence is evident, then, in his sympathetic presentation of two antagonistic perspectives, that of the abnormal individuals, Mortimer and Eduard, and that of the normal mass of people who only want to live in peace, pursuing simpler, more natural pleasures. This ambivalence is mirrored also in the play's style. Brecht uses a variety of techniques to stylise speech and behaviour with a demonstrative gestic boldness which both expresses the emotions of the speaker and, at the same time, contains them aesthetically. With the exception of certain import-ant moments when the pain or exultation of a character is communicated with unusual directness, the techniques of presen-tation ensure that the world of the play is kept at some distance from the world of the audience. The elements from which Brecht fashioned a language markedly distinct from everyday speech and capable of expressing often violent emotions in a controlled manner are too many and varied to be analysed exhaustively here. The following is a summary catalogue of a number of the most important devices he used. They are quoted only in German because their peculiar qualities cannot be rendered in translation. He favoured impersonal constructions which express feelings obliquely or understate them: "Man meint nur, man bricht einen Eid nicht gern" (*E*, 153); archaic word forms: "litt kein Seel in Höllen/Mehr als Arm-Gaveston" (*E*, 154); very formalised sentence structures, often omitting colloquial particles: "Kommt der Mensch übers Wasser, wird viel Eisen blank/In England" (*E*, 153); ellipsis and parallelism: "Bruder, genug!"/"Bruder, still!" (*E*, 154); paradox: "durch günstige Umständ/Erledigt, ausgemerzt durch zuviel Glück" (*E*, 163); aphoristic terseness combined with coarse, unliterary vocabulary: "Verrecken ist Soldatenlos" (*E*, 152). There are frequent deviations from normal modern syntax for the sake of rhetorical emphasis, e.g. "Fielen gegen Mittag in Verwirrung und Absicht/Sämtliche" (*E*, 164). The bold use of syntax permits the co-ordination of speech with gesture, e.g. "Wird Eisen blank in England, Lancaster,/Wirds, Bruder, denk ich, Köpfe geben, auf Pfähle sie/Zu stecken, weil die Zungen ihnen lang sind" (*E*, 153). The medium in which these various elements are embedded is a "roughened" versification which avoids "the oily smoothness of the usual iambic pentameter" (*GW*, **19**, 396), in order to create abrupt, jagged rhythms that will reflect the quality of feeling in this turbulent epoch of civil war.

Brecht's systematic use of metaphors, many of them drawn from the animal kingdom, is a further important means of heightening, yet simultaneously formalising the expression of emotion in the play.[17] The animal imagery in particular also illustrates the ambivalent attitude taken to violence in the play. Here is just one example of the widely flung net of such imagery:

Spencer: Mit Sankt Georg
Zerfleischen Brüder sich, und wie zwei Molche,
Im Kampf zerknäult, zahnt sich Heer in Heer,
Und Englands Dörfer brennen auf für England.
(*E*, 176)

Spencer: By Saint George
Brother butchers brother and like two salamanders

Snarled in struggle army bites at army
And England's hamlets burn in England's name.

(*M*I, 209)

Here and in other, similar passages there is a clearly satirical
description of the tendency of wars to reduce the individual's
importance and function to that of the organ of some bloody animal.
Yet animal metaphors are also used to express qualities of wildness
and strength in a positive manner, as when Eduard likens himself to
a wounded tiger (*E*, 233). These contrasting uses of animal imagery,
on the one hand presenting violence as courageous and
exhilarating, on the other as inhuman and ugly, illustrate well the
emotional indeterminacy of the adaptation. But whether noble or
ugly, the animal imagery represents the net of earth-bound
existence in which all the characters are trapped, and which does
not allow even those with a gentler disposition to escape the struggle
of creature against creature.

The stylisation of language is supported by the stylisation of
gesture to create the same dual effect of dramatic expressiveness and
aesthetic control. Eduard's unswerving refusal to have his will
bounded by any convention or agreement is symbolised by his
gesture of tearing up first the order for Gaveston's banishment, later
the field-reports warning of the advance of Anna and Mortimer,
and finally the document of abdication. His unity of purpose
throughout his career is thus conveyed visually as he tears apart
England, dissipates his military strength, and destroys his own life.
A good illustration of stylised gesture is to be found in the scene
where Anna finally abandons her attempts to win Eduard's love
and joins forces with Mortimer:

> *Anna*: Will ich werden zu einer Wölfin,
> Reißend durchs Gestrüpp mit nackten Zähnen,
> Nicht ruhn,
> Bis Erde deckt den längst entseelten Eduard,
> Eduard Gloster, meinen Gatten von ehdem,
> Vorgestern, Erd deckt.
> [*Sie wirft drei Hände Erde hinter sich*]
>
> (*E*, 188)

> *Anna*: I shall become a she-wolf,
> Ranging bare-toothed through the scrub.

Not resting
Until earth covers Edward long since dead –
Edward Gloucester, my husband sometime
Yesteryear – earth covers him.
[*She throws three lumps of earth behind her*]
                                    (MI, 221)

The gesture of throwing earth should presumably accompany each
of the last three lines of the speech. Thus ritualised, Anna's feelings
are both fully expressed and yet kept within the confines of a clearly
symbolic representation of life.

The theatrical idiom of Brecht's "history" is that of the
fairground theatre or the *Moritat*, a popular type of ballad which
narrated dire or awe-inspiring incidents from history, and appealed
to the same taste for sensationalism as the "yellow press" of the
present day or other forms of popular entertainment. The singer of
the *Moritat* would often illustrate his tale with lurid placards. Such
ballad-mongers were still to be seen at the fairgrounds which Brecht
was fond of frequenting in his youth.[18] His adoption of the style of
the *Moritat* for his life of Eduard is yet another reflection of his
ambivalent attitude to violence. His elaborate care in the staging of
scenes of violence and suffering, such as the preparations for the
hanging of Gaveston, Gaveston digging his own grave, the capture
of the peers, Eduard's torture and murder, attests to his fascination
with such subjects. His own account of his handling of a number of
scenes indicates that he wanted to combine an awareness of artifice
with something similar to the pleasurable involvement in aggression
which the stylised events of farce provide:

Theatrical principles governed the design of the props. The
wooden axes, long sabres and spears of the soldiers forced the
actors to perform certain acrobatic movements. The cloth,
square and wide when unfolded, allowed the traitor Baldock to
underline the cunning of his movements and also to present a
piece of sleight of hand. The executioner and the murderers also
knew their craft. The peers were tied around very smartly with a
rope and pulled off the stage like a bundle. The hanging of
Gaveston was carried out very precisely, it was an attraction in its
own right. One could be saddened by Gaveston's sorry fate and at
the same time take pleasure in the skill with which he is hanged on
the branch.[19]

If on the one hand the *Moritat* gave an opportunity to indulge in vicarious violence, the self-conscious use of this archaic form in a modern theatre was also a way of calling attention to the nature of the entertainment being offered in the play. The style of the play sets the content at an ironic distance by commenting implicitly on the primitiveness of the historical age it described and on the crudity of the emotions to which such a representation appealed. By matching the archaic form to the barbaric subject-matter Brecht was both setting the events of the play at a historical distance and simultaneously raising the question whether the distance in time from Eduard's age had really been matched by an equal degree of moral and emotional development away from late medieval barbarism. If the modern audience felt itself drawn emotionally into the bloody world of the play, how substantial had been the progress of humanity in the intervening six hundred years?

Brecht's adaptation of Marlowe marks a certain advance in theatrical effectiveness as compared with *In the Jungle*. The archaic style of the *Moritat* and the historical distance of the late Middle Ages created effortlessly the element of aesthetic detachment which Brecht needed to counterbalance the violence of the action. Brecht's choice of a more or less contemporary Chicago as the setting for *In the Jungle*, by contrast, had forced him to stylise language and gesture in a far more contrived manner in order to create a similar distancing effect – that of a "cold, unreal Chicago" – with the result that the play became so obscurely metaphorical that it is difficult to stage successfully. Perhaps it was the ease with which he could combine violence with control by "copying" Marlowe, that prompted Brecht to describe the adaptation as a "greedy reminiscence" of a more fortunate dramatic age.

Yet, although *Edward II* is better suited to the demands of the stage than *In the Jungle*, it is not quite such a well balanced play as its predecessor. *In the Jungle* was scrupulously even-handed in its assessment both of the attractions of romantic self-indulgence and of the emotional and moral damage that would ensue from such behaviour. *Edward II*, by contrast, is less rigorous in its presentation of the consequences of the king's existential revolt. If he had adapted the play later in his career Brecht undoubtedly and quite rightly would have paid more attention to the plight of the common people (and, of course, would have interpreted the feudal war quite differently). But just as unsatisfactory as his analysis of the consequences for others of Eduard's sado-masochism, is Brecht's portrayal of the effects on the king himself. His adaptation signally fails to face up to the principal difficulty in giving a "heroic" reinterpretation to Eduard's fate, namely the manner of the king's death. In Marlowe's play Edward's homosexuality is punished in a horrifying, grotesque act of poetic justice when Lightborn (i.e. Lucifer) pierces him through the anus with a red-hot poker. In Brecht's version there is no mention of the red-hot poker, Eduard being merely smothered to death. By making the king's death far less harrowing Brecht leaves as a last impression in the minds of the audience the image of Eduard's heroic–masochistic triumph over his tormentors. The agonised screams that would inevitably have accompanied death by the burning iron would have been bound to make a fierce mockery at the last of Eduard's belief that his masochistic strength would enable him to master even the worst experiences which life might devise for him. Brecht's change in the manner of the king's murder did not stem from squeamishness or concern for the sensibilities of his audience. Rather it is yet another example of the tendency of his imagination to create images of life mastered, rather than render experience in its full harshness and complexity.

6 *A Man's a Man*

If Brecht's early plays are remarkable for their thematic consistency, they are no less so for the formal and dialectical versatility with which the themes are treated. *A Man's a Man* (1926) takes up themes which are familiar from Brecht's earlier plays – questions of the individual's freedom of choice, his ability to master experience, the importance or otherwise of a sense of personal identity – but explores them in a quite novel way.[1] Whereas in *Edward II*, for example, it was the heroic quality of one man's struggle against the limitations on his will that interested Brecht, in *A Man's a Man* the contingent nature of the individual's life, its subordination to forces beyond his control, is seen in its ironical, even farcical aspect. With an abrupt shift of perspective, the concern for personal integrity which led King Edward down his masochistic course is revealed as ridiculous and pointless. In the comic world of *A Man's a Man* no greater mastery of life can be achieved than the satisfaction of basic physical needs, and this is seen to be best achieved by simply adapting oneself to whatever life's changing circumstances demand. Whereas all Brecht's previous plays had more or less active heroes, *A Man's a Man* is a first, ingenious attempt at writing a play with a passive, by usual standards "undramatic" hero. The result is a farce which lucidly combines intellectual sophistication with theatrical concreteness, simplicity and liveliness.

CONTINGENCY AND IRONY

A Man's a Man is a parable on the contingency of human existence. Its characters are subject to a combination of social and biological pressures as they are swept along by an encompassing, supra-individual action, the advance of British imperialism in Asia[2] which constantly hounds and harries them into one conflict after another. Every action the characters take to shape their own destinies leads them increasingly to lose control over their lives, so that the plot takes the form of a series of ironic reversals. This plot chiefly concerns the efforts of a group of British soldiers to create a replacement for the missing member of their machine-gun crew whom they lose during an illicit raid on a native temple. The seemingly unpromising material from which they hope to fashion a substitute for the missing Jeriah Jip is a lumbering, good-natured Irish porter by the name of Galy Gay who (for some unspecified reason) happens to work in the port of Kilkoa. The soldiers are successful in transforming Galy Gay into a "human fighting machine", but the consequences are not entirely as they planned, since the "fool" they have duped learns to exploit the situation they have put him in, and lays claim to their rations and blankets. In the topsy-turvy world of the play calculating activity enslaves while "foolish" passivity proves to be a form of wisdom. The following analysis of the plot will elucidate the connections between contingency and irony in the fates of the characters.

The first demonstration of the individual's lack of freedom is given in the second scene of the play when the machine-gun crew attempt to burgle a native temple. The main concern of these soldiers is to ensure that they have a sufficient supply of whisky to satisfy the vast appetite for liquor which their social role has encouraged them to cultivate. They need beer and whisky in order to march through India, just as much as the queen's tanks need petrol (*MiM*, 9). When the soldiers break into a native temple to obtain money for drink the latent contradiction in their situation, between the appetite and attitudes which the army has encouraged them to develop and the limitations placed by army regulations on their behaviour, begins to unfold its harmful implications for the men. Their attempt to rob the temple is not only a painful experience in itself, since the place is full of booby-traps, but also leads to the loss of one of their number, Jeriah Jip, who leaves a large patch of hair in some tar which has been smeared on the door lintel, and therefore cannot return to camp, lest his bald patch should betray the fact that the unit was guilty of the break-in. Thus the compulsion of their appetites leads the soldiers into a further compulsion, namely the need to devise some stratagem which will save them from the consequences of their original action. Their experiences with the booby-trapped temple prove to be a model of their ensuing fate, for just as every attempt to extricate themselves from one booby-trap in the temple leads them into a worse one, so

every effort to avert one danger simply delivers them up to another.
The other three soldiers decide to hide Jip in a palankeen until the
evening, when they intend to return to shave his head completely in
order to avoid detection. That they must postpone this plan till the
evening again results from their lack of freedom as soldiers – they are
obliged to hurry away from the scene of the crime because they must
be on parade very soon. This postponement in turn leads to another
series of chance events which further illustrates the inability of
individuals such as these to control their own fates. Before pursuing
the chain of conflicts in which the three remaining soldiers become
embroiled, we should first consider the subsequent fate of Jip.

Having been placed dead drunk into the palankeen by his
comrades, Jip is dragged into the temple by its owner when a shower
of rain threatens to soak the basket. His imprisonment in the basket
and his removal to the inside of the temple symbolise the theme of
the lack of freedom which his fate illustrates, for in all this he is
unconscious, the passive object of the interplay of arbitrary forces.
This theme is developed further when the owner of the temple,
finding the drunk in his palankeen, decides Jip's immediate future
by determining to recoup the loss sustained in the robbery through
the transformation of Jip into a "god" whose groans from within a
prayer box will extract money from gullible worshippers (*MiM*,
36). Here again, a situation of physical imprisonment symbolises the
individual's general lack of freedom to shape his own life. Jip's
conversion into a bogus god makes him the first character in the
play to experience a change of identity. Here, as elsewhere in the
play, an involuntary change of identity serves to underline the
dominant theme of the contingency inherent in individual
existence, the character's change of name pointing back in time to
the arbitrariness of his first name and to the contingent origins of so-
called individual identity.[3] Just as Jip's old social role led him into
contradictory situations, so his new function produces its own
contradictions in him, namely a conflict between pleasure at having
his appetites for food and drink well satisfied by Wang, and a sense
of loyalty to his old comrades: ("It's quite wrong for me to be sitting
here, but it's good meat" – *MiM*, 47). Jip's feelings towards his
friends may be seen as a moral impulse, or as a selfish need for
companionship, or most plausibly, as the effect of social condition-
ing by life in an army which makes great play of comradeship (see
the "A-Man's-a-Man-Song" – *MiM*, 128), or as a mixture of such
elements; but whichever aspect of his motives one stresses, the

decision to leave his "flourishing business" with Wang in order to
return to Polly, Jesse and Uria is a tragic one. The consequence of
this decision, his only "free" action in the course of the play, is that
he is left alone in the mountains between India and Tibet, the
victim of life's unconcern for his finer feelings. Jip has failed to
realise that the "personal identity" as the friend of the other
gunners, for which he has sacrificed his material interests, is largely
dependent on contingent circumstances of a material kind which lie
beyond his control. Thus, just as he acquired the identity of Jip,
soldier in the queen's army and comrade of Polly, Jesse and Uria,
because it suited the interests of the army, himself and his friends for
him to have this identity, so he must lose this identity now that the
army's interests are met without his having it. Because of his failure
to recognise the primacy of selfish, material considerations in life he
tries to "rise above" enslavement to his physical appetites, and
suffers as a consequence.

A particularly grotesque variation on the themes of the
individual's lack of freedom and the contingency of identity is
provided by the fate of Charles Fairchild, "known as Bloody Five",
the sergeant in the unit to which the machine-gun crew have been
posted. Fairchild first appears in the role of the irate NCO who is
determined to bring to book the soldiers responsible for robbing the
temple. Ironically, however, the self-same rain-shower which will
prevent the three soldiers rescuing Jip from the palankeen and
which could thus have given Fairchild the satisfaction of arresting
them, leads the sergeant himself into a situation where he is obliged
to change *his* identity and commit offences against the honour of his
uniform. It is Fairchild's misfortune to be "perhaps the most sensual
man under the sun" (*MiM*, 33), whose sexual appetite is aroused
suddenly and violently whenever it rains. This absurdity is not
without deeper significance, for the association of sexuality with
rain (traditionally a fertility symbol) is intended to underline the
impersonal and irrational quality of the force of sexuality, and thus
the extent to which man's life is dictated by "alien" forces beyond
his control. Just before the rain begins, there emerges a conflict
between Fairchild's social identity, as the embodiment of disciplined soldierly virtue, and his appetitive, physical self, which is
expressed in the exaggerated, mechanical stiffness of his movements
as his inner rigidity increases in a vain attempt to resist his sexual
impulses (*MiM*, 33). His ridiculous movements present him as a
marionette of his social and biological compulsions. In order to

resolve the contradiction between his instincts and his conscience, the socially conditioned nature of which is reflected in the mixture of biblical and military idioms in his speech, Fairchild changes his identity, as predicted and later demanded by Leokadja Begbick. The "most dangerous man in the Indian Army" is thus transformed into something as "harmless as a milk-tooth" (*MiM*, 31).

Begbick has the power to bring about this transformation of Bloody Five into "Bloody Gent" because she can determine whether or not Fairchild gains access to her daughters in order to satisfy his sexual craving. Her main motive for insisting on his transformation is her own material gain, for not only does she profit from the drinks which the besotted Fairchild has to buy for the whole bar, but the three soldiers have promised to help fold away her canteen tent in time for the imminent departure of the troop train in return for her help in preventing Bloody Five's interference in their plot to create a replacement for Jip. Thus, as in the case of Jip, business interests are involved in the sergeant's change of identity, so that the temporary release from his accustomed social role does not mean an escape from exploitation but simply the exchange of one situation in which he is exploited for another. Here again the point is made that the effects of man's inherent lack of freedom, represented in this case by Fairchild's irrepressible sexuality, are worsened by the battle of all against all as each person seeks to gratify his own appetites regardless of the cost to others. The characters are pinned down by a net of necessity, woven both from their own needs and those of their "neighbours".

The destruction of Fairchild's public persona during his period as "Bloody Gent" is expressed not only by his being subjected to insults and physical assaults, but also by a symbolic incident in which his reputation as "the most dangerous man in the Indian Army" is destroyed. In his drunken state he reveals that the action which won him the name of "Bloody Five" amounted to no more than the shooting-down at point-blank range of five defenceless natives. When mockingly challenged to demonstrate his renowned marksmanship, he is unable to hit an egg at short range. His failure as a marksman, the outward sign of the failure of his soldierly will, is linked by the egg-motif to the future ascendancy of Galy Gay (of whom it is said that he is "like a raw egg inside"), the man who is at this moment also having his identity changed so that he may serve as a replacement for Jeriah Jip. The drunken failure to hit the egg symbolises Fairchild's failure to perceive the fraud in which Galy

Gay is involved, and foreshadows not only his own castration but
also the time when Galy Gay, and not Bloody Five, is hailed as "the
greatest man the army has" (*MiM*, 126). The next stage in the
destruction of Fairchild's persona as the terrible Bloody Five comes
when he himself denies his identity in order to avoid duties which
would take him away from widow Begbick's daughters ("Don't tell
them that it's me", *MiM*, 93). As happens to Galy Gay, Fairchild's
denial of his identity is only a first step towards its eventual loss.

When Fairchild recovers from his collapse into a drunken stupor
to discover that his sexual appetite has led to the loss of his military
reputation, he decides to prevent any similar conflict in future by
"simply" castrating himself (*MiM*, 112–14). The instrument of
Bloody Five's castration is an army revolver, and the terms in which
he describes it ("Aufständige werden erschossen" – an untranslat-
able pun linking mutiny and sexual erection) are those of a military
reprisal. These symbolic details underline the significance of his
action as a case of self-mutilation through identification with his role
in an exploitative system.[4] The motive of "eating" ("What is
important is not that I should eat, but that I should be Bloody
Five") which really plays no part in his choice, has the function of
reinforcing the parallel between his fate and the fates of Galy Gay
and Jeriah Jip; the motif stands here as a general term for the
appetitive self (the appetites being sexual in his case) which is in
conflict with his social role. Like Jip, he feels obliged to resolve this
contradiction by sacrificing his physical interests to "higher"
considerations. Yet, so mechanical is the morality of military
discipline to which he subordinates his private needs, so insubstantial is the prestige which is his ulterior motive in this decision, so
grotesque, in short, is his fate, that his castration produces a feeling
of shock rather than one of tragic identification. In Bloody Five's
case, the diminution of human freedom as a result of social and
instinctual pressures is the most extreme in the play.

The simple truth which has begun to make itself felt in the
uncomprehending lives of Jip and Bloody Five is summed up in the
familiar wisdom that *tempora mutantur et nos cum illis* ("Times
change and we change with them"). Having no grasp of the
contingent nature of "personal identity", both men try to resist the
flow of time by insisting on remaining "who they are". The only
effect of their attempts at resisting change is to injure themselves
even more than circumstances by themselves would have done:
Bloody Five castrates himself *and* loses his reputation, Jip is left

without food *or* friends in the wastes of Tibet (i.e. in a social no-man's land). In the case of both men it is the internalised compulsion of their social habits which drives them to injure themselves in an attempt to correct the changes wrought by time. The machine-gun crew who lose their fourth man are also driven, by a much more primitive form of "identity crisis", to repair what time and circumstance have damaged: if they do not restore their collective identity as a crew of four by finding a replacement for Jip, they face discovery and punishment as the raiders of the temple. Although the consequences of their actions are less obviously disastrous than in the cases of Jip and Fairchild, their fate again illustrates the harsh law of life that rules the world of the play: whatever you do, life will get the better of you in the end. The vision of life that dominates the play from the beginning is of the world as some enormous mouse-trap. Not surprisingly, the young Brecht greatly admired an author whose work is the antithesis of the kind of optimistic–pragmatic writing Brecht later practised – Franz Kafka.[5]

After losing Jip, the three machine-gunners must quickly find someone to stand in for him on parade that day. In the expectation that they will be able to rescue Jip in the evening, they use enticements and flattery to persuade a stranger, Galy Gay, to don a uniform and play the part of Jip in the meantime. But when they later learn that Jip is being well supplied with steak and whisky by Wang, they realise that they will now have to devise some means of making Galy Gay into Jip's permanent replacement. The outcome of their complicated manoeuvres is that Galy Gay outwardly accepts the new identity which they foist on him, but, by continually threatening to relapse into his old self as Galy Gay (*MiM*, 104–5), and thus to expose their trickery to the military authorities, he ensures that it is he who controls their lives and not the other way round. Thus, the soldiers' resistance to change (the loss of Jip) again leads to unwelcome consequences similar to those experienced by Jip and Bloody Five when they tried to control their own lives. This third illustration of the harmful results of a conflict between appetite and social role again points to the limits of human freedom. Just as Jip chose a course of action which changes in the outside world had made impossible to carry through, namely return to the company, and just as Bloody Five's decision in favour of discipline and prestige was manifestly an involuntary, socially conditioned reflex, so the three soldiers are impelled to take a particular course of action by the absence of an alternative to finding a replacement for Jip. The experiences of Galy Gay, which represent the fourth and central treatment of the theme of freedom, must now be examined.

In an interview given to Bernard Guillemin at the time he was working on this play Brecht described Galy Gay's transformation as having been brought about by "three engineers of the emotions" and as taking the form of a "re-fitting" of the personality (*SzT*, **2**, 271). The mechanical metaphor used here also appears in the play, in the phrase "human fighting machine" (*MiM*, 126) which is applied to Galy Gay, and in a "commentary" spoken by Leokadja Begbick on behalf of the playwright: "Here this evening a man will be re-fitted like a car" (*MiM*, 62). The demonstration of the thesis that man is so unfree that he can be treated like a machine takes the form of showing Galy Gay's characteristics before he is transformed, and then showing how the "engineers of the emotions" use these characteristics as psychological levers with which to manipulate him into behaving as they want him to. As has been indicated already, the demonstration does not entirely bear out the thesis, for, although the soldiers are successful in persuading Galy Gay to adopt the name and role of Jeriah Jip, he is sufficiently cunning to use the tiny room for manoeuvre in his situation to emerge as their leader rather than the will-less robot they had intended to construct. As E. Bentley has observed, "the fable of brain-washing is combined . . . with one that contradicts it: a fable of a sorcerer's apprentice or Frankenstein's monster".[6]

Galy Gay's opening speech, the very first of the play, presents him as a man whose attitude to life is almost perfectly adapted to his material circumstances:

Galy Gay: Liebe Frau, ich habe mich entschlossen heute, entsprechend unserem Einkommen, einen Fisch zu kaufen. Es übersteigt das nicht die Verhältnisse eines Packers, der nicht trinkt, ganz wenig raucht und fast keine Leidenschaften hat. Meinst du, ich soll einen grossen Fisch kaufen, oder benötigst du einen kleinen?

(*MiM*, 7)

Galy Gay: My dear wife, I have decided to-day, as befits our income, to purchase a fish. This does not exceed the

circumstances of a porter who does not drink, who
smokes very little and who has almost no passions.
Do you consider I should buy a large fish or do you
require a small one?

His decision to buy a fish for supper is just what is required of him by
the immediate situation. On the other hand, his rather pompous,
inflated style of speech conflicts with his lowly station in life and
suggests that he may be a little conceited or socially ambitious. This
slight contradiction in his make-up makes possible his subsequent
overstepping of the limits of his life as a stevedore and eventual
transformation into a soldier. His fateful characteristic is described
by his wife as "Großspurigkeit" (roughly: "being too big for his
boots" – *MiM*, 58).[7] The tension in him between natural inertia,
evident in his tendency to simply adapt himself to the immediate
situation in which he finds himself, and a capacity for running out of
control (which is really another form of inertia), is expressed in his
wife's warning that he is like an elephant – naturally clumsy, but as
difficult to halt as a passenger train once he gets moving (*MiM*, 8).

It is his tendency to allow social considerations to outweigh his
material self-interest which first interests the soldiers and earns him
the name of "a man who cannot say no" (*MiM*, 22). Uria is
prompted to say this of him after watching his behaviour with
Leokadja Begbick whose basket he is carrying home in his capacity
as free-lance porter. As they walk along the apparently deserted
road she suggests to him that he might use his strength quite
differently on her behalf; in other words, she tries to cheat him out of
his portering fee by offering him sex instead (*MiM*, 20). During
their exchange Galy Gay cleverly evades Begbick's sexual advances
by keeping up a flow of polite and seemingly inane chatter, thereby
all the time adroitly ignoring her suggestions. He is evidently not so
stupid or defenceless as others think. He continues to defend himself
successfully when Leokadja changes her line of attack from a sexual
to a commercial one by offering to sell him one of her cucumbers for
the money which is intended for the fish. But when she feigns offence
at his refusal of her offer, his defences collapse, and his desire to be
thought a gentleman gains the upper hand over his material self-
interest (*MiM*, 22). It is at this point that the soldiers become
convinced that Galy Gay is "one who cannot say no" (*MiM*, 22).
His polite amenability would certainly seem to warrant this title, as
would his passive yielding to "a whole series of unforeseen

circumstances" ("lauter Unvorhergesehenes"), and the keenness to do business which have led him here. On the other hand, he has effectively said "no" to Begbick's sexual advances, which indicates that he does have some kind of a mind of his own, although admittedly not a highly developed one. The soldiers, however, ignore this potential in him – to their cost, as it later turns out.

The soldiers immediately set to work on Galy Gay, exploiting his politeness, his gullibility, his professional opportunism, his willingness to adapt to new situations and demands, his timidity and his vanity, all of which are aspects of "not saying no", in order to lure him into Widow Begbick's canteen (*MiM*, 23–4). Although up till now a non-smoker and proud of the fact, Galy Gay's conformism and social ambition make him eager to play the role of a man of the world, and so he accepts the cigar which the soldiers offer him. So keen is he to establish himself as their equal, that he actively participates in beating down the price demanded by Begbick for a uniform, by complaining that the clothes are too tight and the boots too small (*MiM*, 30). Unwittingly he thus helps to tie the noose that will eventually be placed around his neck. His first, symbolic assumption of Jip's identity is made with the politeness of a man who is eager to get on good terms with his social "betters" (*MiM*, 31–2). After the roll-call has passed off successfully, the normally temperate Galy Gay gets drunk in the process of showing-off to his new companions and boasting about the favour he has done them (*MiM*, 34). His inability to say "no" is evident not only in his becoming drunk, but also in his offer of further help to the soldiers, which they now feel to be unwelcome meddling in their affairs (*MiM*, 34–5).

Thus, Frau Galy Gay's fears about her husband running out of control because he simply does not know when to stop, are proving to be well founded. While he is developing his own momentum, outside events are doing the same. When these two developments come into interaction, a dialectic of increasing loss of freedom resulting from the effects of past actions begins to unfold. Having come to the canteen to deny his identity "just once", he is immediately obliged to deny it a further three times – with obvious symbolic implications – in order to ward off the unwelcome interest of a recent new acquaintance, the widow Begbick (*MiM*, 35). The scene closes after this thrice repeated denial of identity, with the stevedore Galy Gay left incongruously perched on a wooden chair in an army mess.

When the three soldiers return from their unsuccessful foray to recover Jip, they are astonished to find Galy Gay still asleep on the chair. His remaining there is partly a consequence of his having drunk too much, and partly a symbolic expression of his natural passivity and adaptability: rather than say "no" to the situation in which he has found himself, by returning home to his wife, he simply remains there, and, so adaptable is he, is able to sleep soundly on a wooden bar-chair without falling off and without being disturbed when customers come in to play billiards. Jesse believes that this natural adaptability will make their task of replacing Jip an easy one:

> *Jesse*:   So einer verwandelt sich ganz von selber. Wenn ihr den in einen Tümpel schmeißt, dann wachsen ihm in zwei Tagen zwischen den Fingern Schwimmhäute.
>
> (*MiM*, 49–50)

> *Jesse*:   A man like that will transform himself of his own accord. If you threw him into a pond, he'd grow webbed skin between his fingers in a couple of days.

Galy Gay's sleep and reawakening, a fairy-tale motif which is repeated in the experiences of Jip and Bloody Five, symbolises man's passive exposure to momentous changes in his life; Galy Gay's later terrified faint and reawakening to find himself addressed as Jeriah Jip is foreshadowed in this detail.

At first it seems as if the soldiers have been wrong in judging Galy Gay to be "one who cannot say no", for he initially rejects their invitation to join the army under the name of Jeriah Jip, saying that he would prefer to go home, "Because I'm Galy Gay" (*MiM*, 52). However, when they mention the word "business" (*MiM*, 53), his attitude of "not saying no" breaks through in the form of eager opportunism. Having been thus set in motion again, he once more begins to develop his own momentum: because he is so keen to make the most of the situation, he misunderstands a chance mention of the word "elephant", and he proceeds to wax enthusiastic about the advantages of owning an elephant (*MiM*, 54). The next manifestation of Galy Gay's gathering momentum in his new role as prospective businessman comes when he seizes the opportunity, which is created when Bloody Five enters with Frau Galy Gay, of proving that he is a man "who has a good head on his shoulders"

(*MiM*, 55). Bloody Five's intention is to unmask the fraud perpetrated by the soldiers and Galy Gay on the parade ground, but the latter frustrates this by denying to his own wife that he is Galy Gay. He then boasts to his companions, "You can rely on me. Galy Gay has now tasted blood" (*MiM*, 57), words which are repeated later when, as "the human fighting machine" he sets about the destruction of the fortress Sir el Dschowr (*MiM*, 125).

The "business deal" with which the soldiers trap Galy Gay involves his selling an "elephant" which does not belong to him, allegedly an army-surplus elephant, which is however not a real elephant at all, but a very obviously artificial mock-up. Just as Galy Gay overcame his fear of Bloody Five when it stood in the way of business, so now he suppresses his doubts about the elephant in order to proceed with the transaction: "An elephant's an elephant, especially when it's being bought" (*MiM*, 70–1).[8] As soon as he has sold the elephant to Begbick, Galy Gay is accused of the absurd double crime of selling an elephant which was false and of selling an elephant which did not belong to him. His silly hope of avoiding arrest by dealing anonymously is disappointed. To save himself from execution he is prepared once more to deny being Galy Gay and even to confess to being Jeriah Jip. However, the soldiers feel that he can best be persuaded to accept the name of Jip permanently if he is made to experience the terrors of standing before an execution squad. When the order is given for his pretended execution he faints. On waking up out of this faint he is addressed as Jip and asked to hold a funeral oration for his allegedly dead old self. Like the real Jip and Bloody Five, Galy Gay is now confronted with a conflict between his appetitive self and his sense of personal identity. Unlike them, he decides to accept the new persona which circumstances want to bestow on him, since this is the only way he can satisfy his appetites:

> Einer ist keiner. Es muß ihn einer anrufen,
> Drum
> Hätt ich doch gern hineingesehen in diesen Trog,
> Dieweil das Herz an seinen Eltern hängt, doch
> Ist der Unterschied zwischen ja und nein nicht so groß
> Und hab ich nicht angesehen diesen Elefanten,
> Drück ich ein Auge zu, was mich betrifft, und
> Lege ab, was unbeliebt an mir, und bin
> Angenehm.

[*Er steht auf und geht zu den Gummibäumen hinter*]
Und ich der eine und der andere ich,
Wir sehen nach Wetter und Wind,
Das uns zusammen näßt und trocknet, und
Stärken uns am Essen.

(*MiM*, 99–100)

One is no-one. Someone must summon him,
Therefore
I'd yet have gladly looked into this trough,
For the heart is attached to its parents, but
Between "yes" and "no" the difference is not so great
And I did not this elephant regard,
I'll turn a blind eye as far as I'm concerned, and
Cast off what's unliked in me, and I'll be
Pleasing.
[*He stands up and goes to the rubber trees at the back*]
And I the one and the other I,
We'll look out for weather and wind,
That will first wet then dry the pair of us, and
Strengthen ourselves with food.

The eager conformism which led Galy Gay into this situation
enables him to adapt to its demands. This conformism rests on the
firm foundation of determination to satisfy his physical needs at all
costs. Unlike Jip and Bloody Five, who neglect their appetites in
their attempt to preserve their accustomed social persona, Galy Gay
makes the satisfaction of his appetites his first priority. Throughout
the remainder of the action Galy Gay (alias Jeriah Jip) is shown to
profit from his absurd double identity as "I the one and the other I",
for he is not only able to use Jip's pay-book to draw Jip's rations but
also to force the other three soldiers to give him theirs by holding
over them the threat of his reversion to his old identity.[9]

Although he does not know it, Galy Gay's prudent and pragmatic
decision to opt for the satisfaction of his appetites is a piece of
primitive philosophical wisdom. According to the view of personality taken in the play, namely that a man's "personal identity"
amounts to no more than a social role or persona which he acquires
under certain circumstances and which he may well be obliged to
forsake or alter as circumstances change, there is no sense at all in
trying to cling to one's "character", come what may. A man's fate is

no longer "written in the stars", but is a matter of fitness to survive and is determined by his ability to adapt to changes in his environment. Galy Gay, the embodiment of life's amoral ability to "flow into any given form" (*GW*, **15**, 57) is a triumph of the Darwinian principle of the survival of the best adapted. In his willingness to accept whichever social role will best satisfy his appetites, Galy Gay is merely acting in accordance with the compelling principles of life. Presumably Galy Gay's practical wisdom is what Brecht was driving at when he said the play was intended for an audience, "whose interests were not so much aesthetic as philosophical in a primitive sense".[10]

FARCE

In *A Man's a Man* Brecht continued the practice established in *Drums in the Night, In the Jungle* and *Edward II* of using a popular dramatic form ironically as a vehicle for his view of certain existential and social problems. In this case the form chosen was that of farce, and the style of farce that of the silent film comedies which the young Brecht so greatly admired. Brecht acknowledged this influence when he described the play as "a comedy just made for the screen" ("eine geradezu leinwandgerechte Komödie" – *GW*, **17**, 973). The bold visual effects of silent comedy clearly had a strong appeal to Brecht who was seeking at the time to establish a "naïve" form of theatrical expression. In a note on the play he stated:

> *A Man's a Man* is the representative first attempt of the younger generation to establish the new form of major comedy. It is a clear example of the species of epic theatre which Brecht has called for repeatedly and which has been so vehemently attacked by the supporters of the earlier type of theatre. Every single scene of the comedy is so far removed from the problem-play or the psychological type of play that any naive actor would be bound to be able to reproduce it simply from memory.[11]

The theatrical *Grundgestus* (basic pattern of behaviour, recurring in a variety of forms) chosen by Brecht to give physical expression to relationships amongst the characters, and to illustrate the effect on them of the exploiting system within which they interact, is that of "the catcher caught". All the individual characters prey on one another, but the winner of these individual struggles gains at most a short-term advantage for himself, because in the long run it is the encompassing social system which has its interests served by the individually successful hunters amongst the hunted. Any individual who dares to overstep certain limits in the pursuit of personal goals is likely to find himself at odds with the system and eventually made to suffer for his initiative.

The ironic pattern of catching-only-to-be-caught begins with the burglary of the temple, during which the soldiers become more and more entangled in a series of booby-traps from which they emerge bloody and torn. By trying to "fish" for the riches of the temple they cause themselves to be caught. This event begins a chase (a much used pattern of action in silent film farces)[12] with Bloody Five the pursuer and the soldiers the pursued. In the scene following the burglary Bloody Five hides behind a tree in order to jump out on the soldiers and surprise them with a question about the whereabouts of their fourth man. The soldiers in turn then hide in order to jump out and surprise Galy Gay. In Galy Gay's case the catcher-caught *Gestus* operates through the elephant deal: as he tries to "catch" Begbick by selling her a false elephant, he allows himself to be trapped by the soldiers. In each case Brecht fashions a symbolic *Gestus* from the familiar repertoire of the slapstick film or the circus ring.

The aggressiveness of the characters' behaviour to one another, a characteristic of farce, is barely concealed in such physical gestures as springing out of hiding or holding a person down in a chair (the soldiers do this to Galy Gay at one point when he tries to escape), but elsewhere it is forced into hypocritically contorted and more subtly comic forms of expression. Violence is present in this suppressed form, for example, in the scene where the soldiers try to persuade Herr Wang, the owner of the temple, to reveal the whereabouts of Jip:

Polly: Wir suchen einen Herrn, genauer einen Soldaten, der in einer Lederkiste, die gegenüber diesem reichen und vornehmen Tempel gestanden hat, im Schlaf liegt.

Wang: Sein Erwachen möge ein angenehmes sein.

Polly: Dieser Kasten ist nämlich verschwunden.

Wang: Ich verstehe Ihre Ungeduld, die von der Ungewißheit herrührt; denn ich selber suche einige Leute, im ganzen etwa noch drei, genau gesagt Soldaten, und ich kann sie nicht finden.

Uria: Es wird sehr schwer sein. Ich glaube, sie können es aufgeben. Aber wir dachten, Sie wüßten etwas über den Lederkasten.

Wang: Leider nichts. Das Unangenehme ist, daß die Herren Soldaten alle die gleichen Kleider haben.

(*MiM*, 37)

Polly: We are looking for a gentleman, or to be more precise a soldier, who is lying asleep in a leather chest which was standing earlier opposite this rich and distinguished temple.

Wang: May his awakening be a pleasant one.

Polly: This box to which I referred has disappeared, you see.

Wang: I understand your impatience, which is caused by uncertainty; for I too am looking for some people, about three altogether, soldiers to be precise, and I am unable to find them.

Uriah: It will be very difficult. I think you can give up. But we thought you might know something about the leather trunk.

Wang: Nothing, I'm afraid. The unpleasant thing is that these gentlemen, the soldiers, all wear the same clothes.

Here the oblique style of dialogue developed by Brecht in *In the Jungle* is adapted to the task of adding some finesse to the broad comic style of *A Man's a Man*. Wang's contorted, oblique, excessively polite style of speech throughout the scene also underlines the "false-bottomed" quality of the characters' behaviour. The treacherous nature of the world (first symbolised in the "mouse-trap" temple) is shown to operate most subtly, and comically, in men's mutual hypocrisy.[13]

The physical movements which express the nature of human relations in the play also help to delineate the patterns of irony in the action. The hypocritical bows exchanged by Wang and the soldiers as the latter retire defeated from this encounter, recall the scene where similar bows signalled their initial triumph over Galy Gay (*MiM*, 32). Another such pattern is formed by contrasting states of motion and immobility. As Galy Gay prepares to leave the mess in order to escape permanent transformation into Jeriah Jip, his interest is awakened in the promised "deal", so he sits down again (*MiM*, 54). This voluntary and temporary acceptance of immobility is followed by his being thrown in the chair by the soldiers (*MiM*, 60) and later by his lapse into involuntary immobility and passivity when he faints during his mock execution. As has been indicated already, such states of immobility and passivity also form part of the development of Jeriah Jip's and Bloody Five's respective fates. Because of the urgency imposed by the imminent departure of the troop train (the rapid, mechanical movement of which also belongs to this pattern of contrasts), the soldiers agree that Galy Gay must be transformed "at the double" (*MiM*, 63). But in the last scene of the play it is Galy Gay, here shown charging about "unstoppably, like a war-elephant" (*MiM*, 118), who now forces them to move faster than they would like to in an effort to keep pace with him. The former quarry has now become the leader of the chase.

The ironic transfer of power from the three soldiers to their new recruit which these constrasts of movement with immobility make visible, is also brought out by the repetition of a roll-call amongst the soldiers at different points in the action. When the soldiers first experience a threat to their collective identity during the raid on the temple, Uria collects their military pay-books for safe keeping, "For a man can be replaced at any time, but there's nothing sacred any more if a pay-book isn't" (*MiM*, 13). The pay-books next figure in an unseen but audible roll-call, which takes place in the background on Bloody Five's orders while the latter is conversing with Leokadja Begbick in her mess. His disappointment when no gap occurs during the roll-call (such a gap would have allowed him to put the marauding machine-gunners on a charge), anticipates ironically his own subsequent loss of power and identity, which is foretold during this very interview with Begbick (*MiM*, 33). Fairchild's defeat and loss of identity is thus counterpointed with Galy Gay's change of identity and rise to power, a pattern which is underlined by the recurrence of the ritual of the roll-call at the end of the play, when Fairchild has become impotent in every sense, this time with Galy Gay (alias Jeriah Jip) in charge of it (*MiM*, 127).

As well as underlining the shifts of power between the soldiers, Fairchild and Galy Gay in the course of the action, the ritual pay-book inspections also have the function of symbolising the role played by a powerful, anonymous social system, represented here by the army, as the determining context of their inter-personal conflicts. Regardless of the personal reality of the situation, the roll-call must take place and names be given in the appropriate places.

The person in charge of the ritual may change, there may be no real connection between the men actually involved and the roles they are required to play, but at all events the military/social machine demands that these roles be filled. There are several other such symbols in the play which express the relation of the characters' individual experiences to the encompassing social reality in which they occur. The ridiculous elephant sold by Galy Gay symbolises the fact that the "little man" Galy Gay (who is repeatedly referred to as an "elephant"), by participating in this society's system of mutual exploitation, actually sells *himself*. There is a parallel to this symbolic incident in Bloody Five's use of his army revolver to castrate himself: the system with which he identifies destroys him as a man. While Galy Gay is being transformed into the soldier Jeriah Jip, and Bloody Five humiliated as "Bloody Gent", the widow Begbick's mess is being dismantled for loading on to the next troop-train. The dismantling of the tent symbolises not only the destruction of identity to which these two men are being subjected, but also makes visible the unrelenting pressure of social change, here represented by the army's urgent departure, which is deeply involved in the personal changes which the characters have to sustain, and which makes its interfering presence felt in the "noise of an army breaking camp" (*MiM*, 63) that is constantly audible in the background throughout the scenes of dismantlement and transformation, transmitting its power into the hurried, harried movements of the individuals who serve it. Finally, the encompassing, onward-driving action of society in its headlong pursuit of new areas of conquest, is symbolised in the scene showing the soldiers seated passively inside a troop-train carrying them to the battle-front at the inhuman speed of "one hundred days' marches" per minute (*MiM*, 115).

Brecht's use of the visual resources of the stage ensures that the underlying meaning of the action is given concrete theatrical expression.[14] In his use of language, too, one can see his skill in actually *dramatising* the problems in which he is interested, rather than simply using the stage as a platform for the explicit, abstract, direct exposition of his opinions. The title of the play apparently makes an apodictic assertion, namely "a man's a man", but when this phrase and others which formally resemble it occur in the dialogue, the effect is to reveal the unreliability of all simple apodictic statements of this kind, or to expose the underlying particular interest which a person may have in making such generalisations. In the "A-Man's-a-Man-Song" for example, the words of the title have the function of persuading soldiers to accept an ethos of "manliness" which serves the interests of the army: "Denn Mann ist Mann/Und darauf kommt's an" ("For a man's a man/And that's the important thing" – *MiM*, 68). Incorporated thus into the dramatic context, the phrase is robbed of its general validity by being shown to have a quite particular ideological function. Here it serves as an illustration of how an exploitative social system employs ostensibly "objective" truths to persuade men to accept their position within that system. The phrase is, in effect, made to serve the play's basic *Gestus* of the-catcher-caught, for it is evidently a device with which the military machine catches the minds of its soldiers. This *Grundgestus* is reinforced when the soldiers repeat the phrase, with a changed meaning but still as an ostensible expression of a generally valid truth, in order to convince themselves that it is possible to make a man exchange one identity for another; as they prepare to catch Galy Gay, they are in fact laying a trap for themselves:

> *Polly*: Wird das wirklich gehen, Uria? Einen Mann in einen anderen Mann verwandeln?
> *Uria*: Ja, ein Mann ist wie der andere. Mann ist Mann.
>
> (*MiM*, 60)

> *Polly*: Will that really work, Uriah? Turning one man into another?
> *Uriah*: Yes, one man's like the next. A man's a man.

The same pattern of self-injury resulting from a determination to see life in simple terms occurs when Uria, in his anger, uses a phrase which is identical in form, although different in content, during the raid on the temple:

> *Jesse*: Geben wir es auf. Das ist kein gewöhnlicher Tempel, das ist eine Falle.
> *Uria*: Tempel ist Tempel. Den Helm muß ich noch herausholen.
>
> (*MiM*, 11)

> *Jesse*: Let's give up. This is no ordinary temple, it's a trap.
> *Uriah*: A temple's a temple. I've still to get my helmet out.

The untrustworthiness of such expressions as "a man's a man", which formally are assertions of identity, reflects on a verbal level the instability of identity experienced by various characters, and directs attention to the general unreliability of life, its ubiquitous treachery, of which Jesse complains: "from Benares to Calcutta, under both sun and moon we have seen nothing but treachery" (*MiM*, 104).[15]

An important source of comedy in early silent films is the mechanical quality imparted to human movements either accidentally, as a result of technical inadequacies of film-making or reproduction, or intentionally, by consciously exploiting the mechanical qualities of the apparatus. Although one cannot *prove* that Brecht borrowed directly from early films the notion of having characters behave mechanically, one can see certain similar effects in *A Man's a Man*, which enhance the Chaplinesque qualities of the play. Bloody Five's exaggerated stiffness of movement at the threat of a rain shower is an isolated example of such mechanisation on a physical level. The rapid movements of the soldiers might also be so staged as to enhance this film-like effect. More widespread, however, is the occurrence of mechanical effects in the characters' speech. Galy Gay's opening dialogue with his wife draws its comedy both from the contrast between his inflated style of talking and its banal content, and from the stiff, psychologically improbable, obviously artificial way in which the speeches lead on from one another:

> *Galy Gay*: Meinst du, ich soll einen grossen Fisch kaufen, oder benötigst du einen kleinen?
> *Frau*: Einen kleinen.
> *Galy Gay*: Von welcher Art aber soll der Fisch sein, den du benötigst?
>
> (*MiM*, 7)

> *Galy Gay*: Do you consider I should buy a large fish or do you require a small one?
> *Wife*: A small one.
> *Galy Gay*: But of what kind shall the fish be which you require?

The movement of the dialogue here is as jerky and stiff as the movements of marionettes. The most exaggerated example of verbal mechanisation is to be found in Bloody Five's style of speech.

The patchwork of biblical and military registers in his language helps to suggest the fragmented public persona which he has assumed, and which is now cracking open under pressure from his sexual appetites:

Blody:	Sie lachen. Aber ich sage Ihnen, ich möchte dies alles verbrennen sehen, dieses Sodom mit Bartisch und Schaukelstuhl und dir, die du allein ein Gomorrha bist. Schau mich nicht so verzehrend an, du getünchtes Babylon. . . . Der Zusammenbruch der Menschheit fing damit an, daß der erste dieser Kaffern seinen Knopf nicht zumachte. Halt dein Maul!

(MiM, 32–3)

Bloody Five:	You may laugh. But I say to you, I'd like to see this whole place burn, this Sodom with its bar and rocking chair and you, you who are a Gomorrha on your very own. Don't look at me so ravishingly, you whitewashed Babylon. . . . The collapse of humanity began when the first of these Kaffers didn't do up his button. Shut your mouth!

Further emphasis is given to the mechanical quality of Bloody Five's behaviour by his automatic repetition of the phrase "Johnny pack your kit-bag" whenever, like some grotesque Erinnye, he "smells" crime, or his self-assuring habit of insisting "That's quite simple" whenever he is confronted with a problem. As happens to the other soldiers, his very insistence on regarding life as "simple" makes him fall prey to its unmanageable complexities. By giving the behaviour of his figures this mechanically stylised quality, Brecht gives theatrical expression to the idea that their lives are almost entirely governed by forces beyond their control.

In addition to film comedy Brecht drew on another form of popular entertainment in *A Man's a Man* as a source of techniques of presentation, namely the circus. He had for long argued, in a rather tongue-in-cheek manner, that the salvation of German theatre lay in its being converted from a temple into a circus (*GW*, **15**, 48–9). In this play he began to take his own advice seriously. The circus elements in *A Man's a Man* are mostly to be found in the long tenth scene where Galy Gay's transformation into Jip takes place. The artificial elephant used to trick Galy Gay is a variant on the artificial horse traditionally used by circus clowns. The division of the long scene into a series of "numbers", each introduced by Uria, is reminiscent of the ringmaster's presentation of the various attractions in a circus show:

> Uria: [*Pfeift*] Nummer eins: Das Elefantengeschäft. Die M.-G.-Abteilung überreicht dem Mann, der nicht genannt sein will, einen Elefanten. [*Er führt den Elefanten am Strick vor*] Billy Humph, Champion von Bengalen, Elefant im Dienst der englischen Armee usw.
>
> (*MiM*, 68)

> Uriah: [*whistles*] Number one: The Elephant Deal. The machine-gun crew hands over to the man who does not want to be named an elephant. [*He leads the elephant around on a rope*] Billy Humph, Champion of Bengal, elephant in the service of the English army etc.

If Uria's announcements perform a ringmaster function for the individual "numbers" in the tenth scene, the preceding placard, "The transformation of a living human being in the military barracks of Kilkoa in the year nineteen hundred and twenty five" (*MiM*, 61), and the commentary between scenes spoken by widow Begbick (*MiM*, 62) perform for the whole scene a function analogous to that of a barker who calls attention to the attractions of a sideshow at a fair or circus. In doing this, Brecht is not simply announcing ostentatiously his dislike of the "plaster of Paris"-stiffness of so-called legitimate theatre. He is also seeking to create a form of theatre which will appeal to different sections of an audience simultaneously. His farce can be enjoyed on one level as sheer slapstick, but its subtleties also have something to offer the more sophisticated spectator.·

AESTHETICS AND MORALS

The farcical form and style of *A Man's a Man* commend themselves for both symbolic and emotional reasons. Since the world in general and society in particular are seen in the play as vast, malevolent mechanisms, it is apt that the men acting under such compulsions should be cast in the role of knockabout clowns. The violence of the farce seems appropriate to the play's harsh view of reality and exercises both the fears and the aggressions aroused in us by such a vision of life. The element of amused detachment in our response to farce (which derives from our awareness of its artificiality) is conducive to the perception of symbolic and ironic patterns in the action, and thus helps to create a feeling of superiority over the characters caught up in the thick of events. The laughter produced by the events also helps to make palatable what otherwise would be a bleak perception of the human condition. Our sense of enjoying mastery over life's vicissitudes is enhanced by the relatively simple (and basically melodramatic) division of sympathies with which farce operates: we take sides with the "little man" against his more powerful oppressors (the "bullies"), and rejoice with him at their eventual discomfiture.

The plot and emotional structure of the farce works against the satirical potential of the play, for the balance of aggression and retribution in the relations between the individuals who catch and are caught channels our interest and sympathies in certain directions, so that we tend to forget that two wrongs do not make a right, and to lose sight of the wider context of the characters' struggles for dominance. The parallels and contrasts between the fates of Galy Gay, Jip, Bloody Five and the other soldiers create a see-saw effect which gives the action a certain self-enclosed quality. Thus, because Galy Gay's successful bombardment of the fortress at Sir el Dchowr marks the culmination of his rise to power and displacement of Bloody Five as a figure of importance, it is all too easy to forget that human lives are being sacrificed in the process. In fact in the version we are concerned with, the destruction of the fortress is accompanied only by a "shout of joy" from the victors (*MiM*, 126). This suggests that at the time of writing Brecht was more interested in the internal dynamics of the plot than with issuing moral warnings about militarism or imperialism. When he later decided that the play ought to have a serious moral and satirical purpose he had to import into the text an explicit warning about the terrible consequences of Galy Gay's ability to be transformed into a "butcher"; he also had to make it clear that the destruction of the Tibetan fortress costs the lives of innocent, peaceable people. When he produced the play in Berlin in 1931 he had to omit the original ending and present the soldiers as

enormous, deformed, bloodthirsty monsters rather than as the
bungling Tommies of the 1926 version.[16] These moralising ad-
ditions are very noticeably "stuck on" to the farce, which, taken as a
whole, lacks what one would expect to find in a political satire:
concrete and incisive analysis of the causes of imperialist war, and of
its effects on its own soldiers and on the subjugated peoples. In *A
Man's a Man* mutual exploitation is a *human* characteristic, not a
form of behaviour restricted to one class or social system: the native
temple-owner Wang is adept at fleecing his fellow-countrymen, and
actually ends up profiting from the soldiers' break-in – hardly a
pattern of action well suited to exposing the evils of the British Raj!
Such satire as there is in the original version is "generic" rather than
socially specific; it takes the form of an undertone, which occasionally breaks through the surface of the farce, of despair at human
stupidity and treachery.

Imperialism is not presented in the play as the expression of a
specific form of economic and political organisation which can *and
must* be replaced by a more humane one. There is never any
suggestion that some alternative form of society might be created in
which men might be spared the contradictions of warring
compulsions. Rather, the advance of imperialism (which is only
very vaguely imagined) is an image of the rapid and apparently
inexorable spread of modern civilisation over the face of the natural
world. The troop-train hurtling towards the Tibetan border
symbolises the mechanical, juggernaut-like quality of social
"progress". It is as an accelerator of the rate of change in human life
that modern society functions in the philosophical world of the play.
As it drives men along "at the double" to perform its functions and
to change their social roles suddenly if its functions require this, the
rapidly changing world of modern civilisation exacerbates man's
existential problems by adding its own compulsions to those of
nature. *A Man's a Man* is not a "timeless" comedy, because the
philosophical and existential problem of contingency is seen as
reaching a new stage of acuteness thanks to the hectic pressures
exerted by modern society. On the other hand, it is much more a
piece of wry philosophical contemplation of the human condition
than it is a call for political action to remedy social evils. *A Man's a
Man*, which Brecht described as a "classical comedy",[17] is a modern
descendant of a line of philosophical comedies concerned with the
uncertainty of human identity, of which the most distinguished
German example is Kleist's *Amphitryon*.[18]

The farcical tone and techniques of *A Man's a Man* are rooted, we have argued, in the playwright's desire to adopt an attitude of aloof superiority to the facts of human folly and rapacity. He laughs at men because he does not want to weep over them. Laughter offers at least the illusion of temporary mastery over the absurdity of existence. That his is a determination to laugh *despite* a nagging awareness of life's nastiness becomes apparent at certain moments when the tone of farce suddenly yields to one of pain or anger. Whereas we simply laugh at the injuries sustained by the soldiers during their raid on the temple, both because they deserve to be punished for their aggression and because the form of the punishment so well suits the crime, Bloody Five's self-castration is quite horrifying because its extreme violence causes injury far in excess of his "crimes" and because the "higher value" for which he sacrifices himself is so obviously a chimera. Whereas the soldiers, like all true clowns or characters of farce, will bounce back to fight another day, Bloody Five is grotesquely maimed for life. The non-humorous effect of the castration episode is actually intensified by having Galy Gay laugh at the sergeant's misfortune, and by contrasting his laughter with the awed silence that falls on the rest of the troop train. At this point the farce turns against itself and exposes its own cruelty.

The scene where Jeriah Jip tries to rejoin his old comrades is another instance of pathos suddenly exploding the illusion of harmlessness which is essential to the enjoyment of farce. Jip's curse on his old comrades for their treachery powerfully reminds us of our need for the kind of humane, emotional values which the farcical view of life would have us cast aside with cheerful cynicism:

Jip: Der Eiswind von Tibet soll euer Mark aussaugen, ihr werdet nicht mehr die Hafenglocke von Kilkoa hören, ihr Teufel! Ihr sollt aber marschieren bis ans Ende der Welt; und dann sollt ihr umkehren, mehrere Male. Der Teufel selber, euer Lehrer, wird euch nicht um sich haben wollen, wenn ihr alt seid, und ihr sollt weitermarschieren müssen durch die Wüste Gobi bei Tag und bei Nacht über die grünen wehenden Roggenfelder von Wales, und das wird über euch kommen, weil ihr einen Kameraden in der Not verraten habt.

(*MiM*, 124)

Jip: The ice-wind of Tibet shall suck the marrow from your bones, never again will you hear the harbour bell of Kilkoa, you devils! You shall march to the end of the world, and then you shall turn about, several times over. The devil himself, your teacher, will not want to have you around him when you are old, and you shall be compelled to march on through the Gobi Desert by day and by night over the green blowing rye-fields of Wales, and that shall come upon you because you have betrayed a comrade in his hour of need.

The tone of comedy is mingled with that of tragedy in a quieter, but no less effective manner in the scene where Galy Gay holds a funeral oration for his former self. The gag is an amusing one, but the tone in the middle section of the speech produces a lyrical mixture of comedy and poignancy that would be worthy of Chaplin at his best:

Drum kann ich nicht aufmachen diese Kist.
Weil diese Furcht da ist in mir beiden, denn vielleicht
Bin ich der Beide, der eben erst entstand
Auf der Erde veränderlicher Oberfläch
Ein abgenabelt fledermäusig Ding, hängend
Zwischen Gummibäumen und Hütt, nächtlich
Ein Ding, das gern heiter wär.
                                        (*MiM*, 99)[19]

And so I cannot open this chest.
Because there's this fear in the both of me, for perhaps
I am the both, who shortly was engendered
On the earth's changing surface,
A bat-like thing cut from its mother's cord, hanging
Between rubber-trees and hut, by night
A thing that would fain be merry.

The passage evokes elegiacally, even sentimentally, a theme which is perhaps the most pervasive one of modern literature: Galy Gay taking leave of his old way of life represents man as he is forced to leave behind a comfortable, intimate relationship with the natural world and take his place on the treadmill of modern civilisation. Such passages redeem *A Man's a Man* from being merely a heartless farce and give it some of the emotional richness of tragi-comedy.[20]

7 The Operas

The Threepenny Opera, which had its première in Berlin in 1928, was an immediate and enormous theatrical success, the first Brecht had enjoyed since *Drums in the Night*. This success has puzzled later commentators who wonder why bourgeois audiences should have been so enthusiastic about a work containing passages of Marxist social criticism, and who therefore suppose that the work's popularity must have rested on some "misunderstanding".[1] The fact is that the didactic passages (which, ironically, are the ones most frequently quoted in interpretations) were not even part of the original libretto, but were inserted subsequently by Brecht when, after his adoption of Marxism in 1929, he revised the text in 1931; his misleading Marxist commentary on the opera dates from the same year.[2] In its original form *The Threepenny Opera* was a lightweight picaresque farce with few and feeble socially critical implications.[3] Like Brecht's earlier adaptation of Marlowe's *Edward the Second*, this adaptation of John Gay's *The Beggar's Opera* reduced rather than sharpened the political significance of the original on which it was based.

Like *The Threepenny Opera*, *The Beggar's Opera* (first performance 1728) was a great success which reputedly made "Gay rich and Rich gay" (Rich being the theatrical entrepreneur who staged it). Its popularity was due to a felicitous combination of elements. One of these was the fact that it parodied the Italianate style of *opera seria* imported into England by Handel. In place of the vague mythological or pastoral settings favoured by this courtly form of opera Gay set his action in a precisely observed contemporary London underworld. Not only was the change from a serious to a comic type of opera welcome, so also was the replacement of the foreign style of music with songs set to popular English melodies which appealed to the audience's patriotic tastes. A further reason for the opera's success was the satirical trenchancy with which it drew parallels between the "low life" of the underworld and the "high life" of the country's unpopular ruling cliques, and thus exposed the immorality and corruption rampant in high places. Gay's general social satire of the behaviour of the ladies and gentlemen of court, or of lawyers and the like, was also armed with particular political barbs in its clear allusions to the Prime Minister, Robert Walpole, who is variously recognisable in the guise of Peachum or Macheath and "also through names like 'Bluff Bob', 'Bob Booty' and 'Robin of Bagshot' ".[4] On the other hand, the author's satirical–didactic impulse was held firmly in check by his sense of fun and desire for success as an entertainer. The action in which the political asides are embedded is a comic version of the love-story around which opera conventionally revolved. For all that Polly lacks the refinement of the conventional heroine, she is still basically a charming young girl whose ardent love deserves to be, and is, rewarded with the hand of her beloved. Equally, although Macheath is a satirical reflection of Walpole's rapacity, he is also a dashing young hero with an infectious zest for life; it would be churlish indeed to flout the affections of Polly and the audience by sending such a bold, though rakish, operatic hero to the gallows. Because the plot is centred on a love-story and because the satire is delivered wittily, the overall impression left by the opera is of a mixture of gaiety and sharpness, not one of outrage and bitterness. That this is not a false impression engendered by historical and emotional distance from the events and figures satirised, is borne out by the rebuke of a contemporary critic who considered that Gay had "given up his moral for a joke".[5]

If the same critic had reviewed *The Threepenny Opera* his verdict would undoubtedly have been even sterner, for the specific references to contemporary social and political ills, with which Gay's dialogue was peppered, are few and lacking in vigour in Brecht's adaptation.[6] One can discern some intention of making Gay's material more relevant to Brecht's own society in the fact that he re-sites the action, bringing the milieu forward from the eighteenth to the nineteenth century, although with twentieth-century anachronisms in the dress and in other details of the characters' lives, such as the use of lorries to drive loot to the stable where Macheath is married. The choice of a vaguely Victorian milieu was a means of pointing up the hypocrisy of a society resting on the twin pillars of capitalism and Christianity. By changing Peachum's line of business from receiver of stolen goods to owner of a "firm" of fraudulent beggars operating within the law, Brecht approximates the figure more closely to the type of bourgeois entrepreneur who lives "from" rather than in accordance with morality. Through Peachum, Brecht could express criticism directly of the increasing hard-heartedness of the wealthy whose small capacity for charity obliges Peachum to comb the Bible ever more anxiously for new phrases to touch their consciences. On the other hand, Peachum himself serves to personify the hypocrisy of his society since he expects other people to be moral, but only because he wants to exploit their morality. Peachum's "morning hymn", a parody of the Lutheran chorale, comically expresses the workaday ruthlessness of the "Protestant ethic" in the form normally reserved for its Sunday sanctimoniousness.

Although the remodelling of the figure of Peachum brings the satire somewhat closer to Brecht's own times, it is debatable whether this portrait of Victorian cant had much relevance to German society in the 1920s, where even the show of religiosity had become far less characteristic than in the previous century. Perhaps Brecht came closest to emulating Gay's satire of specific features of contemporary society in his characterisation of Macheath. He followed Gay in portraying Macheath as a young man, adored by all the ladies,[7] but substituted for the aristocratic manners of Gay's hero those of an aspiring bourgeois who wants not only wealth but prestige and "a touch of class" in his life. In this mixture of shady dealing and social pretension he resembles the black-marketeers (*Schieber*) who made quick fortunes in the chaos of post-war Germany. Unfortunately this conception of the character, which was at least compatible with the daredevil quality of some of his behaviour, later became obscured by Brecht's claims that Macheath should be presented as a middle-aged man of inflexible bourgeois habits (*GW*, **17**, 995).

The retouching of these two characters was, however, insufficient to give Brecht's adaptation anything like the satirical relevance and precision of Gay's original. There were various things Brecht could have done to give the piece some serious satirical force, but he failed to do any of them. He neither gives increased weight to the picaresque method by exposing the nature of society as it is *really* experienced by its "asocial" elements,[8] nor does he write new versions of Gay's commentaries on specific failings of the ruling classes, nor does he recast the whole style of the action to make it resemble the behaviour of those presently at the upper end of the social scale. Instead he chooses, on the one hand, to exploit the merely comic potential of the underworld characters' attempts to emulate the manners of the bourgeoisie, while on the other hand keeping the satire on the general level of presenting violence, hypocrisy and selfish materialism, with sardonic resignation, as characteristics of human behaviour which are to be found throughout history and in a variety of relationships. *The Threepenny Opera* does not attempt to demonstrate, as does, say, *Saint Joan of the Stockyards*, that the fundamental goodness of human nature is perverted by the specific property- and production-relations of capitalist society.

These two symptoms of the lack of any serious socially critical intent in *The Threepenny Opera* can be illustrated from the first scene of the opera. Where the introductory caption, which talks of the "increasing hard-heartedness of people", might lead one to expect some historically specific account of this process of emotional hardening, Peachum's actual complaints are directed in the most general terms against man's *capacity* for insensitivity: "For man has the fearful ability to deaden his feelings at will, so to speak" (*DGO*, 7). The ensuing dialogue between Peachum and Filch, a young "free-lance" beggar who has been caught "poaching" on Peachum's territory, so clearly conforms to the comic–brutal stereotype of picaresque behaviour that it has virtually no suggestiveness as an illustration of the way power is exercised elsewhere in society. Filch's opening references to Peachum's "business" and to his store of slogans as his "capital" are insufficient to establish a strong and coherent parallel between the fictional events and the realities of the business world. Nor is the notion that the underworld is organised in a business-like way a startling insight, since it has been part of the stock-in-trade of picaresque literature since Cervantes' *Rinconete y Cortadillo*. What is more, the fact that no-one is really hurt in the encounter (we don't take seriously Peachum's threat of "using the saw" on Filch if he repeats his offence) means that the scene does not even have any bite as an illustration of life in the underworld. Far from disturbing the spectator either emotionally or intellectually, the scene is simply good fun, as "culinary" a piece of entertainment as one is likely to find anywhere.

The same tendency for the action to slide off into harmless farce is also evident in the only wholly original scene in Brecht's adaptation, namely Macheath's wedding scene. If the behaviour of Macheath at his wedding is taken as a lampoon of the tasteless but ambitious *arriviste*, it must again be pointed out that the scene is too insistently and obviously a pastiche of gangster clichés for it to be effective as a satire of the bourgeois way of life. Indeed, because the comic effects rest largely on the farcical *contrast* between Macheath's aspirations and his tendency to think and act in a socially quite unacceptable manner, the basis of satire, the sustained *similarity* between fiction and its model in reality, is constantly being undermined. Instead of being made aware that art is here holding up a mirror to bourgeois life, the spectator is drawn imaginatively into a farcical, make-believe world which is only tenuously connected with the real world of social experience. In short, this "opera for beggars", although parodying conventional opera (or, more precisely, operetta), continues to perform the same psychological function as other operas, namely to provide an escape from the pressures of reality.

The plot as a whole confirms the evidence of the two scenes we have just considered, in that the account it offers of human behaviour is of a very generalised nature. The action takes the form of a struggle for power between Peachum and Macheath as leaders of a gang of beggars and robbers respectively. Peachum fears that Macheath's marriage to his daughter, Polly, will enable the robber-chief to learn Peachum's trade secrets and thus gain control over his little empire. He therefore decides that Macheath must be hanged, and bribes the whores in the Turnbridge brothel frequented by his rival to betray Macheath to the police. Several causes can be adduced for Macheath's downfall: the stupidity of his wife in boastfully revealing his friendship with the chief of police to her father, his own bravado and sexual appetite in visiting the whores twice, despite the warrant for his arrest, the venality and spite of the prostitute Jenny whose pimp he once was and whose betrayal of him involves revenge for misused love.[9] As so often in Brecht's early plays, the paradigmatic nature of Macheath's betrayal is suggested by having it take place on a Thursday, the day of Christ's betrayal by Judas; the blasphemy is heightened when Macheath repays Tiger Brown for his later treachery by looking at him in an accusing way so that the policeman "weeps bitter tears", a trick which Macheath boasts of having learned from the Bible.[10] So widespread are the motives of self-interest and treachery that Macheath is only saved from the gallows by the intervention of the queen, who not only pardons him but also nobilitates him. As in *The Beggar's Opera*, this obviously improbable "happy ending" is not simply a sarcastic parody of the fairy-tale unreality of conventional opera, for it is also the fitting culmination of a piece which is fundamentally escapist in character as it weaves a comic, and at times sentimental, plot from the "eternal verities" of human vice and folly. With cynical amusement it simply registers what Jenny's betrayal of him makes Macheath realise, "that the world does not change" (*DGO*, 77).

To a degree, the tendency of the action to be merely amusing is countered by the songs of the opera, or some of them, when they express protest against social evils. In the most straightforward of these homilies, the third and last finale, the audience is exhorted to be more charitable in the future:

Alle: [*singen zur Orgel, nach vorn gehend*]
        Verfolgt das Unrecht nicht zu sehr, in Bälde
        Erfriert es schon von selbst, denn es ist kalt.
        Bedenkt das Dunkel und die große Kälte
        In diesem Tale, das von Jammer schallt.
                                                    (*DGO*, 80)

[*All come forward, singing to the organ*]
Injustice should be spared from persecution:
Soon it will freeze to death, for it is cold.
Think of the blizzards and the black confusion
Which in this vale of tears we must behold.[11]

Almost all the other songs, however, are ambiguous in their moral attitude.[12] This is true, for example, of the earlier finales at the end of acts one and two. In the first of these, a trio sung by the Peachum family, a pessimistic view is taken of life. Man's desires for justice, peace and goodness are made impossible to realise by the inherent poverty of life and the badness of human nature:

Peachum: Ein guter Mensch sein? Ja, wer wär's nicht gern?
           Doch leider sind auf diesem Sterne eben
           Die Mittel kärglich und die Menschen roh.
           Wer möchte nicht in Fried' und Eintracht leben?
           Doch die Verhältnisse, sie sind nicht so!
                                                    (*DGO*, 39)

Peachum: Be a good man? Who wouldn't like to be one?
           But this planet's means are meagre, sadly,
           And man's unkind to friend and foe.
           Who would not live in peace, and gladly,
           But conditions won't have it so.

There is a characteristic vagueness in the word "conditions" ("Verhältnisse"): on the one hand it could be taken to mean that changeable *social* conditions are responsible for man's behaviour; on the other hand, and more obviously, it seems to indicate that the roots of the problem are buried deep in the conditions of life on earth and inherent in man's nature. The word "Verhältnisse" and the talk of "diesem Sterne" ("this star") recall the phrase "die Verhältnisse dieses Planeten" ("the conditions on this planet"), used by Shlink in *In the Jungle* to refer to the hopelessness of nurturing any ideal ambitions on this bare and (literally) God-forsaken planet. As we have seen, this sweeping view of life, an insistently recurring perspective in Brecht's early work, expresses the despair of the transient individual as he contemplates his world, itself transitory, and his inability to satisfy his hunger for eternity. Man is, in this view, driven to be "roh" ("unkind") not only by specific social pressures but by his own awareness of transience and his consequent determination to satisfy as many of his needs as possible, including his aggressions, in the short time available to him. Macheath is aptly likened to a shark because, like Baal, Shlink, Edward the Second, he embodies the predatory instinct of the lone animal, for whom all other animals are enemies or victims.

The meaning of the first finale is further complicated by its dramatic and musical presentation. On the one hand, the smug cynicism of the Peachums, who profit from crime and are thus only too glad to embrace pessimistic views on man's inherent depravity, has its self-congratulatory aspect underlined by the stage-directions which require that the flint-hearted Peachum hold the Bible as he preaches about man's fundamental rights, and that mother and daughter dance a "silly two-step" as they sing the mocking refrain:

> Da hat er eben leider recht.
> Die Welt ist arm, der Mensch ist schlecht.
> (*DGO*, 39)

> He's right, although it's awfully sad,
> The world is poor and man is bad.

On the other hand, Peachum's dark and cynical generalisations strike home with the force of the self-evident, and the hammering crescendo in the accompanying music invites sympathy with his belief in brutality as the obvious and proper response to the brutality of life.

The second "Threepenny Finale" is a mirror image of the first, in that it adopts an aggressive, socially critical stance, but it has the validity of its position relativised by the fact that it is sung by hardened criminals and not by truly "poor people". The verses of the song place the responsibility for crime on the shoulders of those who deny men the basic material necessities of life:

Ihr, die ihr euren Wanst und uns're Bravheit liebt,
Das eine wisset ein für allemal:
Wie ihr es immer dreht und wie ihr's immer schiebt,
Erst kommt das Fressen, dann kommt die Moral.
(*DGO*, 59)

You who love your paunches and our virtue,
There's one thing we insist upon:
No matter how you twist and turn the issue,
First comes the belly, morals follow on.

However, the refrain, with its insistence that "Der Mensch lebt nur von Missetat allein" ("man lives but from villainy alone") makes one wonder how things could ever be otherwise. There is no indication in the chorus that social conditions are responsible for making man "forget" his humanity; rather the impression is given that under *all* circumstances man must have no aspirations to higher things – "beneidenswert, wer frei davon" ("you're better far, to be free of them") – since these will only distract his attention from the realities of life as a bloody struggle for dominance.

Ambiguous though the songs are, they have a degree of moral seriousness which is almost completely absent from the action of the opera. Each song is sung under special golden lighting which marks it off from the surrounding action and signals its disillusioning function. Almost all the songs have a common object of attack, namely the simple-minded sentimentality in the lyrics and music of operetta. Just as *The Beggar's Opera* had been a broadside fired against the Handelian operas which had been in vogue for a number of years, so Weill and Brecht directed their fire against the worn-out operettas which were being revived, particularly by film-producers, in the late 1920s. Siegfried Kracauer summed up the situation thus: "The more worn-out the operettas are, the more suitable they seem to be for filming – *The Beggar Student, His Highness's Lady* – they swarm over the audiences with their charming princes, their fairy castles and their clichéd couplets."[13] And, just as eighteenth-century audiences were grateful for the change of style offered by Gay and Pepusch, so the Berliners were delighted with the sharply acidic quality of the Brecht–Weill songs after the excess of sugar poured out by such sentimental operettas.

It is usually not difficult to identify the type of standard operetta number parodied by a particular song in *The Threepenny Opera*. The effect repeatedly achieved by Weill is of a cheap, tattered romanticism which completely fails in its attempt to cover the nakedness of an unromantic reality. This ironic relationship to operatic romance is hinted at in an announcement made before the curtain rises:

> "Sie werden heute abend eine Oper für Bettler sehen. Weil diese Oper so prunkvoll gedacht war, wie nur Bettler sie erträumen, und weil sie doch so billig sein sollte, daß Bettler sie bezahlen können, heißt sie *Die Dreigroschenoper*." *(DGO,* 5)

> "This evening you will see an opera for beggars. Because this opera was intended to be as grand as only beggars might dream of, and because, on the other hand, it had to be so cheap that beggars could afford it, it is called *The Threepenny Opera*."

Here are some examples of the way Weill's songs parody their counterparts in standard operetta: the "Wedding Hymn for the Poorer Classes" has a dragging rhythm and melancholy melody where conventional operetta would have served up fulsome optimism, probably with religious overtones; in place of the sweetly romantic song about dreams fulfilled which an operetta bride might sing on her wedding day, Brecht and Weill have Polly sing the bloodthirsty "Song of the Pirate Jenny" (in which an oppressed scullery maid dreams of taking revenge on the men who exploit her) in order to indicate the reservoir of resentment filling up in the heart of a woman whom her husband "and master" regards merely as a prized possession; whereas operetta choruses about soldiers and robbers are rollicking and idealistic, the "Ballad of Mack the Knife" has a repetitive, threadbare melody which keeps falling back on itself and is sung to the cheerful–cheerless monotony of a hurdy-gurdy, while the "Song of the Cannons" not only focuses on the savagery of soldiers but also, with a suddenly accelerating tempo towards the end of each verse, suggests that the soldiers, far from sitting comfortably and masterfully on their cannons, are being hounded along by events completely out of their control.

Although the urge to deflate and undermine is strong in Weill's music, it is far from being consistently hostile to sentiment.[14] His settings of such lines as "Die Liebe dauert oder dauert nicht / An dem oder jenem Ort" ("Love lasts or does not last in this place or in that"), or of parts of the "Barbara-Song", have the kind of hauntingly poignant melody which betrays the later composer of "September Song". It is just that such fragments of melancholy sentiment are put into a musical or dramatic environment which suggests that any satisfaction of the longings expressed by the melodies may be unattainable.

What I have tried to show is that there is no reason to suppose that the success of *The Threepenny Opera* rested on some misunderstanding. Its plot and characters offered an escape from reality into a picaresque world of broad comedy, while its lyrics contained a mixture of acerbic wit and sentiment which arrived at a particularly opportune moment in the Berlin of 1928. That its appeal is not restricted to a particular time and place, however, is demonstrated by repeated successful revivals. In this connection it is interesting to note that the country where *The Threepenny Opera* has enjoyed more productions than almost any other of Brecht's plays is not decadent America or England but the German Democratic Republic.

RISE AND FALL OF THE CITY OF MAHAGONNY

The Threepenny Opera contained little that would seriously spoil the spectator's enjoyment of an evening's fun, for even the moralising songs made their points with so much verbal and musical wit that they could be digested without much difficulty. Despite its darker, aggressive moments, the opera was basically cheerful in character, and was rewarded, accordingly, with immediate and continuing success. The opera *Rise and Fall of the City of Mahagonny* (completed in 1929), also a fruit of Brecht's collaboration with Weill, certainly did not carry the whole audience with it at the Leipzig premiere in 1930,[15] for the reason that it put fun ("Spaß"), at the centre of a penetrating and disturbing analysis of the spiritual and moral condition of contemporary society. In this work the painful awareness of man's inability truly to get the better of his problems, which is present in all Brecht's early plays, but generally pushed into the backgound by his determination to create images of life mastered, forces itself into the centre of attention and calls into question the whole philosophy of *Spaß* which, in one form or another, was Brecht's principal means of dealing with pain in all his previous plays. *Mahagonny* is a last, devastating expression of the central conflict of Brecht's early period, but, in its bitter pessimism, already a prelude to his imminent adoption of a new strategy through which his will to master life might re-assert itself more successfully.

"All who truly seek are disappointed"

As the title of the opera indicates, *Mahagonny* narrates the history of a city. In Weill's words, "The city arises from men's needs, and it is men's needs which bring about its rise and fall".[16] What are these needs, and how do they cause these effects? The city of Mahagonny is founded by a group of fleeing criminals as a last, desperate attempt to make their fortune. They hope to trap men with the offer of fun in their "city of nets" and wring from them their hard-won gold. The predatory intentions of the founders are indicated by the fishing rod on which they hoist the town's flag. Underlying the involvement of all who are party to the city's rise and fall is a sense of disorientation and desolation, symbolised in the desert place where the town is established. Even the founders of the city confess that "this whole Mahagonny only exists because there is nothing else to cling to" (*Mah*, 7.)[17] The prostitutes who come to make a living here are aptly designated as "sharks". Yet, they are also forlorn, vulnerable creatures "who've lost their good old mamma", and whose feelings of existential insecurity make them seek solace in whisky, dollars and "pretty boys". Men come from the great cities to Mahagonny because life in mass society, with its constant change and its reduction of the individual to an anonymous, inter-changeable unit, has given them a keen sense of personal transience and dissatisfaction:

> Wir wohnen in den Städten.
> Unter ihnen sind Gossen,
> In ihnen ist nichts,
> Über ihnen ist Rauch.
> Wir sind noch drin,

Wir haben nichts genossen.
Wir vergehen rasch
Und langsam vergehen sie auch.
             (*Mah*, 9)

We live in the cities,
Under them are sewers,
In them is nothing,
Over them is smoke,
We are still in them,
We have enjoyed nothing.
We are wasting away quickly,
And slowly they are waning too.

The founders of Mahagony "sell" their undertaking to these men by promising them idyllic peace "far from the bustle of the world", and the recognition of their importance as individuals – "only yesterday they were asking for you there" (*Mah*, 9).[18] The promise proves to be a lie, for, once in Mahagonny, each man is treated as just another of the "Jimmys, Jimmys, Jimmys" on whom the founders batten. In other words, the "city of fun" is an organisation which seeks to profit from the exploitation of modern man's existential fears and needs.

The development of the city initially takes the form of a transition from concealed to open anarchy. Underlying the illusion of peace and harmony in the early days of the town is a real conflict of interest between founders and incomers, i.e. owners and customers. This clash of interests is reflected, on the one hand, in the despair of the founders that those customers who are content just to enjoy the peace of the town do not feel any need to spend their money on the amusements on offer, and, on the other hand, in the disappointed departure from the town of those other customers who have expected something more exciting for their money. Peace of mind appears to be incompatible with lively appetites and, by extension, with making profits through the satisfaction or exploitation of appetites. The idyll provided in Mahagonny is illusory, not only because the town offers an artificial haven from the harsh world, where the customers must earn the money necessary to support themselves here, but also because the internal structure of relationships is fundamentally antagonistic. If the customers merely enjoy the peace, the business must fail; if business booms, it can only be because the customers have been persuaded to forget the *spiritual* needs which have brought them here in the first place. Another source of potential conflict lies in the fact that the laws which make the place pleasantly peaceful for some also make it boring for others. The collapse of the undertaking is only averted by the arrival in the town of a group of lumberjacks from the frozen wastes of Alaska. Among their number is a man called Jimmy Mahoney who, like others before him, is dissatisfied with the dull peacefulness of the place, but who, when he tries to leave, is prevented from doing so by his companions. Because he is forced to stay in Mahagonny his boredom and frustration grow until they erupt in angry rebellion. Paradoxically, however, the challenge he poses to the founders of the city proves to be their salvation. In order to understand Jim Mahoney's crucial role in the development of the city, it is necessary to consider his past experience.

Before coming to Mahagonny, Mahoney has endured years of hardship working as a lumberjack in Alaska. This role contains an ambiguity on which the complexity and irony of the rest of the opera depends. On the one hand, Mahoney the lumberjack is an archetypal figure with symbolic connotations which are familiar from Brecht's earlier plays (*Baal, In the Jungle*) and poetry. First, the lumberjack represents man as an exploiter of nature; this function makes him aware that man, like the rest of nature, lives by destroying other life, and that the universal transience of life will dispose of him as coldly as he disposes of the forests. But Mahoney's role as a lumberjack has a social as well as an existential significance. As an *exploited* exploiter of nature he has "sold his skin" in Alaska for money, believing that this will buy pleasures enough to compensate him for the pain of earning it. In other words, having been exploited as a producer, he now looks forward to his rewards as a consumer, unaware that society will also exploit him in this function. Mahoney's view of the world, which has been formed both by a perception of the essential human condition as a transient creature of nature, *and* by the ruling ideology of a materialist, exploitative society, casts him in the tragically ambivalent role of a seer and blind man.[19]

Having lived face to face with the hostility and destructiveness of nature, his own included, Jim Mahoney can find no satisfaction in the all too peaceful town of Mahagonny. At his first angry pistol shot, the mechanical little white cloud that has produced a spurious illusion of timelessness as it drifted to and fro above the town, trembles and scuttles off, leaving the sky to the hurricane which

Jim's outburst has apparently summoned up. Inspired by the approaching hurricane, Jim urges the inhabitants of Mahagonny to emulate its destructiveness by giving free rein to their appetites in the short time available to them: "Do tonight what is forbidden. When the hurricane comes it will do the same" (*Mah*, 29). The song he teaches the others to sing describes all human relations as anarchic, but also carries a suggestion that man lacks any metaphysical comfort in the world:

Denn wie man sich bettet, so liegt man,
Es deckt einen keiner da zu.
(*Mah*, 29)

You must sleep on your bed as you've made it
There's no-one to tuck you in.

What Mahoney does not realise is that the aggression towards other men which he declares to be essential to human happiness, is a socially conditioned reflex; nor is he aware that his idea of fun is above all a reaction to his experiences in Alaska. After years of deprivation he puts his faith in uninhibited consumption, and after years of suffering violence through "selling his skin" he believes pleasure will lie in the exercise of violence. In the course of the opera he has to learn that the "laws of human bliss" which he formulates are not a universal key to happiness.

Yet, despite Brecht's subsequent demonstration of the unhappy consequences of Mahoney's attitude, the hero is presented sympathetically during the hurricane scene itself. As the hurricane approaches, Mahoney shows personal qualities of composure, courage and passionate commitment to the complete and immediate satisfaction of his vital appetites, qualities which give him heroic stature in contrast to the fainthearted mass of people in Mahagonny. The fact that Mahoney's attitudes play into the hands of his exploiters only emerges later, although it is hinted at in Begbick's immediate interest in his proposals. In the hurricane scene Mahoney is seen predominantly in his existential rather than his social aspect, as a man who confronts the fierce truths at the heart of life rather than as a victim of social manipulation. Because Brecht is sympathetic to the absolute and amoral claims of the existential self, and because there is always a suggestion in the opera that social violence is at bottom only another form of the violence inherent in nature, his presentation of Mahoney's fate remains ambivalent to the end.

Under Mahoney's new motto "Du darfst" ("everything is permitted") business begins to boom in Mahagonny. The phrase "Hochbetrieb in Mahagonny" ("Mahagonny in full swing") is an ironic one which suggests that it is not only the staff but also the consumers who are "working" at full stretch as they create profits by consuming ever more frantically. The element of coercion in their hectic pursuit of "fun" is suggested by the chorus as it lists the pleasures to be practised here, in the manner of a set of factory regulations:

> Erstens vergeßt nicht, kommt das Fressen,
> Zweitens kommt die Liebe dran,
> Drittens das Boxen nicht vergessen,
> Viertens saufen, solang man kann.
> Vor allem aber achtet scharf,
> Daß man hier alles dürfen darf.
>
> *(Mah, 31)*

> First, do not forget, you shall guzzle,
> Second, it's the turn of love,
> Thirdly, don't neglect the boxing,
> Fourthly, boozing all you can.
> Above all, observe the strictest rule:
> Permissiveness permitted to the full.

The injunction "daß man alles dürfen darf" sounds like an ironic perversion of the enlightenment dictum, "Kein Mensch muß müssen" ("no man must be obliged"). The suggestion that consumption is simply a form of exploitation complementing that which is practised on the factory floor, is reinforced by the queue of dispirited men as they wait before Begbick's brothel, chanting her instructions on how to treat the prostitute, before being moved, as on a conveyor belt, into the brothel itself. However, the scene also carries other symbolic overtones. Begbick's brothel with its queue of customers is also an image of man's subjection to the mechanisms of appetite, an expression of what in *The Threepenny Opera* was called man's "sexuelle Hörigkeit" ("sexual dependence"). As well as personifying the men's social exploitation, the "madame" Begbick embodies the coercive force of instinct (just as she did towards Bloody Five in *A Man's a Man*). Man's inability to escape the eternally unsatisfying treadmill of desire was conveyed by a detail in the typescript version of the scene which unfortunately was omitted later: as each customer left the brothel by one door, he rejoined the queue at the other.[20]

The same kind of ambiguity emerges in the second part of this scene, where Jim Mahoney and the prostitute Jenny are shown in post-coital mood inside the brothel. They sit some distance apart, each preoccupied with him- or herself; he smokes while she puts on her make-up, in readiness for the next customer. On the one hand, this can be taken to illustrate the destruction of human relations by the capitalist cash-nexus.[21] On the other hand, and more plausibly, the scene is concerned with the brevity of sexual relations and with their failure to satisfy spiritual needs. After they have partially and temporarily taken possession of each other, physically and economically, the two lovers, sunk in their separate thoughts, sing the beautiful "Crane Duet". The "conceit" of this remarkable love song is that two lovers resemble a flock of cranes and a group of clouds drifting at an equal speed and height across the sky. What is so striking about this imagery, particularly in view of the context in which the song is sung, is the quality of ascetic purity symbolised in the relationship of clouds and cranes to one another. The lovers are thought of as physically separate and as having quite distinct natures, and the calm, even harmony of their shared flight as resting on their acceptance of distinctness and distance from one another. Their completely absorbing relationship is a contemplative one which encloses them in a private sphere of seeming timelessness – "Thus does love seem to lovers a support" – until, inevitably, time intrudes and drives the cranes and clouds apart.[22] The ethereal imagery of birds and clouds "flying from one life into another" expresses a desire to transcend the material, instinctual sphere of mutual use and possession, and indicates that Brecht's early reading of Eastern philosophy was rooted in something deeper than mere intellectual curiosity.[23] The poem is the fullest articulation of a feeling that runs through the whole opera, and finds expression in a variety of forms – in the confession "that this whole Mahagonny only exists because everything is so bad", or in the nostalgia of the prostitutes for their "good old mamma", or, by implication, in the nauseating grotesqueness with which Jack the Glutton eats himself to death. Whether it takes the form of angry bitterness or elegiac resignation, as in this poem, the pervasive mood of the opera is one of melancholy.

In the next scene, headed "Fighting", Jim Mahoney gives vent to his growing opposition to the "laws of human bliss", which he proclaimed in Mahagonny during the hurricane, by placing all his money on a bet to back his old companion Alaska Wolf Joe in a boxing match against the much heavier and more powerful Trinity Moses. By backing an obvious loser, Mahoney is rebelling against the hard-headed, self-centred materialism which is fundamental to survival in Mahagonny, and expressing his need for "something more" in life, in this case friendship, to fill the spiritual void he feels here. After Joe's death in the fight Jim's disaffection from Mahagonny leads him to indulge in a wild drinking spree so as to escape, through intoxication at least, to "the land where it is better to live". Fired by whisky, his imagination transforms Alaska nostalgically into a lost paradise to which he and his drinking companions try to "sail" on an improvised raft rigged from a billiard table. Their dream of returning to nature is ended abruptly by Begbick's demand to be paid for the whisky that took them there. Because Jim cannot pay for the drinks, and neither his mistress nor his friends will help him financially, he is tried and sentenced to death for the greatest crime known in Magagonny, poverty.

Mahoney's trial and execution and their consequences are presented as ambiguously as all that has preceded them. One may see in the trial a grotesque reflection of the capitalist worship of money: tickets for admission are sold by the prosecuting counsel; whereas a murderer may bribe his way to freedom, failure to pay a small bill is punished by death; so deeply has capitalism alienated human nature that neither Mahoney's mistress nor his friend will give any of their money to save his life. But, because they only vaguely resemble the everyday reality of capitalism, one can also see those events as evidence that life is a brutal and ultimately hopeless struggle in which the payment exacted from the individual is always out of proportion to the satisfactions gained.[24] Mahoney's desertion by man and woman alike in his hour of need attests as much to the inherent deficiency of human nature as it does to its corruption in a particular form of society; the sacrifice asked of Bill and Jenny is little enough, and yet it is too much. Men may talk and dream of friendship and love, it seems, but, when these are put to the test, they prove to be insubstantial illusions conceived by man for his own comfort, to make the world *appear* to be habitable. Mahoney, at any rate, departs this life, not cursing the laws of capitalism, but accepting death as the inevitable outcome of his reckless self-indulgence and urging others *not* to be deterred by his death from living like him. Perhaps this should be taken as a sign that the capitalist system has so addled his consciousness that even his experiences in Mahagonny have not taught him the error of his ways. Perhaps, on the other hand, his unbroken faith in hedonism, despite all his disappointments, is being recommended as a necessary condition of life in a world where there is no possibility of transcendence. Life, though imperfect, even irredeemably cruel, is all there is and must be made the best of:

Laßt euch nicht vertrösten,
Ihr habt nicht zu viel Zeit,
Laßt Moder den Verwesten,
Das Leben ist am größten,
Es steht nicht mehr bereit.

Laßt euch nicht verführen,
Zu Fron und Ausgezehr,
Was kann euch Angst noch rühren,
Ihr sterbt mit allen Tieren,
Und es kommt nichts nachher.
                              (*Mah*, 54-5)

Daily we grow older
We have but little time
So leave the dead to moulder
To be alive is nobler
To flee from life, a crime.

Take not as your teacher
The tyrant or the slave
And do not dread the preacher:
The end for every creature
Is nothing but the grave.[25]

Mahoney's death is followed by demonstrations against the rising prices in Mahagonny, during which the city goes up in flames. As the city burns, Mahoney's personal effects – his hat, stick, ring, watch, revolver, cheque-book and shirt – are carried around like the *reliquiae* of a saint by men chanting the anarchic verses he had once taught them during the night of the hurricane. At the same time the stage is filled with processions bearing the most contradictory slogans, but all united in singing the same nihilistic dirge, "Können uns und euch und niemand helfen" ("Can't help him or you or me or no-one"). It may be that the fire-raisers will free the citizens and allow them to start their lives afresh, but it seems more likely that the flames simply mark the end of yet another of man's failed attempts to create a paradise on earth. The discord of the closing scene, conveyed visually by the conflicting banners and the milling throngs of demonstrators, and aurally by the growing dissonance of the music, expresses not only the class contradictions of capitalist society, but also the fundamental anarchy in human relations that has emerged repeatedly throughout the opera: men have different natures, each man is isolated within his individual experience and, despite his longings to do otherwise, can only treat his fellow creatures as the objects of his self-centred will. The collapse of Mahagonny in chaos is only the final revelation of the anarchic state of nature underlying and frustrating man's every attempt to form and live in societies.

"You'll laugh – the Bible"

In 1921 Brecht noted in his diary, after a conversation with Caspar Neher concerning the painter Hans von Marées, "A good, decent workman, honest, talented, clean. But there's no metaphysics to his pictures. The perspective stops immediately behind the picture" (*Diaries*, 108–9). Brecht's concern with metaphysical questions, apparent in *Baal*, *In the Jungle* and *A Man's a Man*, was still lively when he came to write *Mahagonny*. One expression of his continuing interest are the biblical allusions which are more extensive in *Mahagonny* than in any of his previous plays. From the evidence of this opera alone it is apparent that he was not being merely facetious when, asked what had made the greatest impression on him, he replied, "You'll laugh – the Bible".[26] At any rate, it was the Bible rather than Marx's model of social development that supplied the narrative structure for the opera's account of the rise and fall of the city. Although Brecht never made any comment on this aspect of the work, possibly because he had already made a sharp change of ideological direction by the time the opera was first performed, Weill drew attention to their use of biblical material, in a note published shortly before the premiere: "The subject matter of an opera can be topical in the same way as, say, the biblical stories of the Prodigal Son, the Wedding Feast, or the Woman taken in Adultery. From the beginning we were determined therefore to show the history of a city, which in this sense is indeed a 'biblical' set of events, only in those stages which lent themselves to a strict, elevated manner of presentation. Since we depict the history of the town through its effects on human relationships, we were led inevitably to the central principles of man's communal life, which have been the subject matter of works of art throughout the ages and throughout the world: friendship and treason, poverty and affluence, contentment and revolt, fear and courage."[27] Of course, this is not to say that *Mahagonny* is a religious work. Its intention, rather, is to explore the implications for the life of the individual and society of Nietzsche's "discovery" and proclamation that "God is dead".

Some of these implications have already been touched on in the foregoing thematic analysis, but now they require fuller consideration. The sweeping pessimism of the inhabitants of Mahagonny, as they march around chanting "Can't help a dead man. Can't help him or you or me or no-one", indicates that the initially latent, but later fully manifest anarchy in the city is rooted in something deeper than class antagonism. These sentences connect the aimless "Durcheinander" of the marching demonstrators with their feelings of despair at the finality of death, and, as an extension of this, despair at man's inability to help himself or any other man to deal with life's most intractable problems. The anarchy in the city is thus related to the fact that death is an isolating existential experience, something which distinctly marks the limits of the social sphere of life. The experience of transience, for which there is no transcendent remedy, now that God is dead, prompts the heroes of Brecht's early plays to view other men merely as objects to be exploited for their pleasure; for them existential isolation generates anarchic self-interest. These characters are also subject to the anarchy arising from natural differentiation. In the early days of Mahagonny, for example, some men were content with the peace there, while others, of a more energetic disposition, were bored and dissatisfied. On an intellectual level, the operation of this *principium individuationis*[28] is evident in the anarchy of competing beliefs or ideologies paraded by the citizens of the collapsing city. These various expressions of anarchy are all consequences of the death of God. The waning of faith in a god in whose image all men are made, and the decay of the church, to whose body all men belong as members, culminate in men's loss of any belief that they share a common spiritual substance. When all men were of one spirit they could (in theory, at least) share common goals and experiences, participate in one another's emotional lives, agree on a hierachy of values and beliefs, bow to common commandments. Bereft of such participation in the transcendental, universal life of the spirit, the opera argues, men's lives collapse into an anarchic state of nature in which each man is irredeemably encapsulated in his individuality. Thus the function of the biblical allusions in *Mahagonny*, which we shall now consider in detail, is to put the opera's "pictures of twentieth-century morality"[29] into a kind of historical perspective. By retelling the Bible stories in a new way, *Mahagonny* reveals the gulf separating the contemporary spiritual condition of Western man from the spiritual ideals which Western civilisation ostensibly embraced for some two thousand years.[30]

In the opening scene of the opera a group of travellers, among them a man called Moses, are shown attempting to flee from their pursuers across a desert. This parody of the Israelites' flight from Egypt lays the basis for the subsequent handling of biblical material in the opera. In bestowing on his Moses the sobriquet "Trinity Moses" Brecht gives to a man the attributes of God, thus implying that it is man who is responsible for the quality of his own life. The lack of any apparent moral direction in the hurricane which threatens to destroy Mahagonny, like some latter-day Babylon, but instead kills the agents of justice while sparing the sinners in this city, presents nature as being ruled by blind chance rather than by a righteous god. The parallels and contrasts with the biblical story of Moses are developed in the foundation of Mahagonny as a "paradise city".[31] Whereas the original Moses was called by God to lead the Israelites away from the fleshpots of Egypt and towards a Promised Land which he himself was forbidden to enter, Trinity Moses establishes his own "Promised Land" in the middle of the desert, offers more in the way of fleshpots than ancient Egypt ever could, and then sets out to recruit his "chosen people" ("they were asking about you there only yesterday") to populate it. Whereas the entry of the Israelites into Canaan was part of God's providential plan for his people, Mahagonny comes into being because of a chance event – the breakdown in the desert of the lorry in which the founders were fleeing from the police. When God looked on his Creation he "saw that it was good"; the founders of Mahagonny, on the other hand have to confess that the city they create "only exists because everything is so bad".

The next stage in Brecht's use of Biblical parallels is in his introduction of Jimmy Mahoney, whose counterpart in the Bible is Christ. A contrast with Christ's lowly station is already implicit in Mahoney's arrival in Mahagonny in the role of a relatively rich man, his "pockets full of dollars". This initial point of difference gradually unfolds its full significance: whereas Jesus's poverty symbolised the gulf separating his kingdom from all worldly concepts of power, Mahoney's wealth defines him as a man who has already absorbed the values of this world, and so prejudices from the outset any possibility of his fulfilling any redemptive function in Mahagonny. This parallel and contrast is developed further when he protests at having to stay in Mahagonny with the words, "Oh, Jungens, ich will doch gar kein Mensch sein" ("Oh, lads, but I do not want to be a man at all" – *Mah*, 21), which contain an ironic echo of God's incarnation as Christ, "des Menschen Sohn" ("the Son of Man"). Although Mahoney does not know it, his desire to leave Mahagonny appears later to have been an attempt to avoid the "redemptive" task which his sense of "something lacking" in life will force on him. Mahoney is an unwitting and unwilling Messiah, a saviour without a god to guide him, a martyr to beliefs from which he later turns away when the "gospel" he brings proves to be as fallible as he is himself. Whereas Christ brought a message of love, Mahoney, having experienced only social conflict and existential fear, knows no better alternative than wild anarchy to the bogus harmony which he first meets in Mahagonny. The "laws of human bliss" which he unleashes on the night of the hurricane are a barbarous parody of the Beatitudes. Yet the ultimate failure of Mahoney's doctrine of self-interest, and his growing, although disappointed, longing for love and friendship, suggest that the opera's scornful rejection of the Biblical view of the world is mingled with great sadness at man's inability to transcend the self through love. When he had accepted the Marxist belief in man's inherent, though corruptible goodness, Brecht did in fact move towards advocating something like charity in his praise of "friendship", both as a goal to be attained and as one of the means of attaining it: the Marian overtones in the maid Grusha's love for the "high-born child" (in the late play *The Caucasian Chalk Circle*) cannot be ignored.[32]

In the course of the scenes depicting the "pleasures" of Mahagonny the relation of Mahoney to Christ becomes one of diminishing contrast and increasing similarity. When he backs an obvious loser simply for the sake of friendship, Mahoney is refusing to conform to the materialistic logic of life in the city. From this point on the resemblance between his fate and Christ's grows, for no-one may behave like this in Mahagonny without being destroyed, as Christ was destroyed, by the self-interest of others. The Last Supper finds its equivalent in Mahoney's invitation to his friends to drink with him. After his betrayal by Jenny and Bill, Mahoney has to experience a night in "Gethsemane", during which he has nothing to comfort him but the darkness that separates him from the coming day of execution, as he sits alone, chained at the foot of a tree. Despite the reversion of the Cross to a pagan life symbol (the living tree), and despite Mahoney's attempts to face death with atheistic stoicism, this scene is not merely a harsh travesty of the biblical original, for, in its own way, it evokes compassion and respect for a man's efforts to meet suffering with dignity.

The parallels with the Passion extend into the scenes of Mahoney's trial and execution. The freeing of Barabbas is echoed in the pardon given to the murderer Toby Higgins, while the fickle emotions of the people of Jerusalem are matched by the vacillating attitudes of the crowds at Mahoney's trial. When Mahoney hands over his girlfriend Jenny to his friend Bill, both of whom have betrayed him, his action is a sardonic perversion of Christ's bringing-together of his best loved disciple and his mother. Whereas Christ died calling on God, Mahoney dies an unrepentant atheist and sensualist. The consequences of their respective deaths are as different as their lives and gospels had been: after the Resurrection Christ's disciples went out into the world with a gospel of hope; Mahoney's death leaves behind pessimism and, as the flames engulf Mahagonny, a suggestion of the Apocalypse arriving.

The term "parody" which, for want of a better one, we have been using to describe Brecht's use of biblical material in *Mahagonny* hardly does justice to the variety of effects produced by it. Clearly, one of the attitudes to the Bible expressed by the opera is the rejection of its "providential" interpretation of the world, its warnings of punishment in Hell, its diatribes against the seductions of this world, and its message of redemption through love. The world inhabited by the men of Mahagonny is ruled, not by divine will, but by chance and human selfishness, it lacks any possibility of transcendence, and offers only the pleasures of the senses as compensation for the pain of life's transience. Along with the rejection of the biblical understanding of the world goes a rejection of biblical values – or some of them, at least. Implied in Mahoney's angry boredom with the tranquillity he meets in Mahagonny is a rejection of heavenly peace, not only as something illusory, but also because it does not fulfil all the needs of the human spirit. There is also clear sympathy for Mahoney's heroic vitality as he rejoices "satanically" in the hurricane's destructiveness, or calls on other men to continue the pursuit of pleasure regardless of the consequences.[33] Yet the Bible is also used in other, contrary ways. The Bible's wrath at the "harlot" Babylon (Rev. 17) is matched by the disgust expressed in the opera both at the exploitation practised in Mahagonny and at the unbridled indulgence of appetite. The dream of transcendence contained in the "Crane Duet" is a secularised version of the biblical ideal of spiritual peace, something which has a growing attraction for Jim Mahoney despite his rejection of it in the hurricane scene. Although no character in the opera shows any real ability to feel for any other person, the opera itself presents Jim Mahoney's "martyrdom" compassionately, thus expressing at least a *need* for transcendence, if not a belief in its attainability. Although the parody of the Israelites' flight from Pharaoh substitutes comedy for the drama of the original, the laughter produced by the collapse of Trinity Moses' lorry is tempered by a growing sense of menace as the fugitives plan their "city of nets". Moreover, the transformation of Moses into a figure of fun (the backfiring, collapsing car is an old circus gag) suggests that the price of liberation from divine providence and wrath is the reduction of man's status to that of a clown, subject to the malevolence of an unreliable world. The biblical model in the background of the opera provides a measure of the loss of human dignity sustained in the transition to the "modern world view". Similarly, in the scenes of Mahoney's trial and execution the overtones of the Passion intensify the grotesqueness of the hero's fate.

The emotionally unsettling, because conflicting, effects created by the use of biblical material in *Mahagonny* are also engendered by other aspects of the opera's style. Just as the moments of farce are undermined by a sense of menace, there are witty details in the language which have a nasty cutting edge. The "Green and lovely Moon of Alabama", for example, suggests that even the symbol of romance has taken on the colour of dollar bills in Mahagonny, but the image also carries the more unpleasant suggestion of gangrenous decay spreading over the world. The joke in the lines "Where civ-civ-il-i-sation/Will lose its scab and heal" *M*, II, iii, 9) turns sour when one realises that syphilis, to which the ills of civilisation are being likened, was an incurable disease when the opera was written. Similarly, Begbick's invitation to "fit yourself out with a fresh girl" is too telling an image of reification to be merely funny. A similar kind of aesthetic ambiguity is also to be found in Weill's music. For example, the song "Oh moon of Alabama", obviously parodies, with its exaggerated *glissandi*, the most sentimental type of popular music, yet it also manages to convey the girls' forlornness and intense longing for the lost security of their "good old mamma".[34] There are moments when Weill's score seems to adopt a mock-baroque style, as in the hurricane scene, which goes back to the *Tempestas* scene commonplace in baroque opera, but which may also be regarded as a daemonic mockery of the "Pastoral Symphony" from Handel's *Messiah* (there being a number of points of similarity between this oratorio and *Mahagonny*).[35] On the other hand, there is as much respect and renewal as there is parody in such musical reminiscences. Weill's comments on the style of the opera reveal a concern for the musical purity and self-enclosure of each musical number, which has a recognisable affinity with the baroque operatic "theory of the affections" (*Affektenlehre*):

> When producing the opera it must always be remembered that these are *enclosed musical forms*. It is therefore essential to establish firmly the purely musical sequence and to group the performers in such a way as to make possible a virtually "concertante" rendering.[36]

We have tried to demonstrate that *Mahagonny* not only depicts conflict, but is itself thoroughly imbued with it. The emergence of anarchy in this man-made paradise is presented ambiguously, so that one is often uncertain whether to regard the violence there as a remediable symptom of capitalist alienation or as an ineradicable characteristic of human nature. There are also sharp conflicts of value in the opera, in that mockery of divine providence goes hand in hand with dreams of transcendence, heroic vitalism alternates with disgust at man's bestiality, and sarcasm jostles pathos. Such stylistic features as the separation of the artistic elements of music, action and decoration, the mixture of farce with tragedy, and the musical eclecticism (Bach, Handel and Wagner alongside jazz and tin-pan alley), are all expressions on an aesthetic level of the conflicts consequent on the disappearance from man's life of the certainty, or hope at least, which was once provided by faith, and of the disintegrative effects this loss has had on man's social and spiritual life. All these forms of discord combine to make *Mahagonny* one of the most complex and disturbing works ever produced by Brecht. In this instance he did not, exceptionally, distort his poetic vision by forcibly imposing simplistic solutions on painful and difficult problems, but sustained the conflicts and ambiguities in his vision to the bitter end. The result was a work of unusual force and integrity. It is, perhaps, significant that this, his most unqualified and "uncensored" expression of perplexity about the human animal was almost the last work he wrote before entering on the commitment to Marxism which gave renewed scope to his desire to see life's problems mastered.[37]

8 The *Lehrstücke* and Beyond

When a writer makes a major change of direction in the course of his development the critic is faced with the tricky problem of accounting for the change and analysing the relationship between the different phases in the writer's work. The simplest way of explaining the fact that in 1929 Brecht began to devote his talents to promoting the cause of the communist revolution is to say that he made a rational and moral choice. He had been interested in Marxism for some years, so that his decision, when it came, was a considered and informed one. The delay between his first serious reading of Marxist theory (1926) and his integration of the methods and values of dialectical materialism into finished imaginative works (1929)[1] may help to explain his lifelong adherence to these principles once he had adopted them. It is reported that the event which precipitated his moral commitment to Marxism–Leninism was the brutal suppression by the police of communist demonstrators on May Day 1929 in Berlin.[2] It is certainly very plausible that the increase in political violence in that year, together with the severe deterioration of social and economic conditions in capitalist countries, made it seem necessary to set aside irony and ambivalence in favour of clear and firm political decisions. However, the commitment to revolutionary communism was only one of a range of options which, in theory at least, could be chosen on moral and rational grounds. Even if one accepts that there was an irreducible element of rational and moral choice in Brecht's change of direction in 1929, it would be contrary to common experience to assert that decisions on issues so fraught with difficulty and obscurity are completely free from the influence of subjective factors. On such large questions the individual's habits of mind and feeling will tend to make one choice more probable than another. In Brecht's imaginative work, which is what interests us here, there are striking continuities of style, attitude and preoccupation reaching across the

ideological divide between his Marxist plays and those written
before his commitment to Marxism. The most persuasive explanation for this is that certain features of Marxism–Leninism
matched certain habitual needs and impulses in Brecht. To put it
another way, his subjectivity appears to have played an important
role in determining the *version* of Marxism he adopted (or
constructed) and the *way* he incorporated the theory of dialectical
materialism into his imaginative work. In this final chapter I shall
argue this view by considering in general terms the points of
correspondence between his earlier attitudes and salient features of
his Marxism (nothing is implied about Marxism "in general" – if
such a varied body of thought can be so described); by examining in
some detail a few of his earliest Marxist experiments; and by
discussing briefly the relations of some of Brecht's best known
"mature" plays to the work he produced in the twenties and early
thirties.

As we have seen, Brecht's pre-Marxist plays were all marked by a
conflict between his will to create a manageable image of reality and
his perception of life's resistance to such attempts at mastery.
Bravado and irony were his chief weapons in the struggle against his
awareness of life's painful aspects. Such imaginative mastery as he
was able to achieve in this way was bought, however, at the cost of
perverting or of relegating to impotence or illusoriness the moral
and idealistic impulses in his make-up. It was also only a very
restricted kind of mastery, since it simply consisted of adopting a
certain emotional or aesthetic attitude to problems which were
accepted as being insoluble in any practical sense. These restrictions
are very evident if one compares his attitudes during his "anarchic"
period with the feelings he had once expressed during his period of
commitment to the cause of imperial Germany. This early commitment had enabled him to integrate more of his needs in an organised
whole: in contributing (in imagination, at least!) to the war-effort he
could find an outlet for aggression, while yet having it sanctioned
morally and religiously; he could work for the community, while yet
retaining his belief in the importance of the individual; he could feel
his life enlarged through his participation in an event of world-
historical importance; he could feel that his life had a definite
purpose and direction. Yet there soon emerged a conflict between
his critical awareness of the reality of the war and the values by
which he had originally justified the sacrifices it entailed. In the
anarchic period that followed the collapse of his early idealism his

critical intelligence could be given freer rein, albeit at the cost of having to suppress other impulses.

Transient though it was, the period of Brecht's early patriotic enthusiasm shows how strongly he could be attracted by a "grand design" for life. This ideal of a comprehensive mastery of life reclaimed his attention and enthusiasm in 1929. As with his commitment to the idea of Germany's spiritual mission, Brecht's commitment to communism took place under circumstances of war, not war between nations on this occasion, but war between social classes and political ideologies. No doubt it appealed to his combative instincts to take sides in the increasingly severe political conflicts of the time, particularly as the parties of the Left (although divided amongst themselves) commanded a degree of active mass-support such as had not been seen in Germany in the last decade, and therefore had a reasonable chance of winning the political battle. Brecht saw no sense in backing a loser. On the other hand, the political battle was attractive not merely because it offered an outlet for his pugnacity (which had been quite successfully channelled into other, non-political directions throughout the twenties), but because engaging in these conflicts would make it possible to release and possibly realise idealistic and collectivist ambitions which he had long suppressed. By committing himself to a vast social movement which demanded of the individual as much heroism, self-sacrifice and discipline as any country going to war, but offered in return not only the solution of pressing material problems, but also a sense of community, of moral justification and historical mission, Brecht was able to re-integrate to a considerable extent moral, emotional and intellectual impulses which had been in constant conflict ever since the collapse of his early idealistic enthusiasm for German nationalism.

Brecht's will to master reality could find satisfaction in many aspects of Marxism. As a very extensive body of theory ranging over many aspects of social life it promised an intellectual mastery of the workings of past and present societies which could be translated into practical mastery of the social and material problems facing mankind. The Marxist theory of alienation was not only concerned with material exploitation, and its abolition, but also held out the assurance that the innate, but hidden goodness of human nature would emerge through man's self-liberation and so justify all the costs inevitably entailed in the revolution. Marxism also provided a means of mastering Brecht's internal conflicts, since commitment to the single goal of revolution necessitated the imposition of a scale of priorities on his various impulses and needs. The conflict between his moral sense and his long-held conviction that "amoral" toughness was needed to survive in this world was resolved (theoretically) by applying the maxim that the end justifies the means: "Embrace the butcher, but/Change the world, it needs it!"[3] The "materialist ethic" of Marxism allowed Brecht to have the cake of idealism while only appearing to eat that of materialism. The impulsive side of Brecht's nature, which had frequently conflicted with his sense of prudence, now had to submit to the discipline of rational control, but only so that man might, in the long term, follow his impulses without self-destructive consequences. Brecht's habitual tendency to think in extremes, which we have seen taking various forms of expression in the plays of the twenties, was at work in the attraction which the argument held for him that *real* change can only be achieved by an uncompromising radicalism which eschews all attempts to reform isolated aspects of society.

Since our concern is mainly with Brecht's creative work, we have to ask in what ways Marxism specifically met, or failed to meet, his artistic needs and the peculiarities of his imagination. The scale and seriousness of the problems tackled by dialectical materialism accorded well with the importance Brecht attached to recovering for the theatre of the modern age the scope and stature (*Größe*) which drama had once enjoyed. The tendency to write in a rhetorical manner, to which Brecht's will to master reality had always made him prone, meant that he was by nature equipped to play the roles of teacher and propagandist. On the other hand, he also had a sense of artistic integrity, which was likely to be brought into sharper conflict with the ulterior motives for his writing once these had acquired a degree of moral or political sanction. Brecht had always had an awareness of the varying needs of different audiences and a desire to satisfy these needs so as to attract large masses of the population back into the theatres. Since it was necessary to enlist the interest and help of all possible groups in order to advance the cause of the revolution, his new role gave him an added incentive to experiment with different levels and modes of writing. His Marxist experiments ranged from the calculated simplicity of pieces written for children, workers' organisations and lay players to complicated analyses of the interaction of "base" and "superstructure" in social processes, which, with their allusions, parodies and verbal subtleties were designed to attack the ideological prejudices of the educated spectator. Not only did the social struggle between exploiters and exploited provide a wide field of conflicts for the dramatic imagination to feed on, but the partisan involvement in this struggle provided an impetus, in the form of an urgent desire to reach and promote clear decisions through dialectics, which could give dramatic life and forward movement to "epic" representations of large social processes that were naturally resistant to being confined within the limits of the "well-made play". On the other hand, his dialectical-materialist analysis of behaviour in terms of the conflict between man's productive potential and the historical limitations placed on its realisation by any given society meant that his plays generally avoid the worst excesses of stereotyped portrayals of wicked capitalists and virtuous workers. The "emancipated sensuality" which is one of the goals of materialist revolution provided a (somewhat deodorised) home for Brecht's love of *Spaß* (fun), and encouraged him to devise theatrical forms combining the values of usefulness and pleasure. The generally cool and controlled atmosphere of his productions (which did not preclude the presentation of heated action), the emphases on wit, elegance, lightness of touch, were all means of creating an aesthetic of mastery, designed to impart to the spectator the pleasure to be derived from adopting a "productive" (i.e. imaginatively active) and "sovereign" attitude to life.[4] An aesthetic of this kind was particularly valuable as a weapon to combat the demoralising effects of the spread of fascism, since the sense of the grotesque and farcical which were part and parcel of it provided a different view of the rise of Hitler from that created by such vague and un-manageable concepts as "the daemonic", "perverted genius" or "the German character". Yet, although there were many ways in which working for the goals of the revolution suited Brecht's talents and inclinations, it cannot be said that, through his adoption of Marxism, he was entirely successful in yoking together his sense of complexity and his determination to master life's problems. While it was the intention of his Marxist work simultaneously to stimulate the spectator's political will and his capacity for "complex seeing", the actual products of his imagination are rather different in effect. All too often the underlying tension between the pragmatic will and his doubts about its exercise results in an imaginative imbalance which tips his writing either in the direction of over-simplification or its opposite. In many of his plays these conflicting tendencies are to be found side by side.

The dramatic first fruits of Brecht's newly acquired faith in man's sociability and rationality were a group of playlets which he described as *Lehrstücke* ("learning plays"). The main characteristic of this type of play is that it is written primarily for the benefit of its performers.[5] The *Lehrstück* is an instrument of political and moral (but also aesthetic) education, designed to help the performers come to terms, in various ways, with the kind of problem represented in the action of the plays. The process of rehearsal and enactment is thought of as a process of reflection and involvement which will provide a training for life in the real world. One of these was an opera for schools, written in collaboration with Kurt Weill, entitled *Der Jasager* (*The Boy who Said Yes*). The text was an adaptation of a Japanese Noh play *Taniko* (*The Valley Hurling*) which celebrated a religious custom of sacrificing the life of any pilgrim who falls ill on a particular pilgrimage into the mountains. The play ends with the appearance of the pilgrims' god, who brings back to life the boy who was sacrificed. Brecht's first version of the play secularises the journey into the mountains by giving the group the motive of wishing to acquire knowledge, and by giving to the boy who joins their party, and falls ill during the journey, the motive of wishing to fetch medicine for his sick mother. Superficially this represents a rationalisation of the plot: the play now celebrates the individual's ethical ability to accept the subordination of his needs to those of the community. However, as some of the school-children to whom the play was first performed objected, there was nothing very rational about the decision to sacrifice the boy's life simply because a "great custom" prescribed that this should happen to anyone falling ill on such a journey. Brecht accepted these criticisms, and reworked the plot again to produce two new versions of it, a pair of plays entitled *Der Jasager* (which, for convenience, we shall call *Jasager II*) and *Der Neinsager* (*The Boy who Said No*).[6] In *Jasager II* the whole party is crossing the mountains for medicine and instruction because an epidemic has broken out in the town. The boy, who has asked to join the expedition because his mother is one of the sick, falls ill in the mountains himself and agrees to be thrown into the valley, so as not to hinder the others in their efforts to save the town. In this case, however, the boy's agreement to the traditional sacrifice is hailed as being in conformity with "necessity" (*J*, 38). The intention is obviously to remove the last traces of apparent "superstition" to which the school-children had objected in the *Jasager I*, and to present a thoroughly rational resolution of the problem. In *Der*

Neinsager the motives are left as in *Jasager I*, with the boy seeking medicine and the others pursuing knowledge, but when the "great tradition" is invoked to justify the killing of the boy, he now *refuses* to acquiesce in his sacrifice. He insists rather that one must "think anew in every new situation" (*J*, 49) and reject customs which appear to have no rational justification. Because the party's quest for knowledge is a lower priority than saving the boy's life, the party must postpone their journey through the mountains in order to carry him home. The others agree that his solution is the most rational one.

The problem with this determined progress towards greater rationality is that it is more apparent than real. The difficulties begin with *Jasager I*: if the party can be asked to fill the boy's jug with medicine for his mother, why was the boy permitted to join them on this difficult journey in the first place? It would surely have been more rational for the teacher to bring back the medicine, leaving the boy to tend his sick mother in the meantime. In *Jasager II* the case against taking the boy along is even stronger, since the party is going to fetch medicine anyway, and would presumably manage better without a young boy in the party. In *Der Neinsager* the problem of conflicting interests and duties, which gave some depth to *Jasager I* is simply swept aside by asserting that the quest for learning is less urgent than the boy's need of help. This facile solution would not apply if the "researches" of the others were of real importance – if, as in the next *Lehrstück*, *Die Maßnahme* (*The Measures Taken*) the "Lehren der Klassiker" ("the doctrines of the classics", i.e. Marxist theory) were at stake. To make things worse, the return of the whole party in this version conveniently ignores the presumably dire illness of the mother which was the motive for the boy's journey.

This little group of plays provides some very instructive insights into the workings of Brecht's mind at the time. His original *Jasager I* exhibits a characteristic tension between the author's perception of life's painful aspects and his will to so master experience as to minimise the sense of tragedy. On the one hand, the playlet ends with a complaint about "the sad ways of the world / And its bitter law" (*J*, 27), which seems refreshingly honest after the death-defying bravado of the heroes of earlier plays; on the other hand, the boy's stoical acceptance of death as the logical outcome of, and punishment for, his foolishness in joining the expedition ("The thought of my mother / Seduced me into making the journey" – *J*,

27) is a rather implausible attempt to minimise the pain of the experience and substitute for the sense of tragic waste a trite moral warning about the danger of allowing one's heart to govern one's head. In fact, the three versions of the plot grow more implausible and facile as Brecht's determination "rationally" to manage away the tragic aspects of life increasingly gains the upper hand over his initial perception of a possible painful divergence of interests between even a well-intentioned individual and his community. This tendency towards over-rationalisation was not one that developed merely because of the pupils' criticisms of his first version, but was inherent in his original decision to convert a religious play into a "learning play" which would educate its performers to understand social problems. As with all his adaptations, there is an evident connection between his current preoccupations and the possibilities he detects in the original. *Jasager I* shares with all the other early "learning plays" a focus on the relations between a dying individual and other men. The persistence of this theme is in turn explained by the fact that it was the sense of individual transience, and of the separateness of men's lives from one another, that had once led Brecht's early heroes on to their anti-social rampages. As he turned to Marxism, with its doctrine that the individual is the sum of his social relationships, Brecht was bound to try to lay the ghost of his earlier conviction that the loneliness produced by the experience of human transitoriness made any real community of feeling unattainable. *The Boy who Said Yes*, *The Baden-Baden Learning-Play on Agreement* and *The Measures Taken* are all exercises in self-assurance that the individual can be disciplined, or has sufficient self-discipline, to accept the subordination of his needs and feelings to those of the community – even to the point of death. In return for this humility, the community is able to help the individual in his dying; in *The Boy who Said Yes* and in *The Measures Taken* the spiritual bond between individual and community is expressed by physical contact at the point of death ("Lean your head on our arm" – *J*, 26). The increasingly shallow manipulations of the Japanese plot are symptomatic of the strength of Brecht's determination to prove that rationality can master even the problem of death.[7]

The Measures Taken (1930)[8] puts the problem of *The Boy who Said Yes* into the concrete situation of class struggle.[9] The plot is constructed a good deal more logically than the adaptation of the Noh play, but the play does not thereby mark an advance towards a more consistently rational and manageable view of life. If anything, the tightening of the plot has the opposite effect. The framework of the play is a hearing by a committee of Moscow's Communist Party (represented by a choir) of four agitators whose task it was to foster the revolution in China. They were successful in this task, but explain that their success necessitated the elimination of a young comrade whom they recruited from a local party-cell to help them; they ask the examining committee to pass judgement on "the measures taken". Their "report" takes the form of a re-enactment of their meeting with the young comrade, his repeated failures to carry out successfully the duties assigned to him, their persistent efforts to correct his impulsiveness and inadequate understanding of revolutionary work, and their eventual decision to bury him in a lime-pit when the consequence of his last and most grievous error threaten the continuation of the whole mission. Brecht once said that the purpose of the play was to teach politically correct behaviour by means of the representation of politically wrong behaviour.[10] It would, however, be more accurate to say that the play attempts to teach both by positive and negative example: the behaviour of the young comrade illustrates the dangers which can arise from an inadequate understanding of the theory and practice of revolutionary work, particularly when combined with emotional excitability; the behaviour of the agitators, on the other hand, shows that successful agitation depends on many talents, but particularly on the ability to subordinate personal feelings to tactical and strategic considerations. Yet, as so often in Brecht's Marxist plays, the intended and the actual effect of the piece are two quite different things. The concatenation of circumstances leading to the death of the young comrade is tragic in its inevitability. Because there is no-one else available, the agitators have no alternative but to accept the young comrade's offer of help, although it is evident at their first meeting that he is not entirely suited to the task, and to continue assigning him necessary tasks despite his repeated failures. But just as it is external circumstances which drive the agitators into the terrible predicament of having either to kill the young comrade or jeopardise the whole mission, so there are equally powerful internal compulsions which prevent the young comrade from learning from his mistakes. The nub of the tragedy lies in the fact that it is his compassion for the exploited and his anger towards those who cause their suffering, the very qualities which attract him to the tasks of the revolution, which make him unable to execute these tasks properly, since his impulsive responses to immediate circumstances constantly undermine the rational self-control needed for strategic effectiveness. The objectively tragic structure of the action is incompatible with the playwright's declared intention of teaching how to behave in a politically correct manner, for it demonstrates repeatedly that the very type of person who needs to be taught the importance of rational self-control is *incapable* of putting what he knows in theory into practice in real life. Quite apart from the contradictions in the conception of this "learning play", *The Measures Taken* represents a very questionable piece of political wisdom when set against the political background of the Weimar Republic. Like Johanna Dark, the naïve heroine of Brecht's *Saint Joan of the Slaughterhouses*, the young comrade may well have been intended to personify the reformism and (in Brecht's view) the lack of intellectual rigour in the policies of the Social Democratic Party.[11] If such were the case, the play's argument for radicalism can only be seen as aggravating these tensions between different factions of the German Left which helped the Right to power. After various attempts at re-writing the play Brecht eventually decided not to permit any further public performances, on the grounds that experience had taught him that it usually provoked "nichts als moralische Affekte für gewöhnlich minderer Art" ("nothing but moral excitement, usually of the poorer sort" – *DM*, 258). One may be forgiven for suspecting that he also had other motives for forbidding its performance.

It is often said that Brecht's "mature" plays show a development away from the disciplined, "anti-individualist" attitude of the *Lehrstücke* and towards a more complex view of the relations between the individual and the community. A number of reasons can be detected for this development. In theatrical terms there was a need for it because the severely functional *Lehrstücke*, although not without their own aesthetic merits, were lacking in the emotional and aesthetic richness which appealed to Brecht's own imagination and which he knew was necessary to sustain the interest of an audience. As a political motive for the change towards greater interest in and sympathy for the fallible individual, one might cite the fact that the real effects of bureaucratic "rationalisation" had become evident in Stalinist Russia. In his public pronouncements Brecht judiciously defended the progress of socialism in the Soviet Union. On the other hand, personal friends of Brecht "disappeared" during the purges, and Brecht preferred to spend the years of his exile in Denmark, Sweden, Finland, even America, the bastion of high capitalism, rather than in Moscow. Both for personal and for tactical reasons it was presumably more difficult for Brecht, as the 1930s unrolled, to sing the praises of the Party as whole-heartedly as he had done in *The Measures Taken* and *The Mother*, even if he still believed that "historical necessity" was a sufficient explanation for the measures taken in Soviet Russia.[12] Instead of showing the consistent toughmindedness and self-denial necessary for revolutionary success, and trusting in the audience's imaginative and dialectical ability to understand that the revolutionaries' "suppression" of their humanity was itself an act done in the name of humanity, Brecht's preferred method was now to show the travails of individualism in a competitive world. This allowed him both to express his admiration for the individual, whose "full and free development" was to be the goal and justification of social revolution, but also to demonstrate the self-destructive consequences of pursuing individual interests in a class society. The tough-minded attitudes of the agitators in *The Measures Taken* continues to be an element in his later work, and comes to prominence again in *The Days of the Commune*, but it is now left to the audience to reach the conclusions which lead on to the choice of disciplined pragmatism. If the audience reached such conclusions by an act of reflection they were more likely to find them acceptable than when confronted with the actual sight of physical liquidation (no matter how well-intentioned) on the stage. Although believing that "the truth is concrete", Brecht often preferred to leave it abstract.

Yet, far from solving the problems evident in the early *Lehrstücke*, the greater sympathy for individualism shown in the "mature" plays inevitably compounds these problems. Again and again they are marked by the same curious combination of over-simplification on the one hand and awkward complexity on the other, as was evident in *The Measures Taken*. And as in that play, the effect is to frustrate, in varying degrees, the rhetorical and didactic intentions of the playwright.

The tendency to over-simplify expresses itself in many ways. It is at work, for example, in the forced atmosphere of jollity, eager rationality and comradely goodwill which enables two groups of peasants, in the opening scene of *The Caucasian Chalk Circle*, to resolve without acrimony and without recourse to arbitration their dispute about the allocation and use of a tract of land. Thus to celebrate the USSR as the land of Reason, particularly with regard to the "solution" of agrarian problems, is to fly in the face of historical facts and to make a mockery of the suffering caused by the Soviets' policy of forced resettlement. Nor is the "Dispute over the Valley" to be defended as an ironically presented Utopia, designed to criticise the reality of rural life in Soviet Russia by holding up an image of how it ought to be. By locating his Utopia quite clearly in post-war Russia Brecht is claiming, at the very least, that reality is closer there to Utopia than anywhere else. This is unlikely to win for the play the sympathy of any but the ignorant or the already converted; the sceptical, those who take to heart Brecht's own "praise of doubt", are more likely to have reservations from the very outset about the playwright's reliability as an interpreter of history, to say nothing of human psychology. Things do not improve much when the stories of Grusche, the naïvely good-hearted servant-girl, and Azdak, the sly, but equally good-hearted village clerk-cum-judge begin to unfold. As personifications of human qualities which could eventually help break the chains of alienation and exploitation, these characters have all the appeal of fairy-tale figures; unfortunately, they also share their implausibility. Anticipating the defeat of Hitler, *The Caucasian Chalk Circle* is perhaps defensible as a celebration of the ability of humanity to survive even the darkest and bloodiest periods of history, but the play's partial attitude towards the other home of totalitarianism vitiates its worth even as a Utopia, since it does not even begin to show the paths leading from present reality towards the ideal.

The Caucasian Chalk Circle contains an unconvincing vision of mastery achieved. Yet, even where Brecht restricted his imagination to the task of defining the problems of attaining mastery over life, his late plays are frequently weakened by the tendency to over-simplification. The problems of evil are too insistently reduced to the status of mere by-products of economic circumstance. Repeatedly Brecht puts "split characters" at the centre of his plays: the kind prostitute Shen Te, "Angel of the Waterfront", who has to transform herself into the tough Shui Ta in order to defend herself from exploitation; the estate-owner Puntila, who, when drunk, is affable and likeable even in his self-centredness, but who becomes harsh when sobriety and his sense of economic priorities return; the brave and fundamentally caring Mother Courage whose role as a business woman forces her to be harsh both towards others and even towards her own family at times. In each case the alternate appearance of the character's good and bad "faces" is explained wholly in terms of the pressure of social circumstances which make their "natural" productivity and goodness destructive and self-destructive. Although not intended to be understood psychologically, these abstract models of behaviour inevitably remind us of just how complicated human beings are in reality. The divisions of Brecht's own personality, which could make him behave cruelly at times and kindly at others, for example, are not explicable in any such straightforward way. Nor were the changing moods of Ruth Berlau, an actress who was Brecht's neurotic, alcoholic, but above all jealous mistress for a number of years, to be reduced to the manageable formulae on which the characters of Puntila and Shen Te/Shui Ta were based. Common experience of the problems of dealing with such complicated characters in reality makes Brecht's overly rational use of the "split personality" seem arbitrary, constructed, even escapist.[13] Much the same can be said of the argument of the play *Roundheads and Pointedheads*, where fascist anti-Semitism is presented as nothing more than a manipulative ideology contrived to distract attention from the "real" (i.e. class-) divisions in society. Here again the rationalisation of the problem seems forced, and may have involved an element of over-reaction against a real awareness of the insidious perennial attractions of all socially approved opportunities for the exercise of irrational aggression. There can be no doubt that Brecht, whose second wife, Helene Weigel, was a Jew, genuinely felt scorn for the anti-Semitism of the Nazis, nor that he would have been thoroughly ashamed by that time of a remark he made to Caspar Neher in 1918, which appears to allude to the supposed "Jewish spirit" in the literature of German Expressionism: "Der Geist siegt auf der ganzen Linie über das Vitale. Das Mystische, Geistreiche, Schwindsüchtige, Ekstatische bläht sich und alles stinkt nach Knoblauch. . . ." ("All along the line spirit is triumphant over vitality. All that is mystical, intellectual, tubercular, overblown and ecstatic is becoming puffed-up, and everything stinks of garlic").[14] One wonders whether he would have been so insistently rationalistic in his later approach to the problem of anti-Semitism if he had not previously felt the attraction of the irrational component in it.

The tendency to over-simplify matters in order to assert and foster man's ability to manage them also influences the presentation of nature in Brecht's later works. There is something wilful and one-sided about Galileo's exultation at the freedom which he thinks is given to man by the discovery that space is much vaster than previously believed, and that, contrary to official wisdom, the earth is not the static centre of an "encapsulating" cosmic order. Even if one grants that his enthusiasm reflects the point-of-view of a somewhat irreverent scientist bursting with excitement about new scientific possibilities, the play offers no genuine corrective to this perspective. The occasional warnings that Galileo's new cosmology will threaten the spiritual peace of faithful and simple Christians everywhere are dismissed as mere obstacles to social change, reflecting on the one hand the timidity and enforced submissiveness of the weak and the self-interest of the powerful on the other. The historical–materialist method, with its exclusive focus on the conflict between "progressive" and "reactionary" social forces, precludes any serious consideration of the existential desolation and revulsion at the thought of the "grauenhaften Sternenhimmel" ("the terrifying star-covered sky" – *Diaries*, 39) which the young Brecht was honest enough to admit to feeling. An implausibly positive and one-sided view of nature is also taken in *Mother Courage*, where nature is talked of as a cornucopia, all man's misery being attributed to the imposition of a false "order" on to the rich anarchy of the natural world. Similarly, in *Schweyk in the Second World War*, man's physical appetites are hymned as the source of all human goodness, whereas all evil is seen as issuing from the lack or suppression of appetite. In these later plays the destructive and ugly aspects of nature, both outside man and within, submerge at times in a wash of sentiment. When reading these plays it is necessary constantly to remind oneself of the historical conditions in which, and above all *against* which, they were written: the dreams of nature's anarchic bounty or of uncomplicated sexual liberation (*The Days of the Commune*) need to be seen as reactions to the discipline, prudishness and personal austerity which were part and parcel of Nazism's enslaving ideology. On the other hand, writing which lacks the ring of truth does not make for persuasive propaganda – far less good poetry. One suspects that, underlying the propagandist reasons for glorifying nature and the appetites, there was a continuing personal reaction against his own lack of powerful appetites[15] and against his awareness of the world's hostility to man. The early plays also represented attempts to put forward an affirmative view of life, but they did at least make clear where the difficulties lie in "living positively".

In the best of Brecht's later plays such over-simplifications are not sufficient to detract seriously from his ability to present a complex view of human behaviour. *Mother Courage and her Children*, for example, makes a much more interesting, persuasive and complicated statement than Brecht's own comments on the play frequently suggest. In his commentaries he repeatedly emphasises the protagonist's profit-seeking connivance in the war, and at one point even suggests that she could have stayed out of it altogether.[16] The play itself, however, shows Mother Courage caught up willy-nilly in the Thirty Years War as it sweeps inexorably back and forth across Europe, bringing death and ruin to active participants and innocent bystanders alike. She chooses to be a camp-follower because she does not believe that there is any sure way of avoiding the war or its effects, and because she believes that this social role gives her the best chance of providing for herself and her family. Her role as a businesswoman in the war is not used to present her as a particularly avaricious person; rather, it shows her as an individual struggling to help her family by living in accordance with the competitive principles operating throughout society. The destruction of her family is not used to point a facile moral about personal greed or blindness, but contributes to a larger indictment of the form of social and economic organisation which condemns her to live as she does. The loss of her children as a result of her very efforts to provide for them illuminates the fundamental contradiction at the heart of a society which turns human productivity into a destructive and self-destructive force. As it stands, the play's dialectical–historical analysis of the hopelessness of Mother Courage's individualist efforts to survive puts the case for *radical* social change much more effectively than Brecht's retrospective comments, with their distorting and simplifying emphasis on individual culpability. By showing that Mother Courage had no alternative but to become "guilty" in the prevailing historical circumstances, Brecht makes an effective plea for collective action to remove the historic causes of such individual tragedy.

In avoiding the perils of over-simplifying the problems of human behaviour, however, such later plays as *Mother Courage, The Life of Galileo* or *Squire Puntila and his Servant Matti* run into the opposite difficulty of raising problems which are very difficult to solve. The conclusion one is supposed to draw from these demonstrations of the destruction or perversion of human energies by the class-structure of society is that a social transformation is required which will allow the productive energies of the individual to benefit both himself and the rest of society. Yet it is hard to imagine that any of these characters, with their unusual appetites, energies and evident pleasure in conflict or deceit, – Mother Courage is attracted to the tough cook rather than the tame parson who is no match for her, Puntila loathes the stiffly correct diplomat destined to marry his daughter and is just as self-centred when drunk as when sober – would feel at home within the confines of the kind of rationally planned, self-disciplined and egalitarian society which, in the Marxist–Leninist view, is necessary to eliminate the evils produced by class-division. The more convincingly the characters are drawn (i.e. as having a strong streak of self-interest), the less probable does it seem that men will create any form of social organisation which will be free from destructive conflict. Perhaps Brecht's hope was that conflicts would at least be kept within tolerable limits.

Brecht's lasting difficulty in accommodating his hopes for social harmony to his intuitive understanding of human nature (a notion which he latterly detested in theory, but never abandoned in practice) is evident from the fragments of a *Lehrstück* entitled *der böse Baal der asoziale* (*Wicked Baal the Asocial*), a project to which his thoughts returned repeatedly from the early 1930s until very shortly before his death. The aim was to think of ways in which a socially useful didactic piece could be built around Brecht's first and most unrestrained personification of anarchy. In the very sketchy scenes produced during his first attempt at the project Brecht's approach was the rather too simple one of demonstrating that "asociality" could be put to positive use as a means of disrupting and exposing the hypocrisy of apparent sociability within class society, or of revealing the anti-social effects of conformist behaviour within such a society (e.g. Baal is shown in the role of a passport-official whose punctilious performance of his duties puts a life at risk – *dbB*, 81). Because the project never developed beyond the stage of some rudimentary fragments Brecht kept returning to the problem of why this should have been the case. In March 1939 he decided that the reason was the fact that: "asocial people are unimportant. They are merely the owners of the means of production and other sources necessary to life, and they are asocial merely by virtue of this fact. Naturally, their aides and satellites are asocial as well, but again only by virtue of their function. It is positively *the* gospel of the enemy of mankind that such things exist as asocial drives, asocial personalities etc." (*dbB*, 109).

However, this reduction of the problem of asociality to a function of a particular kind of social role within a particular type of socioeconomic structure did not satisfy Brecht for long. Brecht knew too well that the figure of Baal, as he had originally conceived it, was no embodiment of institutionalised "asociality" but rather the opposite of this, a personification of elemental energies and appetites which refused to be institutionalised in any shape or form. He knew very well that he was really evading the nagging question as to how a post-revolutionary society might cope with the problem of asociality, if he simply dismissed the phenomenon as a specific characteristic of life under capitalism. In March 1941 he ventured a different explanation for his failure to complete the fragments:

> The major error which prevented me from producing the series of short didactic pieces concerning "Wicked Baal the Asocial" lay in my definition of socialism as a *great form of order*. In contrast to this, it is much more practical to define it as a *great form of production*. Naturally, production must be understood in the broadest sense, and the struggle is concerned with liberating the productivity of all men from all bonds. The products can be bread, lamps, hats, pieces of music, chess-moves, irrigation, complexion, character, games etc. etc. (*dbB*, 110).

Brecht had now begun at least to face up to his real problem with the play, which was how to find a *modus vivendi* to accommodate both the "asocial" tendency of the transient individual to take self-satisfaction as his absolute in life, and the opposite tendency of society to regard each individual only as a function of the social whole, but the solution offered here was still a facile one. It amounted to the simple assertion that the conflict between individual and society would disappear entirely under socialism, since a socialist society would be the spontaneous expression of mutually enriching individual productivity. This dream of an anarchic idyll left the question completely unanswered as to how the "great form of productivity" could emerge without "a great form of order".

Brecht last worked on the fragments in the summer of 1954 in East Berlin, when he remodelled a scene from the very earliest version of *Baal* (1918) for inclusion with others which seek to define Baal's possible role in a workers' state. In its remodelled form the scene shows Baal being given notice to quit his post as clerk in a town hall. As Baal lies back on his bed, the official messenger reads out the letter of dismissal:

Der Amtsdiener:	[*liest*] Werter Herr Baal! Da für Genies Ihrer Sorte eine so ermüdende Arbeit wie die eines Schreibers, der Sie sich ja selbst tagelang entziehen, nicht mit dem Verantwortlichkeitsgefühl der Behörde vereinbar ist, sind Sie ab 1. Juni aus den städtischen Diensten entlassen. Unterschrift: Der Chef selbst. Es tut mir leid, Herr Inzipient.

(*dbB*, 90–1)

The Messenger:	[*reads*] Dear Mr Baal, since for your kind of genius a position as taxing as that of a clerk, from which indeed you yourself absent yourself for days on end, is not compatible with the Authority's sense of responsibility, you are dismissed from the service of the town with effect from 1st June. Signed: the boss himself. I'm sorry, Sir.

Baal's reply is characteristic. He addresses a little prose-poem to the messenger:

Baal:	Baumann, manchmal träume ich von einem See, der ist tief and dunkel und zwischen die Fische lege ich mich und schaue den Himmel an. Tag und Nacht, bis ich verfault bin.
Der Amtsdiener:	Unter diesen Umständen verzichte ich auf die 20 Pfennig, obwohl ich auch leben muß. Habe die Ehre! [*Ab*]
Baal:	[*lacht*]

(*dbB*, 91)

Baal:	Baumann, sometimes I dream of a lake, it is deep and dark and I lay me down amongst the fishes and look at the sky. Day and night, until I've rotted away.
The Messenger:	In these circumstances I'll do without my sixpence, though I've got to live too. Honoured to know you, Sir! [*Leaves*]
Baal:	[*laughs*]

Even to the end Brecht had not forgotten the universal problem contained in Baal's truly asocial vision of life as a slow, but inexorable process of natural decay. The latterly hidden, but unextinguished awareness that each individual must face up to painful experiences which cannot be "mastered", except, perhaps, in some poetic dream of transience accepted with tranquillity, accounts in no small measure for the vitality of Brecht's best work. His continuing sympathy for the transient individual both fuelled his determination to find ways of making the world more "habitable" for man, and, equally important, enabled him to resist the facile solutions to which his pragmatic will was all too readily attracted.

Notes

NOTES TO CHAPTER ONE: INTRODUCTION

1. The difficulties once faced by Schumacher are apparent from the fact that the revised edition of his study (1977) contains a chapter on "Agit-prop Theatre and Workers' Stages" which had to be excluded from the original publication in 1955.
2. Herbert Lüthy, "Vom armen Bert Brecht", *Der Monat*, vol. 4, no. 44 (May 1952) pp. 115-44.
3. These literary–historical terms are defined quite differently by various commentators. Recent essays which attempt to define Brecht's position relative to other writers are A. V. Subiotto, "Neue Sachlichkeit: a Reassessment", in *Deutung und Bedeutung*, ed. B. Schludermann *et al.* (The Hague and Paris, 1973); Thomas Koebner, "Das Drama der Neuen Sachlichkeit und die Krise des Liberalismus" and Ernst Schürer, "Die nach-expressionistische Komödie", both in *Die deutsche Literatur in der Weimarer Republik*, ed. by W. Rothe (Stuttgart, 1974); and Jost Hermand, "Einheit in der Vielheit? Zur Geschichte des Begriffs 'Neue Sachlichkeit'", in J. Hermand, *Stile, Ismen, Etiketten* (Wiesbaden, 1978). Two broader studies of the period are H. Lethen, *Neue Sachlichkeit 1924–1932* (Stuttgart, 1970) and J. Willett, *The New Sobriety* (London, 1978). Inevitably, all such attempts at categorisation fail to do justice to the individuality of authors, particularly when they are as complex as Brecht.
4. The opening lines of Paul Kornfeld's comedy *Palme oder der Gekränkte* (1924) are often quoted to illustrate the abandonment of Expressionist ambitions in the years of "New Sobriety": "Let us hear no more about war and revolution and salvation of the world! Let us be modest and turn our attention to other, smaller things: let us observe a man, a fool, let us play a little, watch a little, and, if we can, laugh or smile a little." It is this kind of attitude which has led some commentators to compare this period with the "Biedermeier" period in the nineteenth century.
5. For examples of Brecht's search for "die große Form des Dramas" see *GW*, **15**, pp. 55, 184-6, 194-5, 197.
6. The term "schwarzer Expressionismus" is used by G. Rühle, *Theater in unserer Zeit* (Frankfurt a.M., 1976) p. 28.
7. The one dramatist of this period whose work shares a comparable degree of complexity with Brecht's is Ödön von Horváth. Horváth's work did not begin to appear until 1929. Like Brecht's, it cannot easily be accommodated within the usual literary–historical categories.

8. Graham Greene, for example, has claimed that the most important experiences for a writer have all been by the age of fourteen.
9. Brecht did not turn into a pacifist after he became disillusioned with
   Germany's role in the war. For an example of his continuing endorsement of
   violence see his bitter commentary on German passivity in the face of the
   atrocities committed by troops occupying the Rhineland in 1920 (*GW*, **20**, 14).
10. The year 1926 is frequently given as that from which Brecht's Marxism is to be
    dated. In the summer of that year he wrote to his assistant Elisabeth
    Hauptmann that he was "fathoms deep" in Marx's *Das Kapital* – see Elisabeth
    Hauptmann, "Notizen über Brechts Arbeit 1926", *Sinn und Form: 2*, Special
    Bertolt Brecht issue (Berlin, 1957) p. 243. However, although there is evidence
    of some knowledge of Marxism in theoretical statements made in the next few
    years, I do not see any evidence of a firm commitment to Marxist theory and
    practice in Brecht's creative work until the latter part of 1929.

NOTES TO CHAPTER TWO: "BAAL" ·

1. The influence of Frank Wedekind's *Erdgeist* (*Earth-Spirit*) on *Baal* was very
   evident in the first version of the play, where Baal's repeated shouts of
   "Hoppla!" were reminiscent of the ringmaster who speaks the prologue to
   Wedekind's play–see *Baal. Drei Fassungen* (Frankfurt a.M., 1966) pp. 16, 30,
   32. In his admiration for Wedekind Brecht went so far as to describe him as one
   of the "greatest educators of the new Europe" (*GW*, **15**, 4).
2. The figure of "Frau Welt" (called "das große Weib Welt" in the Chorale) was
   a popular subject of medieval literature and illustration. She is depicted as
   alluring when seen from the front, but disgusting from behind, and thus serves
   as an allegory of the world's deceitfulness. Brecht's early diaries contain a
   poem which appears to have been influenced by this tradition:

> Sie wandte mir den Rücken
> Da kroch ein großer Wurm heraus
> (Der wollte mich beglücken
> Er wollt die Hand mir drücken . . .)
> Doch war er mir ein Graus. . . .
>   (*T*, 28)

> She turned her back toward me
> A great fat worm appeared
> (He wanted to reward me
> And stood up to applaud me)
> But I was simply scared.
>   (*Diaries*, 17) [free translation]

3. *Theatre of War* (London, 1972). p. 126.
4. *Baal* was not Brecht's only play to be modelled on the medieval "Dance of
   death". The production notes for the *Songspiel Mahagonny* (1927) contain the
   following statement: "If the work is performed in some hall other than a
   theatre or concert-hall this has the advantage of making evident a certain

affinity with the travelling theatres of the medieval period. MAHAGONNY IS A DANCE OF DEATH", *Songspiel Mahagonny*, ed. David Drew (Vienna, 1963) p. 7.

5. Brecht once noted "Life as a passion! That is how I conduct it. It is self-evident that it will destroy me" (*T*, 198). Brecht always lived intensely. In particular he had an extraordinary – and very bourgeois! – appetite for work. Had he not also been so unswervingly devoted to large, strong cigars, he might possibly have been spared a heart-attack at the age of 57. However, like Baal he chose quality rather than quantity of life.

6. In the first version of the play Baal says to a prison chaplain: "I withdraw into enemy territory. Into blossoming country . . . I flee from death into life", *Baal: Drei Fassungen* (Frankfurt a.M., 1966) p. 54. This territory is both blossoming and hostile because it is the domain of both life and death.

7. When Death visits the fool Claudio in Hofmannsthal's *Der Tor und der Tod* (*Death and the Fool*) he says to him "Ein großer Gott der Seele steht vor dir" ("A great god of the soul stands before you"), *Gedichte und kleine Dramen* (Frankfurt a.M., 1966) p. 83. Although one tends to think of the coarse-grained Brecht and the finely-veneered Hofmannsthal as belonging to quite different worlds, Hofmannsthal was sufficiently interested by *Baal* to write a prologue for a performance of the play in Vienna in 1926.

8. One of Brecht's early sonnets takes as its theme the renewed stimulus to love and desire created by a sudden awareness of the first signs of grey in a woman's hair (*GW*, **8**, 160–1).

9. Kenneth Tynan aptly remarked in his review of a London production of *Baal*: "The ideal audience for *Baal* would be entirely composed of people who remember, more than once or twice a day, that they are going to die. Firstnighters, as a group, do not like their noses rubbed in the fact of mortality; they prefer it to keep its distance and speak blank verse", *Observer Weekend Review*, 10 February 1963.

10. In his more cynical or despairing moments, which were not infrequent, the young Brecht would take the (Nietzschean) view that morality is an illusion created by men for their own comfort: "The purpose of morality is to make you believe you have something in common! But in reality there is no-one keeping an eye on you" (*D*, 136); "Almost all bourgeois institutions, almost the whole of morality, virtually the whole Christian legend are founded on man's fear of being alone, they distract his attention from his unutterable desolation on this planet, from his minute significance and his hardly perceptible roots" (*GW*, **15**, 59–60). It must be remembered, however, that Brecht did not hold this view consistently. The liveliness of his early plays stems largely from the clash of competing perspectives in them.

11. In 1922 Brecht expressed the hope that he had succeeded in *Baal* and in *In the Jungle* in avoiding a great mistake of much art, namely the "attempt to whip up the spectator's emotions" ("ihre Bemühung mitzureißen" – *GW*, **15**, 62). He then added, "It is usual for writers of tragedies to take the part of the hero towards the end, or in fact throughout. This is an abomination. They should take sides with nature" (*GW*, **15**, 62). By the time he made these observations Brecht's writing had begun to incorporate an element of critical distance, but he neither had this intention, nor did he create this effect in the composition of *Baal*.

12. Hermann Hesse's "Novelle" *Klingsors letzter Sommer* (*Klingsor's Last Summer*)

(Zurich, n.d.) which was written in 1919, when Brecht was working on the second draft of *Baal*, is remarkably similar to *Baal* in a number of respects. The story responds to the mood of anger and loss produced by the war with a sympathetic portrayal of an artist who throws his whole reserve of vitality into the struggle with his melancholy sense of transience. With symbolic deliberation Klingsor chooses to paint in water colours which will rapidly fade; a much coarser version of the same attitude is to be seen in Baal's decision to hang up his latest poems for use in the lavatory (*B*, 40).

13. Cf. the remark made by Brecht in 1920: "I wish all things to be handed over to me, including power over all animals, and give as the reason for my demand the fact that I am only present *once*" (*T*, 197).

NOTES TO CHAPTER THREE: "DRUMS IN THE NIGHT"

1. For a collection of contemporary reviews see the appendix to R. Steinlein's article, "Expressionismusüberwindung: Restitution bürgerlicher Dramaturgie oder Beginn eines neuen Dramas? Bemerkungen und Materialien zur theater-kritischen Erstrezeption des frühen Brecht (am Beispiel von *Trommeln in der Nacht*, 1922)", in Joachim Dyck *et al.*, *Brechtdiskussion* (Kronberg and Taunus, 1974) pp. 7–51.

2. See the relevant chapter in E. Schumacher, *Die dramatischen Versuche Bertolt Brechts (1918–1933)*, and the article by H. Kaufmann, "Drama der Revolution und des Individualismus", *Weimarer Beiträge*, vol. ii (1961) pp. 316–31. A more recent critic, D. Bathrick, also argues that the play is "in the most fundamental way discontinuous", *The Dialectic and the Early Brecht* (Stuttgart, 1975) p. 67.

3. In 1922 Stefan Großmann characterised the play thus: "A drama of revolution? No. A rather sarcastic popular play about the hysteria of the German Revolution" (quoted by Steinlein, "Expressionismusüberwindung", p. 42). There is a good deal of historical evidence to support Brecht's view that there was widespread political hysteria in the aftermath of the war.

4. It was not the whole of Expressionism, but the tendency of a number of its representative writers to indulge in excessive moralising, allegorical abstractions and neglect of the material, sensual aspects of life that he disliked, as, for example, in the following passage: "This Expressionism is terrible. All feeling for the beautiful roundness and splendid coarseness of the body withers away like the hope for peace. Mind ["der Geist"] routs vitality the whole way along the line", quoted in K. Feilchenfeldt, *Bertolt Brecht: "Trommeln in der Nacht"– Materialien, Abbildungen, Kommentar* (Munich, 1976) p. 158. On the other hand he admired Expressionist intellectuality where this did not lead to crude oversimplification; his repeated praise of Georg Kaiser is evidence of this. *In the Jungle* shows Brecht continuing to experiment with his own brand of Expressionism.

5. See Frisch and Obermeyer, *Brecht in Augsburg* (Berlin and Weimar, 1975) pp. 137–42 for an account of Brecht's period of military service.

6. It is interesting that the metaphor of the "horsefly" or "gadfly" ("Stechfliege") of jealousy which Brecht used to describe Kragler's feelings about Anna also occurs in his diaries in connection with his own fears about Bi Banholzer. In the absence of any further evidence, this detail must remain

simply a suggestive hint that specific biographical experiences may have influenced the way things are seen and evaluated in the play. One can find the same combination of obscurity and suggestiveness in the relation of Brecht's struggle with a man called Recht for possession of Marianne Zoff to the triangle of relationships between Shlink, Garga and Marie in *In the Jungle*.

7. The influence of the ghostly ballad tradition on *Drums in the Night* was first analysed by Kaufmann in his article "Drama der Revolution und des Individualismus". I think that closer examination of this motif would have led him to take a different view of the play's artistic unity. G. Stern's article on parody in *Drums in the Night* curiously makes no reference to this aspect: see "*Trommeln in der Nacht* als literarische Satire", *Monatshefte*, vol. 61 (1969) pp. 241–59.

8. The motif would have been introduced even earlier if Brecht had decided to give the play the title "Das sterbende Gespenst oder Spartakus" ("The Dying Ghost or Spartacus") as he had once considered doing (*BBA*, **213**, 50).

9. By careful use of the variant material supplied in the appendix to the Methuen translation the English reader can reconstruct fairly well the first published version of the play (to which I refer throughout this chapter).

10. It will be recalled that Marx and Engels began their Communist Manifesto with a promise to replace the "spectre of Communism" currently haunting Europe with a statement of the party's real political objectives – K. Marx and F. Engels, *The Communist Manifesto* (New York, 1968) p. 1.

11. I cannot agree with Bathrick's view that the wild natural imagery associated with Kragler "conveys the spirit of revolution", and even less with his assertion that "Kragler is the revolution" (Bathrick, *Dialectic*, p. 40). While it is true that these images refer to experiences which "the world of bourgeois values and order" would exclude, these experiences need not form a motive for revolution. Kragler's story shows that, on the contrary, they can have the effect of inducing a sense of the world's unchangeability and a desire to enjoy the benefit of such protection as the ordered world of civilisation can afford. The connection between Kragler's arrival in Berlin and the outbreak of the revolution is not, as Bathrick argues, "inevitable", but rather fortuitous, and, as such, gives rise to the ironies and confusions which make the play a comedy.

12. A note for the production at the Deutsches Theater in Berlin in 1922 begins thus: "Die Bühne ist klein und besteht aus Holz und Pappendeckel. Die Kartons sind dünn und unvollständig bemalt. Tür, Fenster und Wand, das sieht alles provisorisch aus. Desgleichen wirkt die große revolutionäre Aktion, die hinter der Szene immer stärker wird, im Zuschauerraum nur dünn und gespenstig" (*BBA*, **1569**, 05). ("The set is small and constructed from wood and pasteboard. The flats are thin and incompletely painted. Doors, windows and walls all have a provisional look to them. Similarly, the great revolutionary action, which is getting ever more powerful offstage, only makes a thin, ghostly effect in the auditorium.")

13. In an early review of a sentimental play entitled *Alt-Heidelberg* Brecht was ferociously critical of the play because of the opportunity it gave the bourgeois audience to add, as he believed, emotional exploitation to the financial and social exploitation on which their lives outside the theatre rested (*GW*, **15**, 20–1). He was particularly incensed by one scene, "touching" for the mothers of students, in which an old man, discharged from service to a students' corps,

gratefully kisses the hand of a princely benefactor. This is the kind of emotional exploitation of the socially underprivileged which Brecht has Kragler rebel against in the address to the audience where he refuses to take the "nobler" course of preferring death on the barricades to the dishonour of accepting the pregnant Anna.

NOTES TO CHAPTER FOUR: "IN THE JUNGLE"

1. Brecht's original title for the play was *Im Dickicht* (*In the Jungle*). This early version, which I have followed, is now available in the edition by G. Bahr under the title *Im Dickicht der Städte: Erstfassung und Materialien* (Frankfurt a. M., 1968). All references are indicated by (*D*, page no.) in the text. The title *Im Dickicht der Städte (In the Jungle of the Cities)* was first used for a revised version of the play in 1927, which, like the revised version of *Baal* made in 1926 (*Lebenslauf des Mannes Baal – Biography of the Man Baal*), is written in a much less metaphorical, more sober style.

2. A diary-entry defines the *"Ort"* ("location") of the action as "die Hinterwelt" ("a hidden world" – *T*, 146).

3. Brecht even asserted in general terms that "The enjoyment of solving puzzles ('Rätselraten') is intimately connected with the essential element of aesthetics – 'wonder'" ("Be-Wunderung", *GW*, **15**, 55).

4. Spalter, Kesting and Gray all take this view. Gray, for example, describes the play as "chaotic and incomprehensible", *Brecht* (London, 1961) p. 42.

5. Brecht's early diaries show that he too liked to withdraw, in the imagination at least, to Tahiti or Asia (*Diaries*, 16, 50, 54, 62, 76, 79, 110). A number of dramas written in the immediate post-war years were concerned with a flight from Europe to the South Seas, see H. F. Garten, *Modern German Drama* (London, 1964) p. 174. Brecht's treatment of both "Amerikanismus" and "Asiatismus" in *In the Jungle* is characteristically free of illusions that either the Far East or the Far West hold out any real hope of a better way of life.

6. The theme of man's loss of any transcendental certainty is a recurrent one in Brecht's early work. Shlink alludes to the problem of the "death of God" again later in the play when he reminds Garga that they live "on a planet which is not at the centre. . . . We are flying, Garga! The whole god-forsaken system, with enormous speed towards a star in the Milky Way" (*D*, 100).

7. One of Brecht's working notes comments on this problem, "All forms of suffering can be combated by having a tough hide. Except for the last, incurable form, the suffering of an undamaged skin, boredom" (*D*, 136).

8. The image of the scarab is one of the most puzzling ones in the play. A scarab is a dung-beetle which rolls balls of dung and buries them underground. If this is what Brecht intended it to mean, the image belongs to the complex of references to excreta which express the characters' disgust with life.

9. Brecht shared Garga's attitudes towards comparatives: "Recently my fingers have developed a prejudice against comparatives. They all follow this pattern: a squirrel is smaller than a tree. A bird is more musical than a tree. Each of us is the strongest in his own skin. Characteristics should take off their hats to one another, instead of spitting in each other's faces" (*Diaries*, 48).

10. These repeated confrontations in the original version drag out the action

excessively; the revised version, although marred by the loss of metaphorical richness, is more economical in this respect. Brecht was aware of this weakness in the play: "*Jungle*'s action has ground to a halt; it's too full of literature. The idle chatter of a couple of littérateurs" (*Diaries*, 135).

11. The "fish" referred to (*D*, 102) are Garga, who has just accepted defeat, and Marie, who ostensibly adds to Shlink's victory by coming to offer him her love.

12. This is yet another of the play's allusions to the Bible. Here Garga compares his fight with Shlink to Jacob's wrestling with the angel (Gen. 32:22). As usual, the allusion is ironical, for Jacob was the stronger and was blessed for it, whereas Garga emerges from the struggle for spiritual values defeated and unblessed.

13. The parallel between Marie and Garga is underlined by Shlink's surprised comment, "That is Garga, George Garga" (*D*, 72), at the end of the seduction scene when Marie tries to show her emotional independence from Shlink by demanding money for her "services".

14. Brecht's uncertainty about how to assess the effects on Garga of the outcome of the struggle is reflected in the variety of endings which he considered at various times: Garga going back to the land (*D*, 135), taking over Shlink's timber business in Chicago (*D*, 137) or, as in the revised version of the play, leaving Chicago for New York (*GW*, **1**, 193).

15. This soulless setting anticipates the scene in *Mahagonny* where a drinking and gambling den, referred to as "the dear God's cheap saloon" (*GW*, **2**, 547) is an image of life as Hell-on-Earth.

16. Here Garga is using Moti Gui as a kind of "Voodoo doll" on whom he vents his desire to humiliate Shlink.

17. Brecht thought it quite proper for the theatre to enlarge certain features of life to "pathological" proportions in order to make them more clearly visible: "The only point of pathology is to help you see, since you've such weak eyesight, specially when up against a mirror. All the same, mankind is a lot healthier than tapeworms and priests might think. It is healthy enough to have invented tragedy and algolagnia [a term for masochism]. The pathological element is the true hero. First on account of its vitality and secondly because it stands out head and shoulders (or possibly a phallus's length) above the crowd" (*Diaries*, 130–1).

18. For example, Garga: "A jungle full of muck and a stinking pond to wash in" (*D*, 21), or Marie, "The trees are as if hung with human muck, the sky near enough to touch, how indifferent it leaves me. I'm freezing!" (*D*, 69).

19. Garga's partner in this scene, "Der Grüne" ("the green one") is also part of the scene's symbolism. He mirrors Garga's initial naïveté.

20. The image of the ship is used repeatedly throughout the play (and generally in Brecht's early poetry) as a metaphor of the self. The probable source is Rimbaud's "bateau ivre".

21. The following diary entry is relevant: "One thing is present in *Jungle:* the city. Which has recaptured its wildness, its darkness and its mysteries. . . . We are on the scent of a mythology here" (*Diaries*, 146). In a later essay he described boxing as "one of the great mythical entertainments of the giant cities on the other side of the great pond" (*GW*, **17**, 948). *In the Jungle* interprets these modern "myths" (including the Wild West and the underworld) as typical expressions of the agression which is built up in modern man by the barrenness of life in the great cities.

22. The spiritual significance of the word is quite unambiguous when it is used in the plural; the plural of "face" is "Gesichter", whereas the plural of "vision" is "Gesichte". One instance of this occurs at *D*, 92: "Der Feind in den Wäldern verbirgt seine Gesichte" ("The enemy in the forests hides his visions"); another instance occurs in the *Diaries* (p. 133): "The great dialogue passages are wholly metaphysical, their corporality and full-bloodedness result from the passion with which the fight in question is waged. Nor am I creating visages so much as visions. This is where Expressionism comes in. Not powers in human form, but humans as spiritual beings."

23. A verse from one of the *Mahagonny* songs uses the same imagery:

> On sea / And on land / Everyone has his skin pulled off.
> That's why they're all sitting / And selling their skins /
> For skins are always worth their weight in dollars"   (GW, **2**, 541).

24. R. Pohl, *Strukturelemente und Entwicklung von Pathosformen in der Dramensprache Bertolt Brechts* (Bonn, 1969) p. 83.

25. In his early notebooks Brecht complained about the tendency of words to come between man and his experiences: "Many things have become immobile, their skin has thickened, they have shells around them, these are words. . . . We have nothing inside us but newspaper reports about things. . . . One has one's own underwear, which one occasionally washes. One does not have one's own words, and one never washes them. In the beginning was not the word. The word is at the end. It is the corpse of a thing"   (GW, **20**, 13).

26. *Von Reinhardt bis Brecht*, vol. 1, p. 312.

27. A diary entry indicates that it was Brecht's intention to cultivate such ambivalent effects: "Yes, of course the style [G. Garga's] has got to be dry and matter-of-fact, of course the momentum has to rip through every scene, of course the whole thing has to be as serious as playing can ever be" (*Diaries*, 126).

28. Brecht wrote this as a motto in the copy of the play he gave to Carl Zuckmayer – see Carl Zuckmayer, *Als wärs ein Stück von mir* (Vienna, 1966) p. 381.

29. In an "alienating" description of everyday life Brecht once described people as "parcels of flesh" who withdraw at night into "piles of stones with holes" for protection against the sight of the "endlessness of the terrifying star-covered sky" (*Diaries*, 39).

30. The objectivity of the play is all the more surprising in view of the fact that at the time of writing it Brecht had intimate and acute knowledge in his own life of the problems of the play. The evidence of the diaries suggests that his relationship with Marianne Zoff gave him ample experience of human unpredictability, of his own need for freedom and of his inability to secure it. The relationship with her did nothing to dispel his sense of existential isolation; in fact, it seems to have aggravated it: "I got up, we couldn't sleep, neither Marianne nor I, I'm in my dressing-gown sitting on the sofa with my arms and legs shaking, it's an attack of loneliness" (*Diaries*, 117). In 1927 Brecht dedicated the play to Marianne.

31. A brief working note simply states "*Jungle* – Position" (*T*, 202).

32. Engel's notes on his method are in Erich Engel, *Schriften über Theater und Film* (Berlin, 1971) pp. 75–9. A review of Peter Stein's production is to be found in *Brecht in der Kritik*, ed. Monika Wyss (Munich, 1970) pp. 27–9.
33. Brecht's disagreements with Engel are recalled by the actor Erwin Faber (who played the part of Garga in 1923) in W. Stuart McDowell, "Actors on Brecht: the Munich Years", *The Drama Review*, vol. 20 (1976) pp. 101–16.

NOTES TO CHAPTER FIVE: "THE LIFE OF EDWARD THE SECOND"

1. Brecht's early views on the "Materialwert" of classical works were expressed in various notes and essays around 1926 (*GW*, **15**, 105–19).
2. Throughout this chapter the adaptation is treated as Brecht's own work, despite the fact that he stated in the first edition, "I wrote this play with Lion Feuchtwanger". The only evidence concerning their co-operation indicates that Feuchtwanger's role was to supervise the formal qualities of Brecht's work, ensuring in particular that his versification remained consistently rough and uneven – see Marieluise Fleißer, "Aus der Augustenstraße" (*E*, 265).
3. For an account of Brecht's later adaptations see Arrigo Subiotto, *Bertolt Brecht's Adaptations for the Berliner Ensemble* (London, 1975).
4. For the sake of clarity Brecht's king is referred to throughout this chapter as "Eduard" while Marlowe's king has the English spelling "Edward".
5. Moelwyn Merchant comments in the introduction to his edition of Marlowe's *Edward the Second*, "That suffering and death should bear an appropriate relation to sins committed is a commonplace of medieval thought, theological, literary or aesthetic" (*Mar*, xxi). All references to this edition will be given in this abbreviated form in the text.
6. Eduard's revolt is a variant on the theme of a son's rebellion against his father which was commonplace in Expressionism. In contrast to the typical son of Expressionist drama Eduard's revolt has selfish rather than altruistic motives. Far from being born of the belief that the world could be changed for the better, Eduard's rebellion is directed against the world's unchanging disregard for individual happiness. The "cosmic" or metaphysical nature of Eduard's revolt is conveyed by his determination, 'Krieg zu führen gegen die Kraniche der Luft,/Den Fisch der Tiefsee, rascher nachwachsend als getötet,/Montag gegen den großen Leviathan, Donnerstag gegen die Geier/von Wales" (*E*, 190; "Wage war against the cranes of the air/The fish in the deep sea that faster spawn than die/Monday against the great Leviathan, Thursday in Wales/Against the vultures" – *MI*, 224).
7. The blasphemies principally consist in parallels between Eduard's experiences and Christ's Passion. Eduard is first warned of the peers' probable treachery on a Thursday; in the scene of his final betrayal by Baldock there are allusions to the Last Supper, the crowing of the cock, the bloody sweat and Peter's bitter tears; Eduard's crown which, if removed, would take with it some of his skin and blood, alludes to the crown of thorns. References to the Passion were commonplace in Expressionism, but whereas a writer like Georg Kaiser would make such allusions in order to heighten the pathos of his hero's failed life, Brecht was unique in having his hero take masochistic delight in his personal *via crucis*.

8. The Methuen translation gives "shooting" for "schlendernd", which the translator presumably mistook for "schleudernd". The Methuen translation also loses an important nuance by rendering "du hast nur mich zum Freund" as "thou hast me for thy friend". The "nur" ("only") betrays Eduard's relish at the fact that as Gaveston's sole "friend" he is able to live at odds with the rest of society, and to shape the fate of his dependent creature in whichever way he pleases.

9. Mortimer's attitude to Anna resembles that of Shlink to Marie in *In the Jungle*.

10. The translation "falls on me" does not quite convey all the overtones of "mich anspringt", which suggests an animal jumping aggressively at another, but also carries an echo of "bespringen", meaning "to mount, to mate with, as amongst animals".

11. The diminished importance of the theme of sovereignty leads to the replacement of "the public debates and consultations of Marlowe's play" by "soliloquies and dialogues", a pattern noted by Laboulle in her "A note on Bertolt Brecht's Adaptation of Marlowe's *Edward II*", *Modern Language Review*, vol. 54 (1959) p. 216.

12. H. Ihering, *Von Reinhardt bis Brecht*, vol. II, p. 20.

13. "A note on Bertolt Brecht's Adaptation of Marlowe's *Edward II*", p. 215.

14. The photograph is one of a number published in an article by W. Stuart McDowell, entitled "Actors on Brecht: the Munich Years", *The Drama Review*, vol. 20, no. 3 (1976) pp. 101–16.

15. This is recalled by Marieluise Fleißer in her account of the production (*E*, 266).

16. "In dieser Inszenierung war das Eigentümlichste der Soldat. Er zog unter eintönigem Trommelwirbel in den Kampf. Marschierte unaufhörlich, wenn der Mond am Himmel stand. Er marschierte nach dem Befehl des Eduard II, und er marschierte nach dem Befehl des Mortimer, und der marschierte, nachdem er an einem Donnerstag die Bewegung der großen Politik auf dem Globus nachzog. Indem der Soldat marschierte, war jede Zeit für ihn verloren – er verschwindelte die Zeit mit Singen. Wenn die Friedensglocken läuteten, legte er die Waffen nieder und sich auf den Boden. Wenn die Schlacht wütete, wurde sein Gesicht weiß wie Kalk, wenn die Schlacht verloren ging, so sprang er über Brücken und warf die Waffen weg. Diese Soldaten waren tausend Tommys" (*BBA*, **329**, 21).

17. A detailed account of the play's imagery is to be found in V. Canaris, *"Eduard II" als vormarxistisches Stück Bertolt Brechts* (Bonn, 1973) pp. 65–102.

18. He recalled seeing panoramas depicting such scenes as "The execution of the Anarchist Ferrer in Madrid", or "The flight of Karl the Bold after the Battle of Murten" (*GW*, **17**, 910).

19. "Das Requisit wurde nach theatralischem Prinzip gearbeitet. Die Holzäxte, Schleppsäbel und Speere der Soldaten zwangen dem Schauspieler eine bestimmte akrobatische Bewegung ab. Das Tuch, viereckig und breit auseindergefaltet, gab dem Verräter Baldock Gelegenheit, die verschmitzte Bewegung zu unterstreichen und zugleich ein Taschenspielerkunststück zu liefern. Auch der Henker und die Mörder verstanden ihr Handwerk. Die Peers wurden sehr flink mit einem Seil umschnürt und wie ein Bündel von der Bühne weggezogen. Das Hängen Gavestons wurde sehr präzise ausgeführt, es war eine Nummer für sich. Man konnte sich über das traurige Schicksal Gavestons

betrüben und zugleich sich freuen, wie geschickt er an den Ast gehängt wird" (*BBA*, **329**, 22–3).

Brecht's insistence that his actors should be precise in their execution of such concrete actions as tying a rope to a tree clearly distinguished his theatrical style from that of Expressionism, where intense "inwardness" was cultivated by directors and actors alike.

NOTES TO CHAPTER SIX: "A MAN'S A MAN"

1. One should not be misled by the novelty of the play's style into looking for major ideological changes where none are to be found. F. Ewen, for example, claims that in this play "for the first time in Brecht's writings the element of change begins to play a part. Man *is* changeable", *Bertolt Brecht: His Life, his Art, his Times* (New York, 1967) p. 136. This is simply not true. Kragler was terrified by the changes he underwent as a prisoner of war; one even finds the same metaphor for adaptibility (that of "growing webbed feet") applied to both Kragler (*TN*, 36) and Galy Gay (*MiM*, 50).

2. For a discussion of Kipling's role in shaping Brecht's view of the British in India see James K. Lyon, "Kipling's 'Soldiers Three' and Brecht's *A Man's a Man*", in *Essays on Brecht*, ed. S. Mews and M. Knust (Chapel Hill, N. C., 1974) pp. 99–113.

3. The arbitrary nature of the social persona is well expressed in lines spoken by Begbick to Fairchild in the revised version of the play: "Und in der Beuge meiner Knie vergiß/deinen zufälligen Namen" ("And in the bend of my knees forget/Your chance name" – *GW*, **1**, 317).

4. In Brecht's later adaptation of Lenz's *Der Hofmeister* Läuffer's self-castigation with a ruler, a gesture which foreshadows his self-castration, represents an application of the same idea to the situation of the private tutor.

5. See the brief article "Geziemendes über Franz Kafka" (*GW*, **18**, 61; "Some Fitting Observations on Franz Kafka") for a statement of Brecht's early admiration of this writer. The "rat-trap" temple in *A Man's a Man* recalls the vision of the world as a mouse-trap in Kafka's "Kleine Fabel", *Sämtliche Erzählungen* (Frankfurt a.M., 1969) p.320. The relationship between Brecht's early works and Kafka's stories is one of occasional affinity rather than influence.

6. *Theatre of War* (London, 1972) p. 98.

7. The word "großspurig" actually means "wide-gauged", as of a railway. It is thus another instance of the use of metaphors of mechanisation in the play.

8. See the discussion of phrases of the type "an elephant is an elephant" below, pp. 135–7.

9. Laboulle quotes passages from an early, unpublished version of the play in which Galy Gay's ascendancy over the other soldiers takes the cruder form of physically thrashing them–"Dramatic Theory and Practice of Bertolt Brecht", Ph.D. Diss. (Leicester, 1961) p.115.

10. *BBA*, **348**, 71. Walter Benjamin was the first to point out Galy Gay's wisdom, *Versuche über Brecht* (Frankfurt a.M., 1967) p. 24.

11. "*Mann ist Mann* ist der repräsentative erste Versuch der jüngeren Generation, die neue Form des großen Lustspiels aufzustellen. Deutlich zeigt sich die von

den Anhängern des bisherigen Theaters so heftig angegriffene und von Brecht immer wieder geforderte Spezies des epischen Theaters. Jede einzelne Szene des Lustspiels ist so weit von Problematik und Psychologie entfernt, daß sie der naive Schauspieler noch aus dem Gedächtnis nachspielen können müßte" (*BBA*, **348**, 71).

12. The booby-trapped temple would also be quite at home in a silent screen comedy. One is reminded of Buster Keaton's fondness for elaborate apparatus as a source of gags.

13. The refinement of the comedy only came by stages. According to Laboulle there was much more crudely physical farce in the sketches made before the preparation of the final text – *Dramatic Theory and Practice of Bertolt Brecht*, p. 101.

14. Jakob Geis, who first produced the play in Darmstadt, said that the aim of his production was "To demonstrate the *hidden meaning* ["Hintersinn"] of this play by presenting its *surface meaning* as clearly as possible"–"Meine Inszenierung von Bertolt Brechts *Mann ist Mann*, Darmstadt, Landestheater", in *Die Scene* (Berlin, October 1926) p. 300.

15. Of course, none of these soldiers has any right to complain of treachery since they are more guilty of it than most. They persuade Galy Gay to become Jeriah Jip "just once", arguing that "einmal ist keinmal", but later mock him with the same phrase when he asks to be let off "just once more" (*MiM*, 29). In other words, they are only too glad to exploit the traps in language when it suits them.

16. For detailed discussions of the differences between the first published version of the play and subsequent editions see M. Kesting, "Die Groteske vom Verlust der Identität", in *Das deutsche Lustspiel II*, ed. Steffen (Göttingen, 1969) p. 180 *et seq.*; also J. Onderdelinden, "Brechts *Mann ist Mann*: Lustspiel oder Lehrstück?", *Neophilologus* (1970) pp. 149–66, and the introduction and notes to the Methuen translation.

17. This is reported by Elisabeth Hauptmann in her "Notizen zu Brechts Arbeit, 1926", in *Sinn und Form*: 2, Special Bertolt Brecht issue (Berlin, 1957) p. 242.

18. M. Kesting sees in *A Man's a Man* "an element of artificiality which clearly takes it out of the tradition of German comedy" – "Die Groteske vom Verlust der Identität, p. 193. Yet surely Kleist's *Amphitryon* or Büchner's *Leonce und Lena*, both admittedly influenced by foreign models, also have a strong element of artificiality. For examples nearer to Brecht's own time one might cite Wedekind's *Lulu* or the farces of Iwan Goll or Sternheim's *Bürger Schippel* which has a plot not dissimilar to that of *A Man's a Man*.

19. Galy Gay's bewilderment at his newly acquired "double identity" is strongly reminiscent of such passages in Kleist's *Amphitryon* as the following:

> I swear to you
> That I, who singly left your camp,
> Doubly arrived in Thebes;
> I met me here with staring eyes.
> This I that's standing here before you now
> Is totally worn out with weariness and hunger.
> The other I came from your house,
> Was all refreshed, encountered there a devil of a fellow,

And both these scoundrels, jealous of each other,
Both of them eager to complete your mission,
Began to fight at once, and I,
I had to go back to the camp
Because I was a foolish rascal.

(II. i. 679–91)

(translated by M. Sonnenfeld, published New York, 1962)

20. Brecht once referred to the "monstrous mixture of tragedy and comedy" (*GW* **15**, 57) in *Galgei*, an early conception of the plot of *A Man's a Man*.

NOTES TO CHAPTER SEVEN: THE OPERAS

1. F. Podszus, for example, claims that the opera's success rested on a misunderstanding – "Das Ärgernis Brecht", *Akzente I* (1954) p. 144.
2. For an account of the changes made by Brecht in 1931 see, R. C. Speirs, "A Note on the First Published Version of *Die Dreigroschenoper* and its Relation to the Standard Text", *Forum for Modern Language Studies*, vol. 13, no. 1 (1977) pp. 25–32. For an account of the manuscript version, from which the first edition was developed, see the introduction and notes to the Methuen translation, which make it clear that Macheath's speech from the gallows, in which he describes himself as a "bürgerlicher Handwerker" ("bourgeois artisan"), although not included in the first edition, did exist in the first draft. The play was first published in 1929 by Universal-Edition of Vienna, not in 1931, No. 3 of the "Versuche" series, as is stated in the notes to the Methuen translation (p. 124). The Methuen introduction is also in error when it states that "What we have therefore is the work as it was written and staged just half a century ago in 1928" (p. vii).
3. According to Ernst Robert Aufricht, the entrepreneur who first staged *The Threepenny Opera*, Brecht himself described the opera to him as a *Nebenwerk* ("Minor work") *Erzähle damit du dein Recht erweist* (Berlin, 1966) – p. 64.
4. E. V. Robert's introduction to his edition of *The Beggar's Opera* (London, 1969) pp. xix–xx.
5. Ibid., p. xxv.
6. *The Threepenny Opera* has found one such stern critic in the person of Raymond Williams who, in his *Modern Tragedy* (Stanford, Calif., 1966), argues that the work contributes to the "protection of conventional moral attitudes" because "the thieves and whores are the licensed types, on to whom a repressed immorality can very easily be projected, and through whom a repressed conscience can be safely controlled. There is no real shock, when respectable playgoers confront them, because they are seen, precisely, as a special class, a district" (p. 192). William's strictures would carry more weight if one could believe that the thieves and prostitutes were even meant to be taken seriously *as such* in the piece. The comic tone of the opera is surely the main reason why it does not shock.
7. In a note written in January 1929 Brecht referred to Macheath as "der junge, von den Dämchen vergötterte Gentleman" ("the young Gentleman, idolised

by the ladies" – *GW*,**17**, 989). Erich Engel, who directed the first production in
1928, recalls that Macheath was then presented as a "charming lady-killer and
bon viveur" – *Über Theater und Film* (Berlin, 1971) p. 104.

8. When Giorgio Strehler was preparing his production of *The Threepenny Opera*
for Milan in 1955, Brecht urged him to give the piece a harsh edge by stressing
the ugliness of life for the poor and criminal classes (see the notes to the
Methuen translation, pp. 102–3. This was a case of Brecht being wise after the
event.

9. I do not agree with Boris Singermann that "We do not, in the last analysis,
understand why Jenny betrayed her old friend" – "Brechts *Dreigroschenoper*:
Zur Ästhetik der Montage", in *Brecht-Jahrbuch* (1976) p. 77. Brecht's females
are often motivated by resentment at male domination – particularly where
this is coupled with unfaithfulness or (as happened to Jenny) desertion.
Another example from the opera is provided by Polly Peachum, whose singing
of the "Song of the Pirate Jenny", expresses resentment at her position in
society. Singermann generally looks too hard for discontinuities in the opera in
his effort to present it as a typical example of the technique of montage, which
he considers to be the characteristic form of artistic expression in the Weimar
Republic.

10. The allusion is to Peter's tears of remorse (Luke 22:62).

11. I am indebted to the Methuen translation (p. 79) for this rendering.

12. George Salomon rightly speaks of "the fundamental ambiguity of the play" in
his essay, "Happy Ending, Nice and Tidy", *Kenyon Review*, vol. 24 (1962)
p. 546.

13. "Der heutige Film und sein Publikum", *Frankfurter Zeitung und Handelsblatt* (30
Nov 1928). T. Adorno was quick to notice the relation of *The Threepenny Opera*
to the light music of the 1890s, "Zur Musik der Dreigroschenoper", in *Bertolt
Brechts Dreigroschenbuch* (Frankfurt a.M., 1960). Herbert Jhering, on the other
hand, related it to contemporary musicals, "*The Threepenny Opera* by Brecht
and Weill presents us with the counter-type to *It's in the Air* by Schiffer –
Spoliansky and Reinhardt's *Artistes*" – *Von Reinhardt zu Brecht*, vol. II (1959)
p. 349.

14. Singermann comments: "*The Threepenny Opera* is not only the most sober
mockery of the Twenties, but is also the most sentimental and warm work of
the period" – "Brechts *Dreigroschenoper*: Zur Ästhetik der Montage", p. 68.

15. For an account of the vicissitudes of various productions, see David Drew,
"The History of Mahagonny", *Musical Times* (Jan., 1963) p. 18 *et seq.* The
introduction and notes to the Methuen edition also contain much useful
material.

16. Kurt Weill, *Ausgewahlte Schriften* (Frankfurt a.M., 1975) p. 58.

17. All references in this chapter are to the text published by Universal-Edition
(Vienna), © 1929, publisher's serial number UE 9852. UE 9852 exists in two
printings, catalogued in the Bertolt Brecht Archive as *BBA*, **1258** and *BBA*,
1421, respectively. Both were printed by Otto Maass Söhne (Vienna). *BBA*,
1258, which has 60 pages, bears the printers' number 322, 30, whereas *BBA*,
1421, which has 59 pages, bears the printers' number 1075, 30. I have used
BBA, **1258**, this being the earlier version. The most important change made in
BBA, **1421** was the removal of Jim Mahoney's aria "Laßt euch nicht
verführen" ("yield not to temptation") from Act I to the end of Act II, where

it is sung by a choir of men led by Begbick; in Act III Mahoney was given a speech of repentance in place of this defiant aria. Evidently Weill first suggested that such a note of remorse was needed in a letter to his publisher in 1930 (Methuen translation, p. 20). Other changes were the making of the "Benares Song" (No. 19) optional, and the transfer of the 'Spiel von Gott in Mahagonny" from no. 21 to no. 20, where it is enacted before Mahoney's execution, and followed by his speech of repentance.

18. In view of the many biblical allusions in the opera, it is possible that the ostensibly caring attitude of the city's founders towards each individual is a travesty of the Psalmist's understanding of God as someone who watches over everything: "He will not let your foot be moved, he who keeps you will not slumber. . . . The Lord will keep your going out and your coming in from this time forth and for ever more" (Psalm 121). The same idea is expressed in Matt. 10:30, "But even the hairs of your head are all numbered".

19. Although Brecht refuses, characteristically, to present Mahoney's fate in a straightforwardly pathetic and cathartic manner, I believe that the conception of the character is tragic and do not believe that Mahoney was being held up simply as a warning example of the consequences of irrationality, as claimed by Cotterill, "In defence of *Mahagonny*", in *Culture and Society in the Weimar Republic*, ed. K. Bullivant (Manchester, 1977) p. 190 *et seq*. One simplifies the opera if one looks in it for the kind of "implied answers" which are admittedly to be found in later works by Brecht.

20. Notes to the Methuen translation, p. 111.

21. Adorno comments weightily, "The reification of human relationships is rendered by the image of prostitution" – "*Mahagonny*", *Der Scheinwerfer*, vol. III, Part 14 (Essen, 1930) p. 12.

22. The conflict of longing and disillusionment in the poem is reflected in Weill's setting: "The individual melodic lines soar and fall to final cadences, points of rest which are systematically denied them by the mechanically shifting harmonies beneath" – Cotterill, "In defence of *Mahagonny*", p. 195.

23. Brecht's diaries indicate his early interest in Lao-tzu (p. 50), Rabindrinath Tagore (p. 54) and Buddha (p. 110).

24. The commonplace metaphor of "paying" for life's pleasures occurs in Brecht's preface to the 1919 version of *Baal*: "The play sets out to demonstrate that it is possible to get one's share of things if one is willing to pay for them. And even if one is not willing to pay. If one simply pays" – *Baal: Drei Fassungen* (Frankfurt a.M., 1969) p. 79. *Mahagonny* presents a more pessimistic view of things: even if you do pay, life may still deny you satisfaction.

25. I am indebted to the Methuen translation (p. 28) for this rendering.

26. "Der stärkste Eindruck", *Die losen Blätter* (1 Dec 1928).

27. Weill, *Ausgewählte Schriften*, pp. 60–1.

28. This concept occupies a central position in the philosophy of Arthur Schopenhauer, with whose work Brecht was familiar (see *Brecht in Augsburg*, p. 114). Although Brecht's mood was often close to Schopenhauerian pessimism, his work was mainly inspired by the desire to overcome such tendencies in himself.

29. Weill, *Ausgewählte Schriften*, p. 58.

30. The importance of biblical allusions in *Mahagonny* was first established by W. Gaede in his "Figur and Wirklichkeit im Drama Bertolt Brechts", Ph.D. Diss.

(Freiburg, 1963). Gunter Sehm gives no sign of having read Gaede's study in his article "Moses, Christus und Paul Ackermann: Brechts *Aufstieg und Fall der Stadt Mahagonny*", *Brecht-Jahrbuch* (1976) pp. 83–100.

31. *Mahagonny* drew on ideas and material from two other projects of Brecht's which were concerned with the rise and fall of great cities. The first, entitled *Die Sintflut*, (The Flood), which he considered developing into a radio play, makes use of the biblical accounts of the Flood, the destruction of Sodom and Gomorrha and Noah's prophecy of the destruction of Nineveh, as the basis of a fantasy through which Brecht could vent his fear and hatred of modern civilisation's "rape" of nature. The second project, entitled *Untergang der Paradiesstadt Miami* (Destruction of the Paradise City Miami), barely went beyond the stage of gathering newspaper reports dealing with the building of Miami amid the swamps of Florida and with the many hurricanes which regularly wreaked havoc in the Southern States. One of these reports contained the quirky fact, incorporated in *Mahagonny*, that one small area was left untouched by a hurricane which, presumably because of the lie of the land, simply veered around it. Although both projects shared the theme of the foolishness of civilisation, they were quite distinct, contrary to what is said in the notes to the Methuen translation (p. viii).

32. It is, of course, true that Grusha's "friendliness" would have led to nothing, were it not for the sharp and partisan intellect of Azdak. Equally, however, Azdak could not have found a true mother for the child if Grusha had not been prepared, in the first place, to risk everything out of love for it.

33. Mahoney's final aria originally bore the title "Luzifers Abendlied" ("Lucifer's Evensong").

34. The many religious allusions in the opera make it seem plausible that the "good old mamma", whose loss is mourned by the girls, is intended to connote Mary or "mother church", as symbols of the kind of security they have lost.

35. The suggestion that *Mahagonny* is an "Anti-Messiah" was first made by Gaede, "Figur und Wirklichkeit im Drama Brechts", p. 100. Although the *Messiah* is not nearly as well known in Germany as it is in England, the revival of interest in Handel's operas in the 1920s may have drawn the work to Weill's attention. The Handelian quality of certain passages in *Mahagonny* and in *Die Bürgschaft* has struck commentators. Whatever the facts about this particular influence are, there are suggestive parallels, both in overall structure and in detail, between the texts of each work. The relatively static nature of the scenes in *Mahagonny*, which Weill considered well-suited to concert performance, also makes it more reminiscent of oratorio than of dynamic nineteenth-century "music drama".

36. Weill, *Ausgewählte Schriften*, p. 59.

37. Neither the *Lindberghflug* nor the *lehrstück* (later the *Badener Lehrstück vom Einverständnis*), two short pieces written after *Mahagonny*, were yet Marxist in intention, but they were very soon followed by other *Lehrstücke* which were.

NOTES TO CHAPTER EIGHT: THE "LEHRSTÜCKE" AND BEYOND

1. Brecht's reading of Marxism is reflected before 1929 in certain essays and radio discussions (*GW*, **15**, 126, *et seq.*), but also in some dramatic fragments such as *Joe Fleischhacker* or, possibly, *Fatzer*.

2. See Fritz Sternberg, *Der Dichter und die Ratio* (Göttingen, 1963) p. 24.

3. These lines are taken from *Die Maßnahme* (*The Measures Taken*). (Frankfurt a.M., 1972) p. 25.

4. The *Kleines Organon für das Theater* (*Short Organon for the Theatre*), for example, talks of making "productivity the main source of entertainment" (*GW*, **16**, 672). The word "souverän" belongs to a semantic group including terms like "beherrschen", "meistern", "Meisterschaft", "Meisterung" which recur with great frequency throughout Brecht's theoretical writings, e.g. "und zwar ist es die Meisterung der Wirklichkeit, welche . . . den Zuschauer in Emotion versetzt" ("and it is in fact the mastery of reality which arouses the spectator's emotions" – *GW*, **16**, 652), or "von geduckten Leuten bekommt man nicht leicht souveräne werke – und man braucht souveräne werke" (it is not easy to get sovereign works from servile people – and sovereign works are needed" *Arbeitsjournal*, 422):

5. "Das Lehrstück lehrt dadurch, daß es gespielt, nicht dadurch, daß es gesehen wird" ("The learning play teaches by being played, not by being seen" – *GW*, **17**, 1024).

6. The various versions of the play are available in an edition by Peter Szondi, *Der Jasager und Der Neinsager: Vorlagen, Fassungen, Materialien* (Frankfurt a.M., 1966).

7. Brecht himself wrote, in criticism of the *Badener Lehrstück vom Einverständnis* that "too much emphasis is given to dying, in comparison to its relatively slight use-value", quoted in R. Steinweg, *Das Lehrstück* (Stuttgart, 1972) p. 26. The criticism could equally well be applied to *Der Jasager* and *Die Maßnahme*.

8. The year 1930 was the date of the first version of the play. For a collection of the various versions, see the edition by R. Steinweg, *Die Maßnahme. Kritische Ausgabe mit einer Spielanleitung* (Frankfurt a. M., 1972), referred to here as *DM*.

9. A sketch for the play is headed "der jasager – (konkretisierung)" ["the boy who said yes – (concretization)"], quoted in Steinweg's edition, p. 202.

10. "Der Zweck des Lehrstückes ist also, politisch unrichtiges Verhalten zu zeigen und dadurch richtiges Verhalten zu lehren" (*DM*, 237).

11. In 1929–30 the leadership of the KPD (German Communist Party) also set its face against the reformist tendencies within the ranks of its own party, see Ossip K. Flechtheim, *Die KPD in der Weimarer Republik* (Frankfurt a.M., 1969) pp. 248–89.

12. See Peter Bormans "Brecht und der Stalinismus", in *Brecht-Jahrubuch* (1974) pp. 53–76.

13. A number of younger authors, although sympathetic to Brecht, have complained about his over-simplified models of the world. Peter Handke, for example, has described Brecht's plays as unacceptable "idylls" which "exhibit a simplicity and order that do not exist", in *Theater heute* (March 1968) p. 28.

14. Letter quoted in K. Feilchenfeldt, *Bertolt Brecht Trommeln in der Nacht* (Munich, 1976) p. 158.

15. Brecht noted in 1930, "Great appetites pleased me very much. It seemed to me to be a natural advantage if people could eat a lot and with enjoyment, generally wanted a lot, could get a lot out of things etc. What I disliked about myself was my slight appetite" (*T*, 214).

16. "It is true that the petit bourgeois of today can no longer stay out of the war, as Mother Courage once could do" – *Materialien zu Brechts "Mutter Courage und ihre Kinder"* (Frankfurt a.M., 1967).

Bibliography

A. PRIMARY SOURCES

(i) *Brecht's works*

Arbeitsjournal (1938–55), ed. Werner Hecht (Frankfurt a.M.: Suhrkamp, 1973) 2 vols.

Aufstieg und Fall der Stadt Mahagonny (Vienna: Universal-Edition, 1929) (UE 9852, printer's no. 322,30).

Baal (Potsdam: Kiepenheuer, 1922).

Baal: Der böse Baal der asoziale, ed. Schmidt (Frankfurt a.M.: Suhrkamp, 1968).

Baal: Drei Fassungen, ed. Schmidt (Frankfurt a.M.: Suhrkamp, 1966).

Im Dickicht der Städte, ed. Bahr (Frankfurt a.M.: Suhrkamp, 1968).

Die Dreigroschenoper (Vienna: Universal-Edition, 1929).

Gesammelte Werke (Frankfurt a.M.: Suhrkamp, 1967) 20 vols.

Der Jasager und Der Neinsager, ed. P. Szondi (Frankfurt a.M.: Suhrkamp, 1966).

Leben Eduards des Zweiten von England, ed. R. Grimm (Frankfurt a.M.: Suhrkamp, 1968).

lehrstück (Mainz: Schotts Söhne, 1929).

Der Lindberghflug (Vienna: Universal-Edition, 1930).

Die Maßnahme, ed. R. Steinweg (Frankfurt a.M.: Suhrkamp, 1972).

Mann ist Mann (Berlin: Arcadia, 1926).

Materialien zu Brechts "Mutter Courage und ihre Kinder" (Frankfurt a.M.: Suhrkamp, 1964).

Schriften zum Theater (Frankfurt a.M.: Suhrkamp, 1963) 7 vols.

Songspiel Mahagonny, ed. D. Drew (Vienna: Universal-Edition, 1963).

Tagebücher 1920–1922: Autobiographische Aufzeichnungen 1920–1954, ed. Herta Ramthun (Frankfurt a.M.: Suhrkamp, 1975).

Trommeln in der Nacht (Munich: Drei Masken, 1922).

Fragmentary and unpublished material in the keeping of the Bertolt Brecht Archive, Berlin.

(ii) *Translations*

Collected Plays, ed. J. Willett and R. Mannheim:

Volume I (London: Eyre Methuen, 1970) contains *Baal, Drums in the Night, In the Jungle of the Cities, The Life of Edward the Second of England* and the early one-act plays.

Volumes II i, II ii and II iii (London: Eyre Methuen, 1979) contain *Man equals Man, The Threepenny Opera* and *Rise and Fall of the City of Mahagonny*.

Diaries 1920–1922, trans. J. Willett (London: Eyre Methuen, 1979).

Although I have mostly supplied my own translations, I have occasionally used the

Eyre Methuen versions. These are published with useful introductions and editorial notes, to which I also refer.

(iii) *Works by other authors*

John Gay, *The Beggar's Opera*, ed. Roberts (London, 1969).

Hermann Hesse, *Klingsors letzter Sommer* (Zurich, n.d.).

Hugo von Hofmannsthal, *Gedichte und kleine Dramen* (Frankfurt a.M., 1966).

Heinrich von Kleist, *Amphitryon*, trans. M. Sonnenfeld (New York, 1962).

Christopher Marlowe, *Edward the Second*, ed. Moelwyn Merchant (London, 1967).

B. SECONDARY LITERATURE

(i) *General*

M. Adler "Untersuchungen zum Studium Bert Brechts", *Neue deutsche Hefte*, vol. 13, no. 3 (1966) pp. 118–24.

T. Adorno, "Jene Zwanziger Jahre", *Merkur*, vol. 16 (Jan 1962) pp. 46–51.

M. Alter, "The many Faces of Bertolt Brecht", *American German Review*, vol. 30, no. 6 (1963–4) pp. 25–80.

H. Arendt, "Der Dichter Bertolt Brecht", *Neue Rundschau*, vol. 61 (1950) pp. 53–67; also in *Brecht: A Collection of Critical Essays*, ed. P. Demetz (Englewood Cliffs, N.J., 1962).

R. F. Arnold, *Das deutsche Drama* (Munich, 1925).

J. Bab, *Über den Tag hinaus* (Heidelberg, 1960).

W. Benjamin, *Versuche über Brecht* (Frankfurt a.M., 1966).

E. Bentley, *Theatre of War* (London, 1972).

——, "A Brecht Commentary (continued)", in *Perspectives and Personalities*, ed. R. Ley, Wagner, Ratych and Hughes (Heidelberg, 1978) pp. 15–27.

P. Böckmann, *Provokation und Dialektik in der Dramatik Bertolt Brechts* (Krefeld, 1961).

T. O. Brandt, *Die Vieldeutigkeit Bertolt Brechts* (Heidelberg, 1968).

Brecht Heute/Brecht Today, Jahrbuch der Internationalen Brecht-Gesellschaft (Frankfurt a.M., 1971, 72, 73) 3 vols.

Brecht-Jahrbuch, ed. J. Fuegi, R. Grimm and J. Hermand (Frankfurt a.M., 1974 et seq.).

A. Bronnen, *Tage mit Bertolt Brecht* (Boston, 1962).

D. Bronsen, "'Die Verhältnisse dieses Planeten' in Brechts frühen Stücken", in *Festschrift für Bernhard Blume* (Göttingen, 1967) pp. 348–66.

R. Brustein, *The Theatre of Revolt* (Boston, 1962).

——, "Brecht against Brecht", *Partisan Review*, vol. 30 (1963) pp. 29–54.

G. Buehler, *Bertolt Brecht, Erwin Piscator: Ein Vergleich ihrer theoretischen Schriften* (Bonn, 1978).

K. Bullivant (ed.), *Culture and Society in the Weimar Republic* (Manchester, 1977).

D. Calandra, "Karl Valentin and Bert Brecht", *Drama Review*, vol. 18, no. 1 (1974) pp. 86–98.

P. Chiarini, *Bertolt Brecht* (Bari, 1959).

H. Claas, *Die politische Ästhetik Bertolt Brechts vom Baal zum Caesar* (Frankfurt a.M., 1977).

G. Debiel, "Das Prinzip der Verfremdung in der Sprachgestaltung Bertolt Brechts", Ph.D. Diss. (Bonn, 1960).

P. Demetz (ed.), *Brecht: a Collection of Critical Essays* (Englewood Cliffs, N.J., 1962).

J. Desuche, *Bertolt Brecht* (Paris, 1963).

K. Dickson, "Brecht: an Aristotelian *malgré lui*", *Modern Drama*, vol. II (1968) pp. 111–21.

——, *Towards Utopia: a Study of Brecht* (Oxford, 1978).

M. Dietrich, *Das moderne Drama* (Stuttgart, 1961).

B. Dort, *Lecture de Brecht* (Paris, 1960).

J. Dyck, H. Gossler, H. P. Herrmann, J. Knopf, H.-H. Müller, C. Pietzcher, R. Steinlein and J. Stosch, *Brechtdiskussion* (Kronberg and Taunus, 1974).

W. Eckardt and S. Gilman, *Bertolt Brecht's Berlin: a Scrapbook of the Twenties* (Garden City, N.Y. 1975).

B. Ekmann, *Gesellschaft und Gewissen* (Copenhagen, 1969).

F. Emmel, *Das Ekstatische Theater* (Leipzig, 1924).

E. Engel, *Schriften über Theater und Film* (Berlin, 1971).

M. Esslin, *Brecht: a Choice of Evils* (London, 1965).

——, *Bertolt Brecht* (New York and London, 1969).

——, "Icon and Self-Portrait: Images of Brecht", *Encounter*, vol. 49 (1977) pp. 30–9.

Europe: Revue mensuelle, vol. 133/134, special Brecht issue (Paris, 1957).

F. Ewen, *Bertolt Brecht: His Life, his Art and his Times* (New York, 1967).

F. Fergusson, "Three Allegorists: Brecht, Wilder and Eliot", in F. Fergusson (ed.), *The Human Image in Dramatic Literature* (Garden City, N.Y., 1957).

L. Feuchtwanger, "Bertolt Brecht dargestellt für Engländer", in *Deutsche Literaturkritik im zwanzigsten Jahrhundert*, ed. H. Mayer (Stuttgart, 1965) pp. 516–22.

F. Fischbach, *L'Evolution politique de Bertolt Brecht de 1913 à 1933* (University of Lille, 1976).

I. Fradkin, *Bertolt Brecht: Weg und Methode* (Leipzig, 1974).

E. Franzen, *Formen des modernen Dramas* (Munich, 1961).

W. Frisch and K. W. Obermeier, *Brecht in Augsburg* (Berlin and Weimar, 1975).

J. Fuegi, *The Essential Brecht* (Los Angeles, 1972).

F. W. Gaede, "Figur and Wirklichkeit im Drama Bertolt Brechts", Ph.D. Diss. (Freiburg, 1963).

——, "Bertolt Brecht", in *Expressionismus als Literatur*, ed. W. Rothe (Berne, 1969) pp. 595–605.

H. F. Garten, *Modern German Drama*, 2nd edn (London, 1964).

P. Gay, *Weimar Culture* (London, 1968).

P. Giese, *Das "Gesellschaftlich-Komische"* (Stuttgart, 1974).

R. Gray, *Brecht* (Edinburgh and London, 1961).

——, *Brecht: the Dramatist* (Cambridge, 1976).

R. Grimm, *Bertolt Brecht: Die Struktur seines Werkes* (Nuremberg, 1959).

——, *Bertolt Brecht und die Weltliteratur* (Nuremberg, 1961).

—— (ed.), *Episches Theater* (Cologne and Berlin, 1966).

——, *Bertolt Brecht*, 3rd edn (Stuttgart, 1971).

——, *Brecht und Nietzsche oder Geständnisse eines Dichters* (Frankfurt a.M., 1979).

—— and J. Hermand (eds), *Die sogenannten zwanziger Jahre* (Frankfurt a.M., 1970).

D. Grossvogel, *Four Playwrights and a Postscript* (Ithaca, N.Y., 1962).

W. Haas, *Bert Brecht* (Berlin, 1958).

——, *Die literarische Welt* (Munich, 1958).

W. Hecht, *Brechts Weg zum epischen Theater* (Berlin, 1962).

——, *Aufsätze über Brecht* (Berlin, 1970).

——, *Bertolt Brecht: Sein Leben in Bildern und Texten* (Frankfurt a.M., 1978).

——, *Bertolt Brecht: Vielseitige Betrachtungen* (Berlin, 1978).

——, H.-J. Bunge and K. Rülicke-Weiler, *Bertolt Brecht: Leben und Werk* (Berlin, 1963).

A. Heidsieck, *Das Groteske und das Absurde im modernen Drama* (Stuttgart, 1969).

——, "Psychologische Strukturen im Werk Bertolt Brechts", *Ideologiekritische Studien zur Literatur*, vol. II (1975) pp. 31–71.

P. Heller, "Nihilist into Activist: Two Phases in the Development of Bertolt Brecht", *Germanic Review*, vol. 28 (1953) pp. 144–55.

J. Hermand, *Stile, Ismen, Etiketten: Zur Periodisierung der modernen Kunst* (Wiesbaden, 1978).

H. P. Herrmann, "Von *Baal* zur *Heiligen Johanna der Schlachthöfe* Die dramatische Produktion des jungen Brecht als Ort gesellschaftlicher Erfahrung", *Poetica*, vol. 5 (1972) pp. 191–211.

C. Hill, *Bertolt Brecht* (Boston, Mass., 1975).

W. Hinck, "Bertolt Brecht", in *Deutsche Literatur im zwanzigsten Jahrhundert*, ed. O. Mann and W. Rothe, vol. 2 (Berne and Munich, 1967) pp. 362–84.

M. Högel, *Bertolt Brecht: Ein Porträt* (Augsburg, 1962).

H. E. Holthusen, *Kritisches Verstehen* (Munich, 1961).

H. Hultberg, *Die ästhetischen Anschauungen Bertolt Brechts* (Copenhagen, 1962).

Inter Nationes, *Bertolt Brecht, 1956–1966* (Bad Godesberg, 1966).

W. Jäggi (ed.), *Das Ärgernis Brecht* (Basle and Stuttgart, 1961).

W. Jennrich, "Bemerkungen zu den Anfängen des Stückeschreibers Brecht", *Weimarer Beitrage*, vol. 14 (1968) Special issue, pp. 101–22.

W. Jens, *Statt einer Literaturgeschichte*, 2nd edn (Pfullingen, 1962).

H. Jhering, *Von Reinhardt bis Brecht* (Berlin, 1958–61 3 vols).

——, *Bertolt Brecht und das Theater* (Berlin, 1959).

A. Kaes, "Brecht und der Amerikanismus im Theater der 20er Jahre: Unliterarische Tradition und Publikumsbezug", *Sprache im technischen Zeitalter*, vol. 56 (1975) pp. 359–71.

K. Kändler, *Drama und Klassenkampf* (Berlin and Weimar, 1970).

H. Karasek, *Bertolt Brecht: Der jüngste Fall eines Theaterklassikers* (Munich, 1978).

H. Kaufmann, *Bertolt Brecht: Geschichtsdrama und Parabelstück* (Berlin, 1962).

——, *Krisen und Wandlungen der deutschen Literatur von Wedekind bis Feuchtwanger* (Berlin, 1966).

W. Kenney, *The Major Plays of Bertolt Brecht* (New York, 1964).

M. Kesting, *Bertolt Brecht in Selbstzeugnissen und Bilddokumenten* (Reinbek, 1959).

——, *Das epische Theater* (Stuttgart, 1959).

V. Klotz, *Bertolt Brecht: Versuch über das Werk* (Darmstadt, 1957).

J. Knopf, *Bertolt Brecht: Ein kritischer Forschungsbericht* (Frankfurt a.M., 1974).

——, *Brecht-Handbuch: Theater* (Stuttgart, 1980).

H. Knust, "Piscator and Brecht: Affinity and Alienation", in *Essays on Brecht*, eds. S. Mews and H. Knust (Chapel Hill, N.C., 1974) pp. 44–68.

——, "Brechts Dialektik vom Fressen und von der Moral", *Brecht Heute*, vol. 3 (1973–4) pp. 221–50.

S. Kracauer, *Von Caligari bis Hitler* (Hamburg, 1958).

L. Laboulle, "Dramatic Theory and Practice of Bertolt Brecht – with Particular Reference to the Epic Theatre", Ph.D. Diss. (Leicester, 1961).

——, "Bertolt Brecht's Fun and Games: An Approach to the Epic Theatre?", *German Life and Letters* (1961–2) pp. 285–94.

H. Lethen, *Neue Sachlichkeit 1924–1932* (Stuttgart, 1970).

R. Ley, "Brecht: Science and Cosmic Futility", *The Germanic Review*, vol. 40 (1965) pp. 205–24.

L. Lucas, *Dialogstrukturen und ihre szenischen Elemente im deutschsprachigen Drama des 20. Jahrhunderts* (Bonn, 1969).

H. Lüthy, "Vom armen Bert Brecht", *Der Monat*, vol. 44 (1952) pp. 115–44.

C. R. Lyons, *Bertolt Brecht: the Despair and the Polemic* (Carbondale, Ill., 1968).

S. Maclean, *The "Bänkelsang" and the Work of Bertolt Brecht* (The Hague and Paris, 1972).

S. McDowell, "Actors on Brecht: the Munich Years", *The Drama Review*, vol. 20, no. 3 (1976) pp. 101–16.

O. Mann, *Bertolt Brecht – Maß oder Mythos?* (Heidelberg, 1958).

—— and W. Rothe (eds), *Deutsche Literatur im zwanzigsten Jahrhundert* 5th edn (Berne and Munich, 1967).

K. Marx and F. Engels, *Gesamtausgabe* (Berlin, 1932).

P. v. Matt, "Brecht und der Kälteschock: Das Trauma der Geburt als Strukturprinzip seines Dramas", *Neue Rundschau*, vol. 87 (1976) pp. 613–29.

H. Mayer, *Bertolt Brecht und die Tradition* (Pfullingen, 1961).

——, *Anmerkungen zu Brecht* (Frankfurt a.M., 1965).

——, *Brecht in der Geschichte* (Frankfurt a.M., 1971).

F. N. Mennemeier, *Modernes deutsches Drama I* (Munich, 1973).

T. Metscher, "Brecht and Marxist dialectics", *Oxford German Studies*, vol. 6 (1971–2) pp. 132–44.

J. Milfull, *From 'Baal' to 'Keuner': the "Second Optimism" of Bertolt Brecht* (Berne and Frankfurt a.M., 1974).

W. Mittenzwei, *Kampf der Richtungen* (Leipzig, 1978).

M. Morley, *Brecht: a Study* (London, 1977).

K. D. Müller, *Die Funktion der Geschichte im Werk Bertolt Brechts* (Tubingen, 1967).

H. O. Münsterer, *Bert Brecht: Erinnerungen aus den Jahren 1917–1922* (Zurich, 1963).

G. Murphy, *Brecht and the Bible* (Chapel Hill, N.C., 1980).

W. Muschg, *Von Trakl zu Brecht* (Munich, 1961).

J. Needle and P. Thompson, *Brecht* (Oxford, 1981).

H. Olles, "Von der Anstrengung der Satire", *Akzente*, vol. 1, no. 2 (1954) pp. 154–63.

R. Pascal, *Brecht's Misgivings*, the 1977 Bithell Memorial Lecture (London, 1977).

M. Patterson, *The Revolution in German Theatre 1900–1933* (London, 1981).

W. Paulsen (ed.), *Aspekte des Expressionismus* (Heidelberg, 1968).

H. Plessner, "Die Legende von den zwanziger Jahren", *Merkur*, vol. 16 (Jan 1962) pp. 33–46.

R. Pohl, *Strukturelemente und Entwicklung von Pathosformen in der Dramensprache Bertold* [sic] *Brechts* (Bonn, 1969).

Q. Qureshi, *Pessimismus und Fortschrittsglaube bei Bert Brecht* (Cologne and Vienna, 1971).

H. Ramthun, *Bertolt-Brecht-Archiv: Bestandsverzeichnis des literarischen Nachlasses:* vol. 1 *Stücke* (Berlin and Weimar, 1969).

W. Rasch, "Bertolt Brechts marxistischer Lehrer", *Merkur*, vol. 17 (1963) pp. 988–1003.

L. Reinisch, *Die Zeit ohne Eigenschaften: Eine Bilanz der Zwanziger Jahre* (Stuttgart, 1961).

P. Rilla, *Essays* (Berlin, 1955).

H. Rischbieter, *Bertolt Brecht* (Velber, 1966) 2 vols.

H. Rosenbauer, *Brecht und der Behaviorismus* (Bad Homburg, 1970).

W. Rothe, *Die deutsche Literatur in der Weimarer Republik* (Stuttgart, 1974).

G. Rühle, *Theater für die Republik 1917 bis 1933* (Frankfurt a.M., 1967).

——, *Theater in unserer Zeit* (Frankfurt a.M., 1976).

J. Rühle, *Theater und Revolution* (Munich, 1963).

B. Schärer, *Bertolt Brechts Theater: Sprache und Bühne* (Zurich, 1964).

A. Schöne, "Theatertheorie und dramatische Dichtung", *Euphorion*, vol. 52 (1958) pp. 272–96.

K. H. Schoeps, *Bertolt Brecht* (New York, 1977).

E. Schumacher, *Die dramatischen Versuche Bertolt Brechts 1918–1933* (Berlin, 1955; rev. edn, West Berlin, 1977).

H. Seliger, *Das Amerikabild Bertolt Brechts* (Bonn, 1974).

G. Serreau, *Bertolt Brecht* (Paris, 1955).

Sinn und Form: 1, special Bertolt Brecht issue (Berlin, 1949).

Sinn und Form: 2, special Bertolt Brecht issue (Berlin, 1957).

W. Sokel, "Brecht und der Expressionismus", in *Die sogenannten zwanziger Jahre*, ed. R. Grimm and J. Hermand (Frankfurt a.M., 1970).

——, "Dialogführung und Dialog im expressionistischen Drama", in *Aspekte des Expressionismus*, ed. W. Paulsen (Heidelberg, 1968).

M. Spalter, *Brecht's Tradition* (Baltimore, Md., 1967).

W. A. J. Steer, "Brecht's Epic Theatre: Theory and Practice", *Modern Language Review*, vol. 63 (1968) pp. 636–49.

F. Sternberg, *Der Dichter und die Ratio* (Göttingen, 1963).

J. Strelka, *Brecht Horváth Dürrenmatt* (Vienna, 1962).

J. Styan, *The Dark Comedy* (Cambridge, 1968).

A. Subiotto, "Neue Sachlichkeit: a Re-assessment", in *Deutung und Bedeutung*, ed. B. Schludermann, V. Doerksen, R. Glendinning and E. Firchow (The Hague and Paris, 1973) pp. 248–74.

R. Symington, *Brecht und Shakespeare* (Bonn, 1970).

G. Szczesny, *Das Leben des Galilei und der Fall Bertolt Brecht* (Berlin, 1965).

A. Tatlow, *The Mask of Evil* (Berne, 1977).

Text und Kritik, special issue: *Bertolt Brecht II* (Munich, 1973).

L. Thomas, *Ordnung und Wert der Unordnung bei Bertolt Brecht* (Berne, 1979).

P. Trost, "Die Sprache Bert Brechts", *Germanistica Pragensia*, vol 1 (1960) pp. 73–89.

I. Vinçon, *Die Einakter Bertolt Brechts* (Königstein im Taunus, 1980).

M. Voigts, *Brechts Theaterkonzeptionen: Entstehung und Entwicklung bis 1931* (Munich, 1977).

K. Völker, *Brecht-Chronik* (Munich, 1971).

——, *Bertolt Brecht: eine Biographie* (Munich, 1976).

G. Weales, "Brecht and the Drama of Ideas", in *Ideas in the Drama*, ed. J. Gassner (New York and London, 1964) pp. 125–54.

B. Weber and H. Heinen (eds), *Bertolt Brecht: Political Theory and Literary Practice* (Manchester, 1980).

W. Weideli, *Bertolt Brecht* (Paris, 1961).

U. Weisstein, "From the Dramatic Novel to the Epic Theatre: a Study of the Contemporary Background of Brecht's Theory and Practice", *Germanic Review*, vol. 38 (1963) pp. 257–71.
A. White, *Bertolt Brecht's Great Plays* (London, 1978).
B. von Wiese, *Zwischen Utopie und Wirklichkeit* (Düsseldorf, 1963).
—— (ed.), *Deutsche Dichter der Moderne* (Berlin, 1969).
J. Willett, *The Theatre of Bertolt Brecht* (London, 1959).
——, *The New Sobriety* (London, 1978).
R. Williams, *Modern Tragedy* (Stanford, 1966).
——, *Drama from Ibsen to Brecht* (London, 1968).
R. Wintzen, *Bertolt Brecht* (Paris, 1954).
H. Witt (ed.), *Erinnerungen an Brecht* (Leipzig, 1964).
M. Wyss (ed.), *Brecht in der Kritik* (Munich, 1977).
C. Zuckmayer, *Als wär's ein Stück von mir* (Frankfurt, 1966).

(ii) *Discussion of Individual Plays*

Baal

W. Anders, "Notes sur *Baal*: Première pièce de Bertolt Brecht", *Revue de la société d'histoire du théâtre*, vol. 11 (1959) pp. 213–21.
E. Bentley, "Bertolt Brecht's First Play", *Kenyon Review*, vol. 26 (1964) pp. 82–92; also in E. Bentley, *Theatre of War* (London, 1972).
D. Daphinoff, "*Baal*, die frühe Lyrik und Hanns Johst: Noch einmal über die literarischen Anfänge Bertolt Brechts", *Jahrbuch der deutschen Schiller-Gesellschaft*, vol. 19 (1975) pp. 324–43.
B. Ekmann, "Bert Brecht, vom *Baal* aus gesehen", *Orbis Litterarum*, vol. 20 (1965) pp. 3–18; also in B. Ekmann, *Gesellschaft und Gewissen* (Copenhagen, 1969).
B. Goldstein, "Bertolt Brecht's *Baal*: a Crisis in Poetic Existence", in *Festschrift für Bernhard Blume* (Göttingen, 1967) pp. 333–47.
V. Günther, "Hofmannsthal und Brecht: Bemerkungen zu Brechts *Baal*", in *Festschrift für Benno von Wiese*, ed. V. J. Günther *et al.* (Berlin, 1973).
E. Krispyn, "Brecht and Expressionism: Notes on a Scene from *Baal*", *Revue des langues vivantes*, vol. 31 (1965) pp. 211–17.
C. R. Lyons, "Bertolt Brecht's *Baal*: the Structure of Images", *Modern Drama*, vol. VIII (1965) pp. 311–23; also in C. R. Lyons, *Bertolt Brecht: the Despair and the Polemic* (Carbondale, Ill., 1968).
W. Muschg, "Brechts erstes Stück", in W. Muschg (ed.), *Pamphlet und Bekenntnis* (Olten/Freiburg, 1968).
G. Nelson, "'*Baal*': the Foundation of Brecht's Style", Ph.D. Diss. (Yale, 1968).
D. Norris, "The Rise and Fall of the Individual in the early Brecht, 1918–1932: an Examination of the 'Baal' Plays", Ph.D. Diss. (Columbia, 1971).
K. Sauerland, "Die Grundannahme des Stückes ist mir heute kaum noch zugänglich", *Germanica Wratislavensia* (Wocław), vol. 22 (1975) pp. 57–69.
D. Schmidt, "*Baal*" und der junge Brecht (Stuttgart, 1966).
L. Shaw, "The Morality of Combat: Brecht's Search for a Sparring Partner", *Brecht Heute*, vol. 1 (Berlin, 1971) pp. 80–97.
W. Steer, "*Baal*: a Key to Brecht's Communism", *German Life and Letters*, vol. 19 (1965–6) pp. 40–51.

G. Weales, "Brecht and the Drama of Ideas", in *Ideas in the Drama*, ed. Gassner (New York and London, 1964) pp. 125–54.
U. Weisstein, "The Lonely Baal: Brecht's First Play as a Parody of H. Johst's *Der Einsame*", *Modern Drama*, vol. 13 (1970–1) pp. 284–303.

Drums in the Night

D. Bathrick, " 'Anschauungsmaterial' for Marx: Brecht Returns to *Trommeln in der Nacht*", *Brecht Heute*, vol. 2 (1972) pp. 136–48.
——, *The Dialectic and the Early Brecht* (Stuttgart, 1975).
K. Feilchenfeldt, *Trommeln in der Nacht: Materialien, Abbildungen, Kommentar* (Munich, 1976).
P. Giese, *Das "Gesellschaftlich-Komische"* (Stuttgart, 1974).
G. Hartung, "Brecht und Schiller", *Sinn und Form*, vol. 18, no. 1 (1966) special issue, pp. 743–66.
H. Kaufmann, "Drama der Revolution und des Individualismus: Brechts *Trommeln in der Nacht*", *Weimarer Beiträge*, vol. VII, no. 2 (1961) pp. 316–31.
H. Mayer, "Brecht's *Drums*, a Dog and Beckett's *Godot*", in *Essays on Brecht* ed. S. Mews and H. Knust (Chapel Hill, N.C., 1974) pp. 71–8.
G. Semmer, "*Trommeln in der Nacht*", *Nachrichtenbrief*, no. 63, Arbeitskreis Bertolt Brecht (Cologne, 1968).
R. Steinlein, "Expressionismusüberwindung: Restitution bürgerlicher Dramaturgie oder Beginn eines neuen Dramas? Bemerkungen und Materialien zur theater-kritischen Erstrezeption des frühen Brecht (am Beispiel von *Trommeln in der Nacht* (1922))", in J. Dyck *et al.*, *Brechtdiskussion* (Kronberg im Taunus, 1974) pp. 7–51.
G. Stern, "*Trommeln in der Nacht* als literarische Satire", *Monatshefte*, vol. 61 (1969) pp. 241–59.

The following studies contain useful information for assessing the relation of Brecht's play to the historical reality of the revolution:

O. Braun, *Von Weimar zu Hitler* (New York, 1940).
O. Flechtheim, *Die KPD in der Weimarer Republik* (Frankfurt a.M., 1969).
Historisches Lesebuch 3, 1914–1933, ed. G. Kotowski (Frankfurt a.M., 1968).
E. Kolb, *Die Arbeiterräte in der deutschen Innenpolitik 1918–1919* (Dusseldorf, 1962).
H. Müller-Franken, *Die November-Revolution* (Berlin, 1928).
A. Rosenberg, *Entstehung der Deutschen Republik 1871–1918* (Berlin, 1928).
Völker hört die Signale, ed. B. Weber (Munich, 1967).
R. Watt, *The Kings Depart* (London, 1969).

In the Jungle

G. Bahr, "*Im Dickicht der Städte*: Ein Beitrag zur Bestimmung von Bertolt Brechts dramatischem Frühstil", Ph.D. Diss. (New York, 1966).
E. Engel, "*Im Dickicht der Städte* von Bertolt Brecht", in E. Engel, *Schriften, Über Theater und Film* (Berlin, 1971).
A. Heidsieck, *Das Groteske und das Absurde im modernen Drama* (Stuttgart, 1969).
L. Kahn, "Dialektisches Drama: einige Gedanken zu Brechts *Im Dickicht der*

Städte", in *Perspectives and Personalities* ed. R. Ley *et al.* (Heidelberg, 1978) pp. 176–80.

C. R. Lyons, "Two Projections of the Isolation of the Human Soul: Brecht's *Im Dickicht der Städte* and Albee's *The Zoo Story"*, *Drama Survey*, vol. 4 (1965) pp. 121–38.

S. Mews and R. English, "The 'Jungle' Transcended: Brecht and Zuckmayer", in *Essays on Brecht*, ed. S. Mews and M. Knust (Chapel Hill, N.C., 1974) pp. 79–98.

The Life of Edward the Second of England

G. Allen, "The Role of Adaptation in the Work of Bertolt Brecht as illustrated by 'Leben Eduards des Zweiten von England' ", Ph.D. Diss. (New York, 1970).

R. Beckley, "Adaptation as a Feature of Brecht's Dramatic Technique", *German Life and Letters*, vol. 15 (1961–2) pp. 274–84.

E. Bentley, *Bertolt Brecht: Edward II–a Chronicle Play*, Introduction (New York, 1966); also in E. Bentley, *Theatre of War* (London, 1972) pp. 131–45.

V. Canaris, *"Leben Eduards des Zweiten von England" als vormarxistisches Stück Bertolt Brechts* (Bonn, 1973).

V. Dreimanis Melngailis, *"Leben Eduards des Zweiten von England*: Bertolt Brecht's Adaptation of Marlowe's *Edward II"*, Ph.D. Diss. Cambridge (Harvard, 1966).

H. Grüninger, "Brecht und Marlowe", *Comparative Literature*, vol. 21 (1969) pp. 232–44.

L. Laboulle, "A Note on Bertolt Brecht's Adaptation of Marlowe's *Edward II"*, *Modern Language Review* (1959) pp. 214–20.

C. Leech (ed.), *Marlowe: a Collection of Critical Essays* (Englewood Cliffs, N.J., 1964).

W. Moelwyn Merchant, *Marlowe: Edward the Second*, Introduction (London, 1967).

B. Reich, "Erinnerungen an Brecht", *Theater der Zeit*, vol. 3 (1966) pp. 1–19; substantially reproduced in R. Grimm's edition of the play (Frankfurt, a.M., 1968).

J. Svendsen, "The Queen is Dead: Brecht's *Eduard II"*, *Drama Review*, vol. II (1965–6) pp. 160–76.

R. Symington, *Brecht und Shakespeare* (Bonn, 1970).

U. Weisstein, "Marlowe's Homecoming or *Edward II* Crosses the Atlantic", *Monatshefte für deutschen Unterricht*, vol. LX (1968) pp. 235–42.

——, "The First Version of Brecht/Feuchtwanger's *Leben Eduards des Zweiten von England* and its Relation to the Standard Text", *Journal of English and Germanic Philology*, vol. LXIX (1970) pp. 193–210.

A Man's a Man

E. Bentley, *Bertolt Brecht: Seven Plays*, Introduction (New York, 1961); also in E. Bentley, *Theatre of War* (London, 1972).

J. Geis, "Meine Inszenierung von Bertolt Brechts *Mann ist Mann*, Darmstadt, Landestheater", *Die Scene* (Berlin, October 1926) p. 300.

A. Heidsieck, *Das Groteske und das Absurde im modernen Drama* (Stuttgart, 1969).

M. Kesting, "Die Groteske vom Verlust der Identität", in *Das deutsche Lustspiel*, vol. II, ed. H. Steffen (Göttingen, 1969) pp. 180–99.

V. Klotz, "Engagierte Komik", in V. Klotz, *Kurze Kommentare zu Stücken und Gedichten* (Darmstadt, 1962).

J. Lyon, "Kipling's 'Soldiers Three' and Brecht's *A Man's a Man*", in *Essays on Brecht*, ed. S. Mews and H. Knust (Chapel Hill, N.C., 1974) pp. 99–113.

J. Onderdelinden, "Brechts *Mann ist Mann*: Lustspiel oder Lehrstück?", *Neophilologus* (1970) pp. 149–66.

H. Rosenbauer, *Brecht und der Behaviorismus* (Bad Homburg, 1970).

L. Shaw, *The Playwright and Historical Change* (Madison, Wisc., 1970).

G. Weales, "Brecht and the Drama of Ideas", in *Ideas in the Drama*, ed. Gassner (New York and London, 1964) pp. 125–54.

J. White, "A Note on Brecht and Behaviourism", *Forum for Modern Language Studies*, vol. 7 (1971) pp. 249–58.

The Operas

T. Adorno, "*Mahagonny*", *Der Scheinwerfer*, vol. III, part 14 (Essen, 1930) pp. 12–15.

E. Aufricht, *Erzähle, damit du dein Recht erweist* (Berlin, 1966) pp. 641 ff.

E. Bloch, "Das Experiment in Mahagonny", *Forum*, vol. 14 (1967) pp. 647–51.

R. Cotterill, "In Defence of *Mahagonny*", in *Culture and Society in the Weimar Republic*, ed. K. Bullivant (Manchester, 1977) pp. 190–200.

D. Drew, "The History of *Mahagonny*", *Musical Times* (Jan 1963) pp. 18–24.

—— (ed.), *Über Kurt Weill* (Frankfurt a.M., 1975).

B. Dukore, "The averted crucifixion of Macheath", *Drama Survey*, vol. 4 (1964) pp. 51–6.

E. Engel, "Über die Neuinszenierung der *Dreigroschenoper* von Bertolt Brecht", in E. Engel, *Schriften, Über Theater und Film* (Berlin, 1971) pp. 103–5.

R. Fischetti, "Bertolt Brecht: Die Gestaltung des Dreigroschenstoffes in Stück, Roman and Film", Ph.D. Diss. (Maryland, 1971).

W. Gaede, "Figur und Wirklichkeit im Drama Brechts", Ph.D. Diss. (Freiburg, 1963).

G. Hartung, "Zur epischen Oper Brechts und Weills", *Wissenschaftliche Zeitschrift der Martin-Luther-Universität Halle-Wittenberg*, vol. 8 (1958/59) pp. 659–73.

W. Hecht, "Die *Dreigroschenoper* und ihr Urbild", in W. Hecht, *Sieben Studien über Brecht* (Frankfurt a.M., 1972) pp. 73–107.

H. Kotschenreuter, *Kurt Weill* (Wunsiedel, 1962).

S. Melchinger, "Mahagonny als Mysterienspiel", *Theater Heute* (May 1964) pp. 32–4.

F. Podszus, "Das Ärgernis Brecht", *Akzente*, vol. 1 (1954) pp. 143–9.

G. Salomon, "Happy Ending, Nice and Tidy", *Kenyon Review*, vol. 24 (1962) pp. 542–51.

G. Sehm, "Moses, Christus und Paul Ackermann: Brechts *Aufstieg und Fall der Stadt Mahagonny*", *Brecht-Jahrbuch* (1976) pp. 83–100.

J. Shervin, "The World is Mean and Man Uncouth", *Virginia Quarterly Review*, vol. 35 (1959) pp. 258–70.

B. Singermann, "Brechts *Dreigroschenoper*: Zur Ästhetik der Montage", *Brecht-Jahrbuch* (1976) pp. 61–82.

R. Speirs, "A Note on the First Published Version of *Die Dreigroschenoper* and its Relation to the Standard Text", *Forum for Modern Language Studies*, vol. 13, no. 1 (1977) pp. 25–32.

R. Taylor, "Opera in Berlin in the 1920s: *Wozzeck* and *The Threepenny Opera*", in *Culture and Society in the Weimar Republic*, ed. K. Bullivant (Manchester, 1977).

S. Unseld (ed.), *Bertolt Brechts Dreigroschenbuch: Texte, Materialien, Dokumente* (Frankfurt a.M., 1960). This contains a valuable collection of articles by T. Adorno, W. Benjamin, E. Bloch, H. Jhering, A. Kerr, S. Kracauer, E. Schumacher, K. Tucholsky, Kurt and Lotte (Lenya-) Weill.

G. Wagner, *Weill und Brecht* (Munich, 1977).

K. Weill, *Ausgewählte Schriften* (Frankfurt a.M., 1975).

U. Weisstein, "Brecht's Victorian Version of Gay: Imitation and Originality in the *Dreigroschenoper*", *Comparative Literature Studies*, vol. 7 (1970) pp. 314–34.

The "Lehrstücke"

M. Alter, "Bertolt Brecht and the 'Noh' drama", *Modern Drama*, vol. 11 (1968) pp. 123–31.

H. Berenberg-Gossler, H. H. Müller and J. Stosch, "Das Lehrstück: Rekonstruktion einer Theorie oder Fortsetzung eines Lernprozesses? Eine Auseinandersetzung mit R. Steinweg", in Joachim Dyck *et al.*, *Brechtdiskussion* (Kronberg im Taunus, 1974) pp. 121–71.

P. Beyersdorf, *Bertolt Brecht: Die Heilige Johanna der Schlachthöfe, Der Jasager – Der Neinsager und andere Lehrstücke. Anmerkungen und Untersuchungen* (Hollfeld, 1975).

"Brecht-Materialien I: Zur Lehrstückdiskussion", *Alternative*, vol. 91 (1973).

H. Brenner, "Die Fehldeutung der Lehrstücke, Zum methodischen Vorgehen der Germanistik", *Alternative*, vol. 78/79 (Berlin, 1971) pp. 146–54.

H. Brüggemann, *Literarische Technik und Soziale Revolution* (Reinbek, 1973).

K. Dickson, *Bertolt Brecht: Fünf Lehrstücke*, Introduction (London, 1969).

R. Grimm, "Ideologische Tragödie und Tragödie der Ideologie", *Zeitschrift für deutsche Philologie*, vol. 78 (1959) pp. 394–424; also in *Das Ärgernis Brecht*, ed. W. Jäggi (Basle, Stuttgart, 1961).

P. Horn, "Die Wahrheit ist konkret: Bertolt Brechts *Maßnahme* und die Frage der Parteidisziplin", *Brecht-Jahrbuch* (1978) pp. 36–66.

J. Kaiser, "Brechts *Maßnahme* und die linke Angst: Warum ein 'Lehrstück' so viel Verlegenheit und Verlogenheit provozierte", *Neue Rundschau*, vol. 84 (1973) pp. 96–127.

F. Kroetz, "Über die *Maßnahme* von Bertolt Brecht", *Kürbiskern*, no. 4 (1975) pp. 99–110.

S. K. Lee, "Das Lehrtheater Bertolt Brechts in seiner Beziehung zum japanischen Nô", *Modern Language Notes* (1978) pp. 448–78.

W. Mittenzwei, "Größe und Grenze des Lehrstücks, Bert Brechts Übergang auf die Seite der Arbeiterklasse", *Neue deutsche Literatur*, no. 10 (1960) pp. 90–106.

G. Nelson, "The Birth of Tragedy out of Pedagogy: Brecht's 'learning play' *Die Maßnahme*", *German Quarterly*, vol. 46 (1973) pp. 566–80.

J. Nordhaus, "The Laienspiel Movement and Brecht's *Lehrstücke*", Ph.D. Diss. (Yale, 1969).

W. Schivelbusch, *Sozialistisches Drama nach Brecht* (Darmstadt, 1974).

R. Steinweg, *Das Lehrstück: Brechts Theorie einer politisch ästhetischen Erziehung* (Stuttgart, 1972).

—— (ed.), *Die Maßnahme: Kritische Ausgabe mit einer Spielanleitung* (Frankfurt a.M., 1972).

——, "Brechts *Die Maßnahme* – Übungstext, nicht Tragödie", in *Das deutsche Drama vom Expressionismus bis zur Gegenwart"*, ed. M. Brauneck (Bamberg, 1972) pp. 166–79.

—— (ed.), *Brechts Modell der Lehrstücke: Zeugnisse, Diskussion, Erfahrungen* (Frankfurt a.M., 1976).

—— (ed.), *Auf Anregung Bertolt Brechts: Lehrstücke mit Schülern, Arbeitern, Theaterleuten* (Frankfurt a.M., 1978).

P. Szondi, *Der Jasager und Der Neinsager*, postscript (Frankfurt a.M., 1966).

A. Tatlow, " 'Viele sind einverstanden mit Falschem' – Brechts Lehrstücke und die Lehrstücktheorie", *Akten des V. Internationalen Germanisten-Kongresses* (1976) pp. 376–83.

M. Voss, "Bertolt Brecht: Der Ja- und der Neinsager", *Der Deutschunterricht* (Stuttgart) vol. 21, no. 2 (1969) pp. 54–63.

Index

Index